RELIGION AND TERRORISM

An Interfaith Perspectives

RELIGION AND TERRORISM

An Interfaith Perspectives

BS Chauhan

MD Publications Pvt Ltd
New Delhi
www.mdppl.com

Published by :

MD Publications Pvt Ltd
"MD House", 11, Darya Ganj,
New Delhi - 110 002
Phone : +91-11-45355555
E-mail : contact@mdppl.com
Website: www.mdppl.com

ISBN: 978-81-7533-328-4

Published and Printed by Mr. Pranav Gupta on behalf of **MD Publications Pvt Ltd** at Repro India Limited.

Preface

Religion's importance in contemporary terrorism is as a means of communication. It really shows how religion is being twisted. Bin Laden himself does not have any theological credentials, yet he issues *fatwas* because he knows people will listen to them, that it is an enormously helpful means to enhance his message to attract new support - and truly is a perversion of religion. Now you do of course have clerical figures in Islam, in Judaism, in white supremacist Christian Churches in the United States, using liturgy to justify violence, including Bin Laden citing the Quran again, a perverse interpretation of it.

Religious groups have used terror to help obtain their ends for millennia. The Romans fed Christians to the lions because of their religion. Pharos killed Jews and terrorized them to keep them in slavery. Christians terrorized Native populations during the crusades, Spanish Inquisition, populating the new world to name a few. Christians killed Jews during the holocaust. They also killed Catholic priests in the name of God.

Religion's importance in contemporary terrorism is as a means of communication. It really shows how religion is being twisted. Bin Laden himself does not have any theological credentials, yet he issues *fatwas* because he knows people will listen to them, that it is an enormously helpful means to enhance his message to attract new support - and truly is a perversion of religion. Now you do of course have clerical figures in Islam, in Judaism, in white supremacist Christian

Churches in the United States, using liturgy to justify violence, including Bin Laden citing the Quran again, a perverse interpretation of it.

Many terrorist groups believe that broadening the constituency gives them more strength, as in Bin Laden's trajectory. Pakistani groups are branching out and helping like-minded Muslims in Indonesia. Using religion, they are trying deliberately to spread their revolution beyond their borders in order to create something in which the sum is greater that the parts. This is part of their strategy right now.

Religion and terrorism are incompatible, if a Muslim is fighting with a Hindu or a Hindu is fighting with a Sikh, they are fighting for their own reasons, religion is not involved at all, they lack complete information about their religion and they just think we right and all other religions are wrong. Sometimes religion is not the only reason for fighting or violence, there might be some personal and family or land disputes, and in India it is the major cause of all fighting between Muslims, Sikhs and Hindus. Take Kashmir as an example, Muslims and Hindus there are just fighting over land disputes, religion is not the main reason, they are not even concerned about their religion, and their aim is just occupy the land. Same case is in Palestine, where Jews are fighting and killing Muslims for land dispute, although religion is also involved but is not main reason, so people all over the world take it as religion terrorism.

I am very thankful to Mr. Pranav Gupta, Director of MD Publications Pvt Ltd, New Delhi, for his kind cooperation and support for this book.

BS Chauhan

Contents

1

Introduction

Religion

A religion is an organized approach to human spirituality which usually encompasses a set of narratives, symbols, beliefs and practices, often with a supernatural or transcendent quality, that give meaning to the practitioner's experiences of life through reference to a higher power or truth. It may be expressed through prayer, ritual, meditation, music and art, among other things. It may focus on specific supernatural, metaphysical, and moral claims about reality (the cosmos, and human nature) which may yield a set of religious laws, ethics, and a particular lifestyle. Religion also encompasses ancestral or cultural traditions, writings, history, and mythology, as well as personal faith and religious experience.

The term "religion" refers to both the personal practices related to communal faith and to group rituals and communication stemming from shared conviction. "Religion" is sometimes used interchangeably with "faith" or "belief system," but it is more socially defined than personal convictions, and it entails specific behaviours, respectively. The development of religion has taken many forms in various cultures. It considers psychological and social roots, along with origins and historical development. In the frame of western religious thought, religions present a common quality, the "hallmark of patriarchal religious thought": the division of the world in two comprehensive domains, one sacred, the other profane. Religion is often described as a communal system for the coherence of belief focusing on a system of thought, unseen being, person, or object, that is considered to be supernatural, sacred, divine, or of the highest truth.

Moral codes, practices, values, institutions, tradition, rituals, and scriptures are often traditionally associated with the core belief, and these may have some overlap with concepts in secular philosophy. Religion is also often described as a "way of life" or a life stance. Religion has been defined in a wide variety of ways. Most definitions attempt to find a balance somewhere between overly sharp definition and meaningless generalities. Some sources have tried to use formalistic, doctrinal definitions while others have emphasized experiential, emotive, intuitive, volitional and ethical factors.

Definitions mostly includes :

- A notion of the transcendent or numinous, often, but not always, in the form of theism.
- A cultural or behavioural aspect of ritual, liturgy and organized worship, often involving a priesthood, and societal norms of morality (ethos) and virtue (arete).
- A set of myths or sacred truths held in reverence or believed by adherents.

Sociologists and anthropologists tend to see religion as an abstract set of ideas, values, or experiences developed as part of a cultural matrix. For example, in Lindbeck's Nature of Doctrine, religion does not refer to belief in "God" or a transcendent Absolute. Instead, Lindbeck defines religion as, "a kind of cultural and/or linguistic framework or medium that shapes the entirety of life and thought... it is similar to an idiom that makes possible the description of realities, the formulation of beliefs, and the experiencing of inner attitudes, feelings, and sentiments." According to this definition, religion refers to one's primary worldview and how this dictates one's thoughts and actions.

There is a tendency in the sociology of religion to emphasize the problems of any definition of religion. Talal

Asad has gone so far as to say"there cannot be a universal definition of religion because that definition is itself the historical product of discursive processes." Other religious scholars have put forward a definition of religion that avoids the reductionism of the various sociological and psychological disciplines that reduce religion to its component factors. Religion may be defined as the presence of a belief in the sacred or the holy. For example Rudolf Otto's "The Idea of the Holy," formulated in 1917, defines the essence of religious awareness as awe, a unique blend of fear and fascination before the divine. Friedrich Schleiermacher in the late 18th century defined religion as a "feeling of absolute dependence."

Religion and Superstition

While superstitions and magical thinking refer to nonscientific causal reasoning, applied to specific things or actions, a religion is a more complex system about general or ultimate things, involving morality, history and community. Because religions may include and exploit certain superstitions or make use of magical thinking, while mixing them with broader considerations, the division between superstition and religious faith is hard to specify and subjective. Religious believers have often seen other religions as superstition. Likewise, some atheists, agnostics, deists, and skeptics regard religious belief as superstition. Religious practices are most likely to be labeled "superstitious" by outsiders when they include belief in extraordinary events (miracles), an afterlife, supernatural interventions, apparitions or the efficacy of prayer, charms, incantations, the meaningfulness of omens, and prognostications.

Greek and Roman pagans, who modeled their relations with the gods on political and social terms, scorned the man who constantly trembled with fear at the thought of the gods, as a slave feared a cruel and capricious master. Such fear of the gods (deisidaimonia) was what the Romans meant by superstitio. Early Christianity was outlawed as a superstitio Iudaica, a "Jewish superstition", by Domitian in the 80s AD, and by AD 425, Theodosius II outlawed pagan traditions as superstitious. The Roman Catholic Church considers superstition to be sinful in the sense that it denotes a lack of trust in the divine providence of God and, as such, is a violation of the first of the Ten Commandments.

The Catechism of the Catholic Church states superstition "in some sense represents a perverse excess of religion." The history of religion refers to the written record of human religious experiences and ideas. This period of religious history typically begins with the invention of writing about 5,000 years ago (3,000 BCE) in the Near East.

Development of Religion

There are a number of models regarding the ways in which religions come into being and develop. Broadly speaking, these models fall into three categories:

- Models which see religions as social constructions;
- Models which see religions as progressing toward higher, objective truth;
- Models which see a particular religion as absolutely true.

In premodern (preurban) societies, religion is one defining factor of ethnicity, along with language, regional customs, national costume, etc. As Xenophanes famously comments:

Ethnic religions may include officially sanctioned and organized civil religions with an organized clergy, but they are characterized in that adherents generally are defined by their ethnicity, and conversion essentially equates to cultural assimilation to the people in question. The notion of gentiles ("nations") in Judaism reflects this state of affairs, the implicit assumption that each nation will have its own religion. Historical examples include Germanic polytheism, Celtic polytheism, Slavic polytheism and preHellenistic Greek religion.

The "Axial Age"

Karl Jaspers, in his Vom Ursprung und Ziel der Geschichte (The Origin and Goal of History), identified a number of key

Axial Age thinkers as having had a profound influence on future philosophy and religion, and identified characteristics common to each area from which those thinkers emerged. Jaspers saw in these developments in religion and philosophy a striking parallel without any obvious direct transmission of ideas from one region to the other, having found very little recorded proof of extensive intercommunication between the ancient Near East, Greece, India and China.

Jaspers held up this age as unique, and one which to compare the rest of the history of human thought to. Jaspers' approach to the culture of the middle of the first millennium BCE has been adopted by other scholars and academics, and has become a point of discussion in the history of religion. In its later part, the "Axial Age" culminated in the development of monism and monotheism, notably of Platonic realism and Neoplatonism in Hellenistic philosophy, the notion of atman in Vedanta Hindu philosophy, and the notion of Tao in Taoism.

Middle Ages

Newer presentday world religions established themselves throughout Eurasia during the Middle Ages by: Christianization of the Western world; Buddhist missions to East Asia; the decline of Buddhism in the Indian subcontinent; and the spread of Islam throughout the Middle East, Central Asia, North Africa and parts of Europe and India. During the Middle Ages, Muslims were in conflict with Zoroastrians during the Islamic conquest of Persia; Christians were in conflict with Muslims during the ByzantineArab Wars, Crusades, Reconquista and Ottoman wars in Europe; Christians were in conflict with Jews during the Crusades, Reconquista and Inquisition; Shamans were in conflict with Buddhists, Taoists, Muslims and Christians during the Mongol invasions; and Muslims were in conflict with Hindus and Sikhs during Muslim conquest in the Indian subcontinent.

Many medieval religious movements emphasized mysticism, such as the Cathars and related movements in the

West, the Bhakti movement in India and Sufism in Islam. Monotheism reached definite forms in Christian Christology and in Islamic Tawhid. Hindu monotheist notions of Brahman likewise reached their classical form with the teaching of Adi Shankara.

Modern Period

European colonisation during the 15th to 19th centuries resulted in the spread of Christianity to SubSaharan Africa, the Americas, Australia and the Philippines. The 18th century saw the beginning of secularisation in Europe, rising to notability in the wake of the French Revolution. In the 20th century, the regimes of Communist Eastern Europe and Communist China were explicitly antireligious. A great variety of new religious movements originated in the 20th century, many proposing syncretism of elements of established religions.

Adherence to such new movements is limited, however, remaining below 2% worldwide in the 2000s. Adherents of the classical world religions account for more than 75% of the world's population, while adherence to indigenous tribal religions has fallen to 4%. As of 2005, an estimated 14% of the world's population identifies as nonreligious.

Classification

Religious traditions fall into supergroups in comparative religion, arranged by historical origin and mutual influence. Abrahamic religions originate in the Middle East, Indian religions in India and Far Eastern religions in East Asia. Another group with supraregional influence is African diasporic religions, which have their origins in Central and West Africa.

- Abrahamic religions are by far the largest group, and these consist primarily of Christianity, Islam and Judaism (sometimes the Bahá'í Faith is also included). They are named for the patriarch Abraham, and are unified by the practice of monotheism. Today, around 3.4 billion people are followers of Abrahamic religions and are spread widely around the world apart from the regions around SouthEast Asia. Several Abrahamic organizations are vigorous proselytizers.

- Indian religions originated in Greater India and tend to share a number of key concepts, such as dharma and karma. They are of the most influence across the Indian subcontinent, East Asia, South East Asia, as well as isolated parts of Russia. The main Indian religions are Hinduism, Buddhism, Sikhism, and Jainism. Indian religions mutually influenced each other. Sikhism was also influenced by the Abrahamic tradition of Sufism.
- East Asian religions consist of several East Asian religions which make use of the concept of Tao (in Chinese) or Do (in Japanese or Korean), namely Taoism and Confucianism, both of which are asserted by some scholars to be nonreligious in nature.
- African diasporic religions practiced in the Americas, imported as a result of the Atlantic slave trade of the 16th to 18th centuries, building of traditional religions of Central and West Africa.
- Indigenous tribal religions, formerly found on every continent, now marginalized by the major organized faiths, but persisting as undercurrents of folk religion. Includes African traditional religions, Asian Shamanism, Native American religions, Austronesian and Australian Aboriginal traditions, Chinese folk religion, and postwar Shinto. Under more traditional listings, this has been referred to as "Paganism" along with historical polytheism.
- Iranic religions originated in Iran and include Zoroastrianism, Yazdanism, Ahle Haqq and historical traditions of Gnosticism (Mandaeanism, Manichaeism). It has significant overlaps with Abrahamic traditions, e.g. in Sufism and in recent movements such as Bábísm and the Bahá'í Faith.
- New religious movement is the term applied to any religious faith which has emerged since the 19th century,

often syncretizing, reinterpreting or reviving aspects of older traditions: Bahá'í, Hindu revivalism, Ayyavazhi, Pentecostalism, polytheistic reconstructionism, and so forth.

Religious Belief

Religious belief usually relates to the existence, nature and worship of a deity or deities and divine involvement in the universe and human life. Alternately, it may also relate to values and practices transmitted by a spiritual leader. Unlike other belief systems, which may be passed on orally, religious belief tends to be codified in literate societies (religion in nonliterate societies is still largely passed on orally). In some religions, like the Abrahamic religions, it is held that most of the core beliefs have been divinely revealed.

Religion in India

India, the land of spirituality and philosophy considers religion as an integral part of its entire tradition. The worship of various religions and its rituals play a significant role in every aspect of human life in the country. India is the birthplace of two great religions of the world, namely, Hinduism and Buddhism. It is also the birthplace of one of the oldest religions of the world, Zoroastrianism, and home to an ancient religion, Jainism. Sikhism is another very recognizable religion which began here bringing together the best aspects of Hinduism and Islam.

Followers of religions originated in other countries such as Islam, Christianity, Bahaism and Judaism also form a part of the population of secular nation, India. Hinduism is the dominant faith. According to 2001 Census, 80.5% of the population of the country are designated 'Hindu'. It is one of the ancient religions in the world, which began about 6000 years ago. Besides Hindus, Muslims are the most prominent religious group and are an integral part of Indian society. There are approximately13.4% Muslims (over 100 million), 2.3% Christians (over 20 million), 1.9 % Sikhs (18 million) and others including Buddhists (6 million), Jains, Parsis (Zoroastrians),

Jews, and Bahais, less than 2 percent. Hindus and Muslims are spread throughout the country.

Muslims are found mostly in the states of Uttar Pradesh, Bihar, Maharashtra, West Bengal, Andhra Pradesh, and Kerala. They represent a majority in Jammu and Kashmir and Lakshadweep. Christian concentrations are found in the northeastern states like Nagaland, Mizoram and Meghalaya and the southern states of Kerala, Tamil Nadu, and Goa. Sikhs are a majority in the state of Punjab whereas Buddhists are found in large numbers in Arunachal Pradesh, Ladakh, Bengal and Sikkim. Though a tiny minority, Jains are found all over India. Majority of Jains live in the states of Maharashtra, Rajasthan, Karnataka and Gujarat.

A religion is a set of faithbased beliefs and practices, which may involve following rituals, as well as ancestral or cultural traditions, writings, history, or mythology. Group rituals and communication may result from shared principles and may provide mystic experiences for followers. Religion is often described as a system of thought based on belief in an unseen being, person, or object that is considered to be supernatural, sacred, divine, or of the highest truth. Moral codes, practices, values, institutions, tradition, rituals, and scriptures are often traditionally associated with the core belief in this entity. Beliefs about the influence of the divine or ordering entity may influence nonreligious codes of morals and ideas of appropriate behaviour. Religion is also often described as a "way of life," a set of rules that a person and community may live by in order to lead what is considered a fulfilled life.

The development of religion has taken many forms. "Organized religion" generally refers to a community of people who regularly gather to exercise, acknowledge, or honour some aspect of their belief system in a divine or ordered entity. Other religions are more centered on individual practice, and in these religions the practice of worship may not require sharing these experiences with others. Religion has been defined in a wide variety of ways. While some sources focus on the rules for personal and community conduct based upon or modelled after an ordering divine power or ordered force, others have emphasized the experiential and emotional aspects. For instance, some sources emphasize religion for its role in instructing individuals on how to behave and treat one another while other sources may view the same practice of religion as a way to grow closer to the divine power.

Religion may be defined as the presence of a belief in the sacred or the holy. Sociologists and anthropologists tend to view religion as an abstract set of ideas, values, or experiences developed as part of a cultural matrix. Understanding a patient's religious belief system may be crucial in providing culturallyappropriate medical consultation. For instance, some individuals' religious beliefs may require healing practices which are given as an adjunct to or sometimes instead of what may be considered standard care. For instance, a religious practice may dictate that a newborn's placenta is taken home for burial under a corner of the house due to beliefs about the afterlife when the standard protocol is to dispose of it in a biohazard container after giving birth. In other situations, a person's religious beliefs may forbid such medical procedures as a blood transfusion.

Abrahamic Religions

The Abrahamic religions are the cluster of faiths with the largest number of followers in the contemporary world. The religions in this group are united by their belief in Abraham and in a single higher power. As a group, the Abrahamic religions include 3.4 billion followers worldwide. Abraham is considered the father of the Christian, Islamic, and Jewish faiths because he is believed to be brought from Mesopotamia to Canaan and to have entered into a covenant with god. This covenant dictated that if Yahweh was recognized as the supreme universal authority and deity, then Abraham would be blessed with innumerably progeny.

Christianity

Christianity is an umbrella term that includes a variety of faiths, including the Roman Catholic Church, Eastern

Orthodox Church, Pentecostalism, Jehovah's Witnesses, Latterday Saints, Adventists, Apostolic Brethren, Christian Scientists, Mennonites, Quakers, and all Protestants. The different sects of Christians are very diverse in their belief systems and may not recognize the beliefs or religious authorities of others who fall into other Christian categories. Christianity has an estimated 2.1 billion followers worldwide, and it is considered the world's largest religion.

Christianity began as an offshoot of Judaism, and Christians believe that its founder, Jesus of Nazareth, is the son of god and the Messiah that was prophesized in a holy book called the Old Testament. Christian beliefs center on the idea that through the death and rebirth of Jesus, all humans were reconciled with god and will therefore receive eternal life upon their death. Christians believe that every person will be judged by god and will be rewarded with eternal occupancy in either heaven or hell upon their death. The Bible is the holy book of Christianity, and it is considered to have been written by humans who were directly inspired by the Holy Spirit. In Christianity, God is considered a trinity of three unique manifestations of three entities who are united and act in concert.

Judaism

Judaism has its origin in the man named Abraham through his covenant with God and currently has 14 million followers worldwide. Judaism centers on the belief that god holds a covenant with the Jewish people, whose ancestor is Abraham. Religious Judaic practice involves observing god's laws as discussed in the holy books, known as the Torah and the Talmud. Judaism does not have a centralized authority dictating religious beliefs and practices, but communities follow a variety of long standing traditions of worship.

Islam

Major groups include the Ahmadi, Druze, Sunni, and Shia. Islam has its origin in the teachings of the 7th century political and religious figure Muhammad. Islam has between 0.9 and 1.4 billion followers worldwide and is considered the world's second largest religion. Muslims believe that Jesus was a prophet of many religions, and that the ultimately powerful god, known as Allah, sends prophets to bring his revelations to those who believe. The religious text of the Muslims is the Qu'ran. Most Muslims follow the Five Pillars of Islam as a guide for how they should conduct their lives. Muslims believe in god, his revelations, his messengers, his prophets, his angels, and in a day of judgment. Muslims believe that there will be a time, unknown to humans, when god will resurrect all of his followers and subject them to judgment. This concept differs from the Christian concept of rapture in that individuals are considered to be judged by god as they die, and only those who are alive at the moment of god's return to earth will meet him on this planet.

Dharmic Religions

Dharmic religions are all centered on the concept of dharma, a belief in the existence of an underlying order in human existence. This family of religions has its origin in India and is most prominent across East Asia, South East Asia, and the Indian subcontinent. These religions include Buddhism, Hinduism, Jainism, and Sikhism.

Buddhism

Theravada, East Asian Buddhism, Zen Buddhism, and Tibetan Buddhism are the primary sects of Buddhism. Buddhism was founded by Siddhartha Gautama in the 5th Century BC. His teachings focused on the holy life and liberation from suffering. Though Siddhartha Gautama is often referred to as the Buddha, he is recognized as being but one of many Buddhas. Buddhas are defined as teachers who have liberated themselves from the cycle of rebirth and suffering by following the practices of Buddhism and achieving supreme awakening.

These Buddhas are considered role models and teachers for other adherents of this religion. Buddhist teachings are aimed at helping individuals reach what is considered a form of supreme awakening, called enlightenment. Perfect enlightenment is said to occur when all dualities fuse and separate entities cease to exist. Buddhism stresses moderation and flexibility as ways of achieving this state of enlightenment. Meditation is also practiced as a way of liberating the mind from suffering. Enlightenment is thought to eliminate the person's suffering. The Buddhist body of scripture is known as the Tripitaka in Sanskrit and as the Tipitaka in Pali.

Hinduism

Hinduism is not based on one belief, but a variety of beliefs, traditions, and practices. It is the world's third largest religion. While some Hindus worship one god, others worship multiple gods. Examples of gods which may be worshiped in Hinduism include Brahma, Shakti, Ganesh, Tara, Vishnu, Durga, and Devi. There is no one deity that is worshiped by all Hindus. It is impossible to identify one universal belief system for Hinduism, but all of its variants have their origins in the Indian subcontinent. Most Hindus believe that the true self of every person is eternal, and that a person is reincarnated or reborn into another person or entity after each physical death.

Karma is central to the belief systems of most Hindus. This concept, broadly defined, relates to the idea that actions of past lives affect circumstances in the next life, and that a person should act correctly in their current life in order to improve the situation of the next. Many Hindus have shrines and icons dedicated to their god or gods, which serve as a tangible link to their believed higher power. Hinduism is commonly thought to be the oldest religion in the history of human civilization. It is a religion that gets its guidance from the Vedas, Upanishads, Sutras, Epics, Granthas, and Prabhandhams. The third largest religion after Christianity and Islam Hinduism is also known as Sanatana Dharma that is "eternal religion" and Vaidika Dharma meaning "religion of the Vedas".

Hinduism does not have any one founder and is perhaps the only religious tradition that is so diverse in its theoretical premises and practical expressions that it is like a compilation of religions. Hinduism believes in idol worship, casteism, reincarnation, 'karma', 'dharma' and 'moksha'. Some moral ideals in Hinduism include nonviolence, truthfulness, friendship, compassion, fortitude, selfcontrol, purity and generosity. According to historians, the origin of Hinduism dates back to 5000 or more years.

The word "Hindu" is derived from the name of river Indus, which flows through northern India. In ancient times the river was called the 'Sindhu', but the Persians who migrated to India called the river 'Hindu', the land 'Hindustan' and its inhabitants 'Hindus'. Thus the religion followed by the Hindus came to be known as 'Hinduism'. Two types of sacred writings constitute the Hindu scriptures: heard (Sruti) and memorized (Smriti). Sruti literature is of two parts: the Vedas and Upanishads.

There are four Vedas: 1) The Rig Veda "Royal Knowledge" 2) The Sama Veda "Knowledge of Chants" 3) The Yajur Veda "Knowledge of Sacrificial Rituals" 4) The Atharva Veda "Knowledge of Incarnations" and there are 108 extant Upanishads.

Smriti Literature refers to 'memorized' or 'remembered' poetry and epics. They are more popular with Hindus, because they are easy to understand, explains universal truths through symbolism and mythology, and contain some of the most beautiful and exciting stories in the history of religion world literature. The three most important of Smriti literature are:

1. *The Bhagavad Gita:* The most well known of the Hindu scriptures, called the "Song of the Adorable One", written about the 2nd century BC and forms the sixth part of Mahabharata. It contains some of the most brilliant theological lessons about the nature of God and of life ever written.
2. *The Mahabharata:* The world's longest epic poem written in about 9th century BC, and deals with the power struggle between the Pandava and the Kaurava families,

with an intertwining of numerous episodes that make up life.

3. *The Ramayana:* The most popular of Hindu epics, composed by Valmiki around 4th or 2nd centuries BC with later additions up to about 300 CE. It depicts the story of the royal couple of Ayodha Ram and Sita and a host of other characters and their exploits. Hinduism is supposed to be 'apauruseya', i.e., of impersonal origin and so also are the Gods of Hinduism. They are eternal & though the deities appear to be different and independent, they are really facets of the same Brahman, the Supreme God.

From the Rig Veda, we come to know of the vedic gods eight Vasus, eleven Rudras, twelve Adityas, Indra & Prajapathi, being the Gods of earth, the heavens and the space. The main Hindu Gods as we accept today can be broadly classified as Saiva Gods (Siva, His consort, His sons, His other forms), Vaishnava Gods (Vishnu, His consort, His various avatharams) & Sakthi or Saktha (Forms of Goddess Sakthi).

Hinduism differs from Christianity and other Western religions in that it does not have a single founder, a specific theological system, a single system of morality, or a central religious organization. It consists of "thousands of different religious groups that have evolved in India since 1500 BCE." Hinduism has grown to become the world's third largest religion, after Christianity and Islam. It claims about 837 million followers 13% of the world's population. It is the dominant religion in India, Nepal, and among the Tamils in Sri Lanka. According to the "Yearbook of American & Canadian Churches," there are about 1.1 million Hindus in the U.S.

The "American Religious Identification Survey" is believed to be more accurate. They estimated smaller number: 766,000 Hindus in 2001. Still, this is a very significant increase from 227,000 in 1990. Statistics Canada estimates that there are about 157,015 Hindus in Canada. Hinduism is generally regarded as the world's oldest organized religion. Most forms of Hinduism are henotheistic religions. They recognize a single deity, and view other Gods and Goddesses as manifestations or aspects of that supreme God. Henotheistic and polytheistic religions have traditionally been among the world's most religiously tolerant faiths. However, until recently, a Hindu nationalistic political party controlled the government of India. The linkage of religion, the national government, and nationalism led to a degeneration of the separation of church and state in India. This, in turn, has decreased the level of religious tolerance in that country. The escalation of antiChristian violence was one manifestation of this linkage. With the recent change in government, the level of violence will diminish.

Name of the Religion

This religion is called:

- Sanatana Dharma, "eternal religion," and
- Vaidika Dharma, "religion of the Vedas," and
- Hinduism—the most commonly used name in North America. Various origins for the word "Hinduism" have been suggested:
    - It may be derived from an ancient inscription translated as: "The country lying between the Himalayan mountain and Bindu Sarovara is known as Hindusthan by combination of the first letter 'hi' of 'Himalaya' and the last compound letter 'ndu' of the word `Bindu.'" Bindu Sarovara is called the Cape Comorin Sea in modern times.
    - It may be derived from the Persian word for Indian.
    - It may be a Persian corruption of the word Sindhu (the river Indus).
    - It was a name invented by the British administration in India during colonial times.

Sikhism

Sikhism was first practiced in the Punjab region of northwest India. It is influenced by ideas of Bhakti Hinduism and Islamic Sufism. Practicing this religion involves a quest for salvation by practicing a personal and disciplined meditation on the message and name of god. By doing this, a person is able to conquer the ego and join with god. The aim of this practice is to free one's self from the cycle of karmic rebirths in order to merge with the spirit of god. However, Sikhs believe that completely understanding god is beyond the ability of any human because their religion was directly inspired by god. Communication with god is considered possible by the rigorous practice of meditation.

Taoic Religions

Taoist religions all have their origins in East Asian religions, which believe in a natural life force, called the Tao or Dao.

Taoism

Taoism is a broad term applied to a diverse body of Chinese folk religions, which together have about 225 million followers worldwide. The founding of Taoism is attributed to Lao Zi (also written Lao Tzu) in 500 BC Lao Zi stressed living in harmony and synchronicity with the natural world and believed that encountering the Tao could occur directly through mystical experience. The Tao is not a god, but rather a universal ordering principle involving two opposing but inseparable forces, the yin and the yang, which are believed to interact and thereby guide everything that occurs.

Taoist religion stresses living in harmony with the life force that it thought to direct both the outer world and the individual's inner world. The human body is seen as a microcosm of the forces of the Tao in the universe. Many practices of Taoism have esoteric, mystical, and sectarian aspects. For instance, these practices may involve astrology. They also emphasize health and healing as a way to gain a long life or even achieve immortality. The most recognized religious text in Taoism is the Dao De Jing, but the Taoist canon is much larger.

Other Religions

Bahai

Bahai (also written Baha'i) is a religion derived from Babism, which is in turn derived from a sect of Islam. This faith has about 6 million followers worldwide and was founded in the midnineteenth century by Marza Husayn Ali, also known as Baha'ulla. Bahai has no formal set of scriptures, and it also has no formal ritual or priesthood. However, Baha'ulla's writings, called Kitab alAqdas or "The Most Holy Book", provide direction on Bahai life. Followers of this religion believe that all of the world's religions are manifestations of god, and that new religions arise which are appropriate for a certain time and place.

Because the Bahai faith promotes the unity of all humankind, it does not encourage prejudices and stresses ethical practices, which include world peace and education. Bahai believes that the twelfth in the series of great imams (religious leaders) will return to establish an era of peace and justice.

New Thought

The New Thought movement is a broad, unorganized, and practically oriented spiritual practice. Encounters with god are accomplished by meditation, prayer, constructive thinking, and realization of the living presence of god. New Thought borrows from the belief systems and histories of many Eastern religions, such as Taoism, but does not embrace a particular dogma.

God is seen as a principle, an allknowing entity, from which the universe unfolds. Suffering is believed to result from failure or lack of knowledge of a person's true nature from what is known as a Perfect Mind and Love, a manifestation of god. Some New Thought followers are licensed practitioners who may offer spiritual healing services, such as intercessory prayer.

Pagan and Earthbased Religions

This is a broad term for a series of cultic or spiritual practices and belief systems, which view a god or multiple gods as a living mythology that orders, explains, and directs phenomena in the world. Connection with nature is often emphasized as a way to live in synchronicity with god. Many indigenous nonAbrahamic religious practices fall into this category. Neopaganism is a term applied to those who practice some form of Paganism in industrialized countries, but which may borrow from the faith traditions of peoples in other times and places.

If we apply the appropriate methods, they can be completely eliminated and we will experience the supreme happiness of full enlightenment. After attaining enlightenment, we will have all the necessary qualities universal love and compassion, omniscient wisdom and boundless spiritual power to lead all living beings to the same exalted state. This is the ultimate aim of Mahayana Buddhism. India, being the birthplace of Gautam Buddha, figures as one of the most important places in Buddhism.

Terrorism

Terrorism, according to the MerriamWebster online dictionary, is the systematic use of terror, "violent or destructive acts (as bombing) committed by groups in order to intimidate a population or government into granting their demands." At present, there is no internationally agreed upon definition of terrorism. Common definitions of terrorism refer only to those acts which (1) are intended to create fear (terror), (2) are perpetrated for an ideological goal (as opposed to a materialistic goal or a lone attack), and (3) deliberately target (or disregard the safety of) noncombatants. Some definitions also include acts of unlawful violence or unconventional warfare.

A person who practices terrorism is a terrorist. Acts of terrorism are criminal acts according to United Nations Security Council Resolution 1373 and the domestic jurisprudence of almost all nations. The word "terrorism" is politically and emotionally charged, and this greatly compounds the difficulty of providing a precise definition. A 1988 study by the United States Army found that over 100 definitions of the word "terrorism" have been used. The concept of terrorism is itself controversial because it is often used by states to delegitimize political or foreign opponents, and potentially legitimize the state's own use of terror against them. A more neutral description, with less emotional connotations, would be Violent NonState Actor (VNSA).

The presence of nonstate actors in widespread armed conflict has created controversy regarding the application of the laws of war. The history of terrorist organizations suggests that they do not practice terrorism only for its political effectiveness. Individual terrorists are also motivated by a desire for social solidarity with other members of their organisation. Terrorism has been practiced by a broad array of political organizations for furthering their objectives. It has been practiced by rightwing and leftwing political parties, nationalistic groups, religious groups, revolutionaries, and ruling governments.

Origin of Term

"Terror" comes from a Latin word meaning "to frighten". The terror cimbricus was a panic and state of emergency in Rome in response to the approach of warriors of the Cimbri tribe in 105BC. The Jacobins cited this precedent when imposing a Reign of Terror during the French Revolution. After the Jacobins lost power, the word "terrorist" became a term of abuse. Although the Reign of Terror was imposed by a government, in modern times "terrorism" usually refers to the killing of innocent people by a private group in such a way as to create a media spectacle.

This meaning can be traced back to Sergey Nechayev, who described himself as a "terrorist". Nechayev founded the Russian terrorist group "People's Retribution" in 1869. In November 2004, a United Nations Security Council report described terrorism as any act "intended to cause death or serious bodily harm to civilians or noncombatants with the purpose of intimidating a population or compelling a government or an international organization to do or abstain from doing any act". In many countries, acts of terrorism are legally distinguished from criminal acts done for other purposes, and "terrorism" is defined by statute; see definition of terrorism for particular definitions.

Common principles among legal definitions of terrorism provide an emerging consensus as to meaning and also foster cooperation between law enforcement personnel in different countries. Among these definitions there are several that do not recognize the possibility of legitimate use of violence by civilians against an invader in an occupied country and would, thus label all resistance movements as terrorist groups. Others make a distinction between lawful and unlawful use of violence. Ultimately, the distinction is a political judgment.

Types

In the spring of 1975, the Law Enforcement Assistant Administration in the United States formed the National Advisory Committee on Criminal Justice Standards and Goals. One of the five volumes that the committee was entitled Disorders and Terrorism, produced by the Task Force on Disorders and Terrorism under the direction H.H.A. Cooper, Director of the Task Force staff. The Task Force classified terrorism into six categories.

- Civil Disorders : A form of collective violence interfering with the peace, security, and normal functioning of the community.
- Political Terrorism : Violent criminal behaviour designed primarily to generate fear in the community, or substantial segment of it, for political purposes.
- NonPolitical Terrorism : Terrorism that is not aimed at political purposes but which exhibits "conscious design to create and maintain high degree of fear for coercive purposes, but the end is individual or collective gain rather than the achievement of a political objective."

- QuasiTerrorism : The activities incidental to the commission of crimes of violence that are similar in form and method to genuine terrorism but which nevertheless lack its essential ingredient. It is not the main purpose of the quasiterrorists to induce terror in the immediate victim as in the case of genuine terrorism, but the quasiterrorist uses the modalities and techniques of the genuine terrorist and produces similar consequences and reaction. For example, the fleeing felon who takes hostages is a quasiterrorist, whose methods are similar to those of the genuine terrorist but whose purposes are quite different.
- Limited Political Terrorism : Genuine political terrorism is characterized by a revolutionary approach; limited political terrorism refers to "acts of terrorism which are committed for ideological or political motives but which are not part of a concerted campaign to capture control of the State.
- Official or State Terrorism : "Referring to nations whose rule is based upon fear and oppression that reach similar to terrorism or such proportions." It may also be referred to as Structural Terrorism defined broadly as terrorist acts carried out by governments in pursuit of political objectives, often as part of their foreign policy.

In an analysis prepared for U.S. Intelligence four typologies are mentioned:

- Nationalist Separatist
- Religious Fundamentalist
- New Religious
- Social Revolutionary

2

Democracy and Domestic Terrorism

The relationship between domestic terrorism and democracy is complex. Such terrorism is most common in nations with intermediate political freedom and that the nations with the least terrorism are the most democratic nations. However, one study suggests that suicide terrorism may be an exception to this general rule. Evidence regarding this particular method of terrorism reveals that every modern suicide campaign has targeted a democracy a state with a considerable degree of political freedom. The study suggests that concessions awarded to terrorists during the 1980s and 1990s for suicide attacks increased their frequency.

Some examples of "terrorism" in nondemocracies include ETA in Spain under Francisco Franco, the Shining Path in Peru under Alberto Fujimori, the Kurdistan Workers Party when Turkey was ruled by military leaders and the ANC in South Africa. Democracies, such as the United States, Israel, and the Philippines, also have experienced domestic terrorism. While a democratic nation espousing civil liberties may claim a sense of higher moral ground than other regimes, an act of terrorism within such a state may cause a perceived dilemma: whether to maintain its civil liberties and thus risk being perceived as ineffective in dealing with the problem; or alternatively to restrict its civil liberties and thus risk delegitimizing its claim of supporting civil liberties. This dilemma, some social theorists would conclude, may very well play into the initial plans of the acting terrorist(s); namely, to delegitimize the state.

Religious Terrorism

Religious terrorism is terrorism by those whose motivations and aims have a predominant religious character or influence. According to Mark Juergensmeyer, religious terrorism consists of acts that terrify, the definition of which is provided by the witnesses the ones terrified and not by the party committing the act; accompanied by a religious motivation, justification, organization, or world view. Religion is sometimes used in combination with other factors, and sometimes as the primary motivation. Religious terrorism is intimately connected to current forces of geopolitics.

According to Bruce Hoffman, to be considered religious terrorism the perpetrators must use religious scriptures to justify or explain their violent acts or to gain recruits and there must be some sort of clerical figures involved in some leadership roles. In the modern age, after the decline of ideas such as the divine right of kings and with the rise of nationalism, terrorism more often involved anarchism, nihilism and revolutionary politics, but since 1980 there has been an increase in activity motivated by religion.

Former United States Secretary of State Warren Christopher said that terrorist acts in the name of religion and ethnic identity have become "one of the most important security challenges we face in the wake of the Cold War." Stephen Weinberg has argued that religion is the most important factor, famously saying "for good people to do evil things that take religion". However, Robert Pape, Rogers et al, Nardin, and Juergensmeyer have all argued that religion should be considered only one incidental factor, and that so called "religious" terrorism is primarily geopolitical.

The Concept of "Religious Terrorism"

Robert Pape, political science professor of the University of Chicago, compiled the first complete database of every documented suicide bombing from 1980-2003. He argues that the news reports about suicide attacks are profoundly misleading "There is little connection between suicide terrorism and Islamic fundamentalism, or any one of the world's religions". After studying 315 suicide attacks carried out over the last two decades, he concludes that suicide bombers' actions stem from political conflict, not religion.

Michael A. Sheehan stated in 2000, "A number of terrorist groups have portrayed their causes in religious and cultural terms. This is often a transparent tactic designed to conceal political goals, generate popular support and silence opposition." Terry Nardin wrote, "A basic problem is whether religious terrorism really differs, in its character and causes, from political terrorism... defenders of religious terrorism typically reason by applying commonly acknowledged moral principles... But the use (or misuse) of moral arguments does not in fact distinguish religious from nonreligious terrorists, for the latter also rely upon such arguments to justify their acts... political terrorism can also be symbolic... alienation and dispossession... are important in other kinds of violence as well. In short, one wonders whether the expression 'religious terrorism' is more than a journalistic convenience".

Professor Mark Juergensmeyer wrote, "Religion is not innocent. But it does not ordinarily lead to violence. That happens only with the coalescence of a peculiar set of circumstances political, social, and ideological when religion becomes fused with violent expressions of social aspirations, personal pride, and movements for political change." and "Whether or not one uses 'terrorist' to describe violent acts depends on whether one thinks that the acts are warranted. To a large extent the use of the term depends on one's world view: if the world is perceived as peaceful, violent acts appear to be terrorism. If the world is thought to be at war, violent acts may be regarded as legitimate. They may be seen as preemptive strikes, as defensive tactics in ongoing battles, or as symbols indicating to the world that it is indeed in a state of grave and ultimate conflict".

Martyrdom and Suicide Terrorism

Important symbolic acts such as the blood sacrifice link acts of violence to religion and terrorism. Suicide terrorism, selfsacrifice, or martyrdom has throughout history been organized and perpetrated by groups with both political and religious motivations. Suicide terrorism or martyrdom is efficient, inexpensive, easily organized, and extremely difficult to counter, delivering maximum damage for little cost. The shocking nature of a suicide attack also attracts public attention. Glorifying the culture of martyrdom benefits the terrorist organization and inspires more people to join the group.

According to Julian Madsen, retaliation against suicide attacks further increases the group's sense of victimization and commitment to adhere to doctrine and policy. This process serves to encourage martyrdom. Suicide terrorism, selfsacrifice, or martyrdom therefore represents "value for money". The world's great religions all have both peaceful and violent messages from which believers can choose. Religious terrorists and violent extremists share the decision to interpret religion to justify violence, whether they are Buddhist, Christian, Hindu, Jewish, Muslim, or Sikh.

Buddhism and Terrorism

Buddhism is a religion or approach to an enlightened life based on the teachings of the Buddha Siddhartha Gautama twenty five centuries ago in northern India. The edict not to kill or inflict pain on others is integral to Buddhist thought. Periodically, however, Buddist monks have encouraged violence or initiated it. The primary example in the 20th and 21st century is in Sri Lanka, where Sinhala Buddhist groups have committed and encouraged violence against local Christians and Tamils. The leader of Aum Shinrikyo, a Japanese cult that committed a lethal sarin gas attack in the mid1990s, drew on Buddhist as well as Hindu ideas to justify his beliefs.

Christianity and Terrorism

Christianity is a monotheistic religion centered on the teachings of Jesus of Nazareth, whose resurrection, as understood by Christians, provided salvation for all mankind. Christianity's teachings, like those of other religions, contain messages of love and peace, and those that can be used to justify violence. The fifteenth century Spanish inquisition is sometimes considered an early form of state terrorism. These Churchsanctioned tribunals aimed to root out Jews and Muslims who had not converted to Catholicism, often through severe torture. Today in the United States, reconstruction theology and the Christian Identity movement have provided justification for attacks on abortion providers.

Hinduism and Terrorism

Hinduism, the world's third largest religion after Christianity and Islam, and the oldest, takes many forms in practice among its adherents. Hinduism valorizes nonviolence as a virtue, but advocates war when it is necessary in the face of injustice. A fellow Hindu assassinated Mohandas Ghandi, whose nonviolent resistance helped bring about Indian independence, in 1948. Violence between Hindus and Muslims in India has been endemic since then. However, the role of nationalism is inextricable from Hindu violence in this context.

Islam and Terrorism

Adherents of Islam describe themselves as believing in the same Abrahamic God as Jews and Christians, whose instructions to humankind were perfected when delivered to the last prophet, Muhammad. Like those of Judaisim and Christianity, Islam's texts offer both peaceful and warring messages. Many consider the 11th century "hashishiyin," to be Islam's first terrorists. These members of a Shiite sect assassinated their Saljuq enemies. In the late 20th century, groups motivated by religious and nationalist goals committed attacks, such as the assassination of Egyptian president Anwar Sadat, and suicide bombings in Israel. In the early 21st century, Al-Qaeda "internationalized" jihad to attack targets in Europe and the United States.

Judaism and Terrorism

Judaism began around 2000 BCE when, according to Jews, God established a special covenant with Abraham. The monotheistic religion focuses on the importance of action as an expression of belief. Judaism's central tenets involve a respect for life's sanctity, but like other religions, its texts can be used to justify violence. Some consider the Sicarii, who used murder by dagger to protest Roman rule in first century Judea, to be the first Jewish terrorists. In the 1940s, Zionist militants such as Lehi (known also as the Stern Gang) carried out terrorist attacks against the British in Palestine. In the late 20th century, militant messianic Zionists use religious claims to the historical land of Israel to justify acts of violence.

Without passion and prejudice, religion is a complicated subject matter the writer is hesitant always to discuss. The situation is made more loathsome and in fact precarious, when talking of religion in juxtaposition with strange bedfellows like politics and terrorism. Universally, religion is the belief in the existence of a God or gods, especially the belief they created the universe and gave human beings a spiritual nature, which continues to exist, after the death of the body. Supplementing this theory further, religion is also a source and indeed a way to moral, emotional and spiritual healing. Here on planet earth, without this dynamic faith, humanity is doomed.

Mosques, churches, sanctuaries, temples, etc are the only institutions in human society, which is totally committed to keeping faith alive in the hearts of men. Hence, Religion is "man in darkness in search of God": religious feelings and sentiments are therefore personal and private issues and by implication no religion is superior to others. Globally there exist many types of religion like Islam, Christianity, Hinduism,

Confucianism, Mazdaism, Taoism, Traditional religions, Judaism, Voodoo religion and many more. In another vein, we have still atheists, whose belief is that God is nonexistent. These religions have adherents, who react variedly and peculiarly to sociopolitical and sundry injustice in their respective polities.

Some of these religionists are docile and prayerful in helpless situations when confronted with cases of injustice; but others sometimes refuse to see eye to eye with any grain of injustice. Thus Islam as a great religion does not cherish any measure of injustice and it abhors imperial designs or urges to lord it over her faithful, particularly by those outside their religious fold. The intelligentsias have all concluded that the peculiar behavioural patterns of Muslims, makes "an injury to one, an injury to all." "Islam is not a violent religion, nor is Muslims violence prone. Rather, the truth is the faith is strongly committed to justice, and since Islam regarded justice as absolute, the believers could go to any length to defend, uphold and secure justice, and such a pursuit could result in hostilities which are antithetical to peace." The moral codes of the religion taught that peace and justice went together. Islam and Arab civilization is not appearing clearly on the radar of western Scourge nations. It still puzzles them; that they dubbed its adherents as fundamentalists and the faith as fanatical. On the other side of the spectrum, Muslims proclaim Americans and the West as terrorists gunning to destroy their culture and desecrate their religion.

Hear Usama in one of his fatwas: "Allah ordered us in this region to purify the Muslim land of all nonbelievers, and especially in the Arabian Peninsula... we believe that the biggest thieves in the world and the terrorists are the Americans..." "Islam could provide a language of opposition: to western power and influence, and those who could be accused of being subservient to them; to governments regarded as corrupt and the instruments of private interests, or devoid of morality; and to a society which seemed to have lost its unity with its moral principles and directions."

Counterterrorism pundits, harbor the opinion that except for the Middle East political palaver, America and Arab countries may well have been the best of friends. Particularly since most Arab countries are all members of the oilproducing club of nations. For where the nectar is, the butterfly and bees perch. Islam as a religion is peace and love. The respected standpoint of religious experts is that when the Middle East political crisis is sorted out; to the satisfaction of stakeholders and justice dispensed: America and the rest of the West will have a rethink about the religion and possibly begin to see Islam positively more than they do now.

The nagging question begging for a soothing answer today is: why is Islamic militancy and hooliganism on an exponential rise and why is America and the West, targets of Muslim charlatanism around the world? Islam is not about violence, rather what Muslims seem to be saying is that there will be: "no peace for the wicked and the oppressor." In Biblical history you will remember that the first religious and political independence of Israel, when they escaped captivity from Egypt crossed the Red Sea, under Moses and later Aaron was discussed in Exodus, chapter fourteen of the Holy Bible.

Soon after that, between the 78 A.D the Jewish Diaspora began and Israel ceased to exist as a nation for too long a time; with the Israelites migrating all over the world, until the middle of the nineteenth century. By 1948, the state of Israel was created with the instrumentality of the United Nations; as it were more than 3.5 million Palestinians became refugees as a concomitant. America and Britain's role in this episode and subsequently the billions of dollars every year aid to Israel by them; was viewed by Palestinians and their Arab instigators as a ploy and tacit support to the Jews: to uphold and occupy their lands and territory.

And for this, America and her allies incurred the hatred of Muslims around the globe. And ever since the occurrence of these events, in 1948 the U.S, the West and Islamic extremists of variegated conceptions, has been at each other's jugular.

Some of these events led to violent struggles by Palestinians and other Israel's neighbors, Syria, Jordan and Egypt to regain their lands from Israel. Of course this yielded more problems in the region as militant groups began to emerge in dozens. The arrowheads of these panIslamic fundamentalist groups became overnight heroes in the Muslim world, called the *Mujahideen* holy warriors. Whilst America and the international community insist they are terrorists.

To be seriously deprecated without reservation are the role of some vicious clerics, who often deceive their followers by turning them one against another for an imaginary place in heaven. It is criminal and immoral inciting innocent worshippers ignorantly to violence. Time after time some religious leaders ungodly set their members upon others; when if we critically reconcile the ends and means of ecumenism: we discover all religions are professing one and same Creator. God is one and not divided in denominations. We as His creatures are often habitual in employing and nomenclatures to name or identify this Creator.

Neither Islam nor Muslims is against democracy, instead I want to believe the contrary, which is that the religion endorsed the rule of law. Out of the 1.4 billion Muslims worldwide, many live in democracies. In short there is no inbuilt friction or inherent acrimony or even discord between Islam and democracy. Contrary to some views prevalent in Western societies, Islam does not preclude countries from embracing democracy or installing representative governments either. That democracy fails or is failing in Muslim nations: it is not Islam that necessitates its demise. But an admixture of historical, cultural, economic and political considerations: could be accountable for the backwardness. A recently conducted survey by Pew Global Attitude indicates majorities in the Arab world, favour democracy as a form of government.

For an instance, we have Muslim democratic nations like Turkey, Indonesia, Bangladesh, Mali, and even Senegal. Other partial democracies are Malaysia, Iran; and in the early 1970s Lebanon was a full democracy, until it was plundered by religion and political destabilizations. Around the world today, there are 47 Muslimmajority nations; most conduct free and fair elections, however some don't. It is also crucial you know that 18% of Muslims worldwide are Arabs. Again take heed, that there is no democracy in the Arab world, and this is the crux of the matter. Libya, Syria, Tunisia, and Saudi Arabia are the least democratic of Arab countries. Experts suggests, other Arab government and administrative systems, fall in between autocracy and democracy, because they may have legislatures, labour unions, political parties but the ruling parties, king or president exercises authority.

"These are countries with "parliaments", "national assemblies" or "people's assemblies", but they are no more than phony structures created to provide the ruling elite with an aura of legitimacy". Pseudodemocracy if you fancy the expression is the dominant rule in those countries and barely the exception. In the last thirty years or thereabout, in Muslim nations if anything, democracy tremendous setbacks, experts have surmised. It is simply for this reason some writers are harboring the view that the democracy gap, which separates Muslim nations from the rest in the world, applies only to Arab nations. Outside Arab countries democracy is gaining a foothold, albeit gradually.

The reasons few Arab countries democratize is thus:

- Oil in the Arab countries belonged to families, elites and rulers: so those having oil concessions and economic advantages don't want to develop market economies or grant political freedom, but had been scrupulously maintaining the status quo.
- Tribalism and patriarchal systems of government inhibits democratic developments and ideals in the Arab world.
- The leaders of Arab countries tend to over the significance of Israeli debacle; using it as a tool to hoodwink Arab masses and divert their attention away from autocratic misrule and leadership ineptitude at home.

- Repressions by monarchies or military dictators also do stymie democracy in Arab nations.
- The absence of secular political parties and organs conduced to democratic reforms in that region.
- Typical traditional hatred against Western-style democracy or nonIslamic system of government by average Arabs: is a major contributing dimension to the dearth of democracy in the Arab land.
- At the base of it all, is the policy attitude of the U.S and other democracies, to support Arab autocrats: felling out of power or clinging to it. This also equates for the failure of democracy to rear its good head in Arab countries. But why are the U.S and other superior democracies supporting Arab autocrats? Because of:
    - National security imperatives
    - Oil

Diplomacy and fear of the unknown of the autocrats are being booted out only to be replaced by radical regimes. Some social thinkers have argued that Islam and its Holy Book have some areas friendly and admissible of democratic virtues and ideals. For instance "Shura"or consultative decisionmaking, and "ijima" or the principles of consensus are in the Qur'an. Others according to Muqtedar Khan, Director of International studies, Adrian College, Michigan are:

- The Constitution of Medina, by Prophet Mohammed in 622 A.D. A document that set down the rules of the community of Medina: being the agreement of Muslims and Jews of the city. It grants equal rights to Jews and Muslims who followed its laws.

Discussants are positing that the areas Islam clashes with democracy tend to lay in the literal interpretation of sharia laws. In the scriptural sense, Muslims believe only Allah give laws whilst man is to implement and obey. This law is sharia, and its doctrine has been severally subjected to complicating interpretations by Muslims of various schools, to the confusion of the wider society. As there are elements of democracy in Islam, so we have aspects of the religion, which disfavours the concept; just like the subjection of women, corporal punishments, i.e. stoning female adulterers to death, amputation and so on. By trying to give these laws human face, most modern Islamic democracies have at best chosen not to enforce those critical sections of the laws.

Some have even opted to reinterpret entirely those sections of it that public morality. The reason some Arab religious scholars and leaders refuse to see meaning in democracy; is to evade checks and balances which are the beacons of a representative government: they are afraid the source of law will be repositioned in the people, if democracy becomes the norm. Separation of powers, and the sister collective responsibility detracts from the entrenched positions of Arab leaders and Muslim scholars: and for this reason they abhorred "a government of the people by the people and for the people". In summary, let everyone bore in mind he is a part of an inseparable humanity; and dutifully strive in constancy to pull down barriers holding him down from loving his neighbor, no matter his cultural and religious backgrounds.

Also, should we realize how vendetta regularly begets injustice and misapprehension; we would learn how to forgive one another. Since we live in a socioeconomical and political atmosphere where begin in the minds of the people, it is also within the minds of these people that structures of peace and unity must be constructed. Let us struggle to live in peace and worship with wisdom: for we are all pilgrims in this world. This presupposes, prudentially that we must join as a formidable collective, making to create a world free from poverty, racism and other forms of injustice, which often necessitate terrorist attacks. It is only a world of justice and peace that can provide a reliable and guaranteed form of security for America, the West and the globe in general.

Religious bigotry or fanaticism has been a permanent element of human history. Religious terrorism was not part of that phenomenon but it is a new and the most terrible development in this regard. Although human history is replete with the horrible tales of torture and violence yet the acts of large scale terrorism were not allowed by any religion. Now a day things have changed and the religious zealots do not spare the slightest opposition. They are so intense in their false beliefs that they do not even spare their coreligionists. All the major religions of the world teach the lesson of tolerance and peaceful living. The irony of the situation is that all the religious communities are at daggers drawn at one another.

According to the Christian teachings you should present your second cheek if some one slaps you at the first. What can be the bigger example of love and tolerance than this? Same is the case with the Islam. The very name of the religion represents the peace. It stresses the brotherhood and peaceful living. Hinduism absolutely denies the violent acts even to the animals. In this religion each and every creature is worshipped and considered as having some spiritual powers. Buddhism is based on the nonviolence and forbids killing of any living being even the ants. Judaism is also the religion of peace and respect.

If we include the secularism in this list we find that it is also a philosophy of peaceful living. Contradictory to the basic teachings of all the religions we find an element of terrorism present in all of them. First of all we find that element of superiority is the fundamental cause of these phenomena. Each religious community has supposed that it is on the right path and all others are wrong. This instinct of loftiness was consciously created in the masses by the clever clergies of all the religions.

The time servers and selfish political leaders exploited the same feelings of superiority and made one community the enemy of the other. When they were not able to control the affairs of the state by true means they used religion as the weapon. This is definitely the most powerful weapon even stronger than the weapons of mass destruction. The sham cultural and moral values were created to gain control over the publics and republics. For their vested interests people were be fooled to fight for their preservation. Muslims fought with the Christians and in return the Christians waged crusades to take their revenge. When one new and wrong custom or rite becomes the social or cultural value, it is very difficult to eradicate it completely. It always becomes the part and parcel of the people's lives.

The Hindu Muslim riots in the Indian subcontinent are also the part of the same serial of wars that are fought for maintaining hegemony over the others. Secondly the political aims of different religious communities are the base of this kind of terrorism. The crook leaders styled themselves as the saviors of the particular religions and communalities and the common folk followed them blindly. This insane following was exploited to make the people fight for the defense of their religion. In fact that was an intrigue or deceit for achieving the covert aims. Same is the case with all religious factions. Their clever leaders or rulers inscribe in the minds of the people that their religion is in danger, fight for its revival. Not only the state machinery but also the general public is mobilized for this purpose. From here begins the terrorism if this particular community is defeated.

Last but not the least reason behind the religious terrorism is the ambition of the rulers and the states to control the world affairs according to their own wishes. The recent example from history is the war against Russia. Russia invaded Afghanistan in 80,s. The non communist world was mobilized to fight against the evil designs of the infidels. The front line beleaguered were the Muslims so they were preached to fight a holy war or Jihad against the atheists of USSR. The idea of jihad or the holy war was propagated by the media and it became the word of the day. The religious sentiments were exploited and Russia was defeated.

Those holly warriors were termed as terrorists when they established their own government. The saviors of the humanity were labeled as terrorists and the west thought it necessary to clear the Augean stables. The west again came forward. This time it was Islam under siege. They presented the most terrific form of this religion and defamed it as the terrorist religion. Those who were the cat's paw were named as al Qaeda and became a pretext to indulge in different states.

The Relation between Religion and Terrorism

Many people say that to be religious is easy. It is an easier road to heaven rather than to hell. Nevertheless, the fact is different since to be religious can become very hard. The road to heaven is not taken by worship or siding with the weak people, but by exploding bombs and killing other people. Unlike the Sufi who attempt to reach Allah and heaven by (practices and rituals within mysticism performed in order to know Allah), we recently view the fact that God and heaven must be redeemed by blood and soul. Rationally, it's hard for us to say that the last one is the road to God.

Nevertheless, it is the latest reality of our religiosity. Religion which should be a holy place now is accused as being the mastermind behind terrorism. It is experienced also by the recent Muslim community. The tragedy of 11th September, 12th October in Bali and Jakarta's JW Marriot Hotel's bombing has dragged the Muslim community into a hard position. Now, many people called as "Muslim activists" by the media are caught by police as suspects behind terrorism. Islam is not a religion of terrorism. But this explanation is unable to reduce the impression that Islam is a terrorist's net.

This ethical-normative argument is true although it hides many facts behind, not only related to the behaviour of religious community, but also related to the religious doctrine. We must admit that several religious doctrines can be used to legitimate terrorism, regardless whether it is right or not. Hence, religion's involvement within terrorism is a problem of interpretation upon a fact. Explanation separating religion from its disciples is the inability of viewing the reality of a religious community's life which is far of its ethicalnormative teaching. The question is this: when should the behaviours of religious disciples be related or distinguished from its disciples? If the good behaviour is accepted as part of religion, why is its bad behaviour rejected?

In social science studies, interrelation between doctrine and its disciples has been an important topic. Taufik Abdullah (1987) might never imagine that terrorism would be a crucial issue in Islam, hence he simply said:"… it's not a paradox when Islam, as the universal revelation and started from the perfect and eternal doctrine, show itself in diversity painted by the history and social cultural situations of its disciples. Tension between eternal doctrine and manifestation in private and social life is the main factor in the Islamic dynamic. That statement may be rightly related to the world of idea or thought. However radical a thought, it would not be called as terrorism if it's not followed by physical violence etc.

But the destruction over humanitarian value and dignity is hard to be observed as "Islamic dynamic" and not as a paradox. It obviously paradox if religious manifestation is against the sacred doctrine of religion.

An adage states that a textual interpretation started from certain philosophy should produce any "social structure" and behaviour mode which is a pure reproduction of "Islamic doctrine". But there has often been an apology within muslim intellectuals by treating the doctrine and the religious disciples differently. Both are separated not because of methodological obligation, but because of an ethical push in order to protect religious "holiness". Briefly, doctrine is never mistaken; it is human's error who believes in such doctrine. This way of thinking, is looked at as "protecting the holiness of religious doctrine". But on the other hand this way of thinking is demonstrating how the religious doctrine's holiness has no influence upon its disciple.

Hence, what is being religious for? Here is the weak point of assumption that textual study tradition is the only way to see phenomena of Muslim society. Hence, we have to realize the importance of Islamic study starting from reality. However, religion is a social reality although it came from divine doctrine. In academic tradition, positioning Islam as the object of scientific study is actually new, since there is no "reluctance" therefore Islam can be approached as merely a 'religion of revelation'.

Yet, scientific study should place Islam as a "historical religion" rather than as a divine religion. Therefore, "religion" has to be open for criticism. From the description above, this question arises: is it true that terrorism has no relation with religion? It's hard to say precisely. If we say 'yes', it seemed to drag religion into the dirty world against the meaning of religion itself. But if we say 'no', it seemed to cover the fact that the actor often uses religious symbol and spirit. The fact that religion is always involved in terrorism should not be covered. It is a bitter fact we should accept. Courage to admit does not always mean making religion "black faced" since there is other community out of it who comprehend their religious doctrine differently.

Hence, the problem is not always laid on religious doctrine but more on interpretation over that doctrine. Some explanation might be used to capture the relation between religion and terrorism. Firstly, on the doctrinal level, religion has the potency to raise "fundamentalist" group. The fact indicates that the extreme movements are almost there in all religion. Here, Amrozi's confession one of Bali's blast suspects is interesting. To him, Bali's bombing was in order to maintain religious life. "What would happen to Bali in the next 15 years if I didn't explode the bomb? People complain about losing material, but actually religion and morality are more important.

Secondly, religion in post modern era is noted by the appearance of "spiritual violence" which later is expressed as "social violence". It appears due to the failure of modernism like the pledge of freedom and pluralism emerging from the mist of vagueness and ambiguity. Due to rational hesitation which is paralyzed by the spirit of post modernism, the chosen way out is running from freedom to enter the 'definite' world which soothes hearts. The chosen way is by submitting the self toward a transcendental authority promising eschatological happiness. Thirdly, response upon the western hegemony and secularism is considered to threaten the Muslim community. A western secular thought which has come into the Muslim world is considered as a serious threat from the "infidel" and should be fought back.

This hegemony is gripping stronger with capitalist ideology which shackles economic principles of Muslim community. The Muslim world will be increasingly buried by the high dependence on the west. Out of those three matters, many people agree with the conspiracy theory. The basic assumption of conspiracy theory is that terrorism addressed toward Islam is the conspiracy of US and its allies which seemed to be threatened by Islam. The conspiracy theory's follower believe that US also responsible upon the emergence of terrorism in various region.

This theory used to be connected to Samuel P Huntington's clash of civilization. It is the fact that after the cold war won by US and its allies, the Eastern power including Islam are potential to be a threat. Based on the above illustration, terrorism is not a "single" phenomenon which emerges suddenly. However, it is a camouflage if religion is not responsible upon the tragedy of terrorism. It is impossible to separate diametrically between the normative teachings of religion with the expression of its disciples. That confession also obliges us as the religious people to do a critical observation upon religious doctrines which is comprehended arbitrarily.

3

Interfaith Dialogue
Religious Diversity and Local Responsibility

The idea of interfaith dialogue is now acknowledged by international agencies such as UNESCO to be a key factor in promoting mutual understanding, solidarity and cooperation for building multicultural societies that respect pluralism, and guided by the principles of democracy and human rights. Diverse faith communities have engaged in dialogue to understand more deeply each other's traditions thereby promoting greater harmony and goodwill. Most importantly, interfaith dialogue also seeks to critically engage participants in revealing common values and principles that may lead to collaboration in personal and social action towards building a more peaceful world for all humanity. Globally, the significant progress and accomplishments of interfaith dialogue is reflected in the growth of various networks and coalitions, such as the World Conference on Religions for Peace, the Parliament of the World's Religions, and the United Religions Initiative.

Through the frequent gatherings and specific projects of these networks, diverse faiths have shown that it is possible for dialogue to establish deeper mutual respect and understanding. It is equally possible to join hands, minds, heart and spirit in overcoming common societal, international and global problems (e.g. wars, militarization, intercultural conflicts, racism, poverty, North South inequalities, human rights, ecological destruction). Such international interfaith dialogue movements draw their inspiration and strength from many inspiring exemplars of local community and grassroots efforts. Interfaith dialogue, if it is to be fruitful and authentic, rests on several assumptions and principles. These include openness to learning about and from each other's wisdom and knowledge about faith and spirituality and a spirit of humility and willingness to be self critical, acknowledging contradictions between theory and practice.

In dialogue, there is also openness within each faith to engage in reinterpretation of beliefs in the context of contemporary societal realities, and to challenge any tendencies towards extremism and intolerance by any leader or followers. In this regard, as many faith leaders have emphasized, interfaith dialogue needs to complement interfaith dialogue. Importantly too, interfaith dialogue needs to involve not only leaders but also ordinary citizens from all walks of life and sectors, including professionals, civil servants, media and educators. Finally, the role of education in promoting interfaith dialogue is essential and vital, so that children and youth who will be future leaders and adult citizens can also grow up to promote a culture of respect, harmony, justice and nonviolence.

Building a Culture of Peace

In this new century, realities worldwide clearly reveal the vast realities of peacelessness and conflict facing humanity. Every minute, we are bombarded by stories of violence, conflicts, and suffering: new wars~ old wars that drag on~ millions of refugees~ ongoing hunger, homelessness and poverty of billions~ resurgence of older diseases and newer ones like HIV/AIDS~ and natural disasters. In the face of such "gloom and doom" news, it can be easy to feel great despair, and for some people, hopelessness or perhaps even indifference. But despite the suffering, destruction and understandable feelings of despair, the good news is that there are growing signs of hope. These conflicts and violence in all levels and forms are being challenged courageously and hopefully by peoples, communities, movements and initiatives working to create a culture of peace through active nonviolence. Amidst the pain, suffering and hardships endured by billions of human beings on planet Earth today, countless voices can still be heard and many inspiring actions witnessed that collectively reflect a global yearning for peace.

For example, ordinary peoples have courageously established zones of peace free from armed conflicts between the Government and armed insurgent groups. Many rural and urban poor people have organized themselves to promote alternative, reliant, just and sustainable communities, while women are struggling worldwide for their human rights and for development that overcomes gendered inequities. Furthermore, teachers, parents, citizens and students in North and South contexts have been implementing programs of conflict resolution and peer mediation to build school environments free from violence. Indigenous peoples have also succeeded, through active nonviolence, to realize their rights to self-determination and cultural survival in the face of development aggression.

Last but not least, North and South citizens have joined hands to promote just and sustainable people centred development policies rather than the current world order dominated by powerful elites, organizations and structures. These exemplars clearly show that the human spirit remains undiminished in the face of multiple conflicts and challenges steeped in all forms of violence and peacelessness. Despite the ending of the "Cold War" and the opportunities provided by the so called "peace dividend," there is widespread consensus that we are still living within a deeprooted culture of violence. It was therefore very meaningful and vital that the United Nations declared 2000 as the International Year for the Culture of Peace, followed by the International Decade for a Culture of Peace and Nonviolence for the Children of the World. We still have another six years left of this International Decade, and so much more needs to be done to fulfil the vision and goals of the Decade.

Besides the numerous UNESCO initiated conference and forums and efforts by some governments to implement National Culture of Peace programmes, there have been inspiring demonstrations of how a culture of peace is being weaved slowly but surely all over the world. For example, at the 1999 Hague Appeal for Peace in the Netherlands, over 7000 peoples representing groups, movements, communities, institutions and agencies, including the UN Secretary General, several Nobel Peace laureates, and NGOs from every sector, shared ideas, strategies, lessons, and hopes for building a more peaceful, just, sustainable and compassionate world. Another 8000 participants from diverse faiths and spirituality traditions gathered in Barcelona at the Parliament of the World's Religions to share many common values and principles which are vital to the building of peaceful individuals, communities, societies and world.

In this peace building, it is clear that diverse faiths and spirituality traditions provide inspirational sources of values and principles that guide action and transformation from a culture of violence to a culture of peace. However, such values and principles may often need to be reawakened as peoples and believers are entrapped by a culture of competitive materialism and egocentric attachments, whether it is attachment to greed, power or identity. At the same time, we also need to be mindful that all faiths need to face the challenge of intrafaith dialogue, being willing to query and transform doctrines and perspectives that may act as barriers to the building of a culture of peace.

Furthermore, the weaving of a culture of peace is necessarily multidimensional and holistic. It is no longer meaningful to see peace as just an absence of war, as popular awareness has tended to emphasize. Rather, from the perspective of peace education and increasingly among interfaith dialogue practitioners, peace also implies justice, human rights, environmental care, intercultural respect and a deep sense of inner peace. We are being called to acknowledge and to overcome violence in all its multiple physical and nonphysical forms and levels.

The Role of Peace Education

Education plays a most vital role in both interfaith dialogues as well as in weaving or building a culture of peace. Without education, interfaith dialogue and peace building will not be effective or sustainable. How can we enter into authentic interfaith dialogue unless we have been educated about the basic beliefs of each other's faiths? How can we build peaceful individuals, communities and the wider world unless we critically understand the realities of violence and conflicts – their nature, why and how they happen, and the consequences?

The goals of educating for a culture of peace are reflected in two related questions: How can education promote a critical awareness and understanding of the root causes of all forms of conflicts and violence at all levels of life (personal, interpersonal, family, community, societies and world)? How can education simultaneously cultivate values and attitudes that move individuals, families, communities, nations and the world to translate their critical understanding into personal and social action for building peaceful persons, families, communities, societies and world? Communities, institutions, civil society organizations, and international/global agencies including UNESCO, have therefore been implementing educational projects and programs that seek to address the root causes of violence and conflicts, and to build societies and ultimately a world based on principles and values of active nonviolence, local/global justice, human rights, intercultural respect and reconciliation, ecological sustainability and inner peace.

As the UNESCO Medium Term Strategy (20022007) (31C/4) stated, it is vital for education to promote universally shared values for the development of peaceful, democratic and pluralistic societies, including values such as human rights, democracy, tolerance, nonviolence, solidarity, intercultural understanding and dialogue among cultures and civilizations. It is also necessary to focus on a number of key pedagogical principles to enhance the effectiveness of multifaith education toward a culture of peace. How we educate for peace or how we conduct interfaith dialogue, is as important as the content ('what" and "why") of educating for peace. It is now appropriate to turn to specific themes of interfaith dialogue in weaving a culture of peace and to draw out implications and challenges for educational institutions and educators.

Dismantling the Culture of War

Despite the ending of the Cold War, reduced tensions and nuclear arms race between the former two superpowers, the world today is still experiencing symptoms of a culture of war yielding untold suffering, hardships, pain, and death. Millions, notably civilians and children, have died in conflicts or become refugees and/or internally displaced persons. Wars, acts of terrorism followed by deadly responses of state sponsored counterterrorism violence, armed intervention and military occupation, are grim reminders of the willingness by which nations and groups resort to armed violence to "settle" conflicts and disputes. In the field of nuclear arms, we also saw how some countries have been spending precious national resources on racing to build up their nuclear weapons. Horizontal proliferation in nuclear weapons, as well as other weapons of mass destruction (mostly chemical and biological) is now a major problem to be resolved nonviolently.

In the meantime, the United States' abandonment of key disarmament accords and its plan to install a new antimissile shield threatens to reescalate the arms race which could lead to an intensified militarization of space. Clearly, in the face of these ongoing manifestations of a culture of war, there is a great need for peace education that focuses on nonviolent resolution of armed conflicts and disputes. As practiced by successive generations of peace builders inspired by Gandhi, conflicts need to be settled through negotiation where all governments and citizens can help to create peace accords. The role of the UN and other multilateral agencies in settling conflicts and disputes through negotiations and mediation, and in post conflict peace building programs need to be fully supported and strengthened. While the participation of Governments and official bodies is crucial in dismantling the culture of war, the increasing role of citizen peacemakers in the peaceful resolution and transformation of conflicts needs to be acknowledged as inspiring role models in building a culture of peace.

Critical education and empowerment of ordinary citizens to be active in the peace building process (e.g., building zones of peace) have been vital in the successful steps towards building nonviolent societies. Another specific dimension of disarmament education and advocacy lies in the campaign to abolish the arms trade that fuels the engines of wars while diverting scarce national resources into weapons instead of into meeting basic human needs. The historic treaty banning land mines also crystallizes how ordinary citizens can mobilize, together with state agencies, to enhance the safety of innumerable peoples worldwide. The culture of war not only persists in such "macro" contexts, but also in the more "micro" spheres of life in all societies.

Domestic violence and physically harmful practices at interpersonal, familial, institutional and community levels have also been challenged by non formal and formal educational campaigns and programs, as has the proliferation of gun ownership and a deepening vigilante mentality in many societies. The role of media, other cultural and social agencies (e.g., entertainment and sports) and even the toy industry likewise are demystified for their explicit or indirect support of a culture of war and physical violence. Through public and school based critical literacy, adults and children are empowered to not consume media violence or war toys, while pressuring governmental and private sectors to enforce relevant policies and regulations.

There has also been increasing concern, especially in North countries, over attitudes, conduct, and relationships within schools which sanction a culture of violence (e.g., bullying, assaults, corporal punishment, "gang" fighting, and teacher victimization). Consequently, in many formal schooling systems, the integration of nonviolence principles in policies, programs, curricula, and teaching learning environments has expanded in recent decades. These programs essentially promote values and practices of conflict resolution and violence prevention to overcome a culture of violence in schools and communities. When children grow up learning values, habits and ways of resolving their daily conflicts through nonviolent resolution and mediation, we are more likely to have a next generation of adult citizens who approach conflicts constructively and peacefully.

When we turn to interfaith dialogue, this theme of education to dismantle a culture of war in all its macro and micro expressions clearly resonates well with core values and principles found in diverse faiths and spirituality traditions. The teachings of many faiths call on their believers to build peace in their daily lives and communities, and to resolve conflicts through negotiation and mediation nonviolently rather than the use of force and coercion. A number of traditions explicitly endorse ahimsa or no killing, and therefore encourage active nonviolence as a way of life. There are now many inspiring exemplars of local initiatives in which different faiths are collaborating to overcome longstanding armed conflicts.

Through interfaith dialogue, many faith leaders and followers have also contributed to campaigns for nuclear disarmament, abolition of the deadly arms trade, nonviolent strategies to deal with the root causes of 9/11 and related political problems, including terrorism. The Decade to Overcome Violence project of the World Council of Churches is a meaningful example of an ecumenical community's contribution to raise awareness of the ubiquitous problem of militarization and wars worldwide and to catalyze action for overcoming such violence and militarism. Many faiths are calling on their believers to reject domestic violence and violence against women, which is a serious problem worldwide.

Nonetheless, while acknowledging these positive outcomes of interfaith dialogue to help dismantle a culture of war, there is also a challenge of interfaith dialogue that many faith leaders and communities are now facing. This concerns the doctrine of "just war" in its various expressions, whereby strategies of war or violent force under some conditions are justifiable. The dialogue on this issue is necessarily complex and difficult, but from the perspective of educating for a culture of peace, its complexity should not slow down the urgent task of promoting the active nonviolence dimension found in each faith. In this way, all faiths are educating and guiding their followers to tirelessly seek nonviolent resolution or transformation of conflicts.

Living with Justice and Compassion

Since the beginning of the modern era propelled by the industrial, technological and lately the information revolution, the dominant voices about human "progress" have envisioned and implemented the concept of "development" in very specific ways. This modernization paradigm of "development" embraces some basic uninterrupted assumptions and themes including the faith that economic growth especially via the "free market" system is central to development, producing wealth that will "trickle down" to all citizens~ And that the North can help the South catch up through aid, trade and investments which collectively integrate the South in the growth centred global economy, marketplace and political order. In recent years, these modernization themes have been boosted even more vigorously by the forces of "globalization from above" and liberalization controlled by the powerful nation states, transnational corporations and international agencies or regimes.

Yet, as the countless voices of ordinary peoples in marginalized contexts worldwide have passionately revealed, such modernization and globalization have accentuated structural violence against the poor majorities. It is estimated that some 1.2 billion human beings live on less then $1 a day. More than 30,000 children die daily from preventable causes.

More than 1 billion people live in inadequate housing, while many millions are homeless worldwide. There are over 250 million child labourers suffering exploitation and poverty. In the area of health, apart from continual and even worsening symptoms of preventable diseases, the HIV/AIDS pandemic has afflicted millions of human beings with tragic long term social legacies. A number of modernization "successes" especially the so called NICs, may be cited, though even these have now suffered major setbacks and economic crisis. But within most societies, the income wealth gaps have worsened between the elites and the marginalized sectors.

Structural injustices and economic exploitation have combined with political systems to undermine entitlements and opportunities for the majorities to meet even their basic needs. These structures and relationships of internal inequities within the South (and increasingly North as well) are interconnected simultaneously with international and global injustices whereby the North disproportionately benefit from regimes of trade, investment, debt, structural adjustment and even aid. The income gap between the richest and poorest countries has increased from 35 to 1 in 1950, 44 to 1 in 1973, and 72 to 1 in 1992. Over 198097, the total debt of the poorest nations grew from US$568 billion to over $2 trillion~ yet in that same period, these same nations repaid $2.9 trillion in principal and interest rates. We must therefore face the challenges of world poverty and recognize that the root causes are inequalities and injustices.

As the former UN Secretary General, Kofi Annan stated: "true peace is far more than the absence of war. It is a phenomenon that encompasses economic development and social justice." Respected religious leaders like Pope John Paul II and the Dalai Lama have constantly reminded the world that there is no peace without justice. More recently, the ILO (International Labour Organization) sponsored the World Commission on the Social Dimensions of Globalization: A Fair Globalization. In its report, the Commission noted that "while wealth is being created ... too many countries and people are not sharing in its benefits." The Commission therefore calls for globalization that is "fair, inclusive, democratically governed, and provides Opportunities and tangible benefits for all countries and peoples."

Confronted with these realities of a structurally violent paradigm of "development", ordinary peoples, NGOs, peoples' organizations, social institutions (e.g. religious, education), global networks of advocates, and some critical political and governmental representatives have been Mobilizing and implementing alternative thinking and strategies for a development paradigm that one acronym PEACE refers to as participatory, equitable, appropriate (in values and technology), critically empowering and ecologically sustainable. Education for such more peaceful development that meets as its central priority the basic needs of all citizens and rethinks the goals of high consumerist, technologically advanced "progress" is clearly a major pillar of peace. From rural to urban contexts, the poor and solidarity groups are empowering themselves through self reliant, and sustainable projects. Worldwide, there is an intensifying campaign to persuade states and banks to cancel the crippling debts of South nations. Holistic framework of peace education, it is therefore important to relate the principle of justice with the ethics of compassion.

In many civilizations and faiths, compassion is an ethical principle for guiding all interrelationships from micro to macro levels of life. Unlike pity, compassion means Being able to express authentic feelings for the suffering of others and then being moved by one's conscience and spirituality to help transform the conditions that lead to such suffering, such as unjust relationships and structures. Also, the "giver" needs to look self critically at him/her and ask if he/she may be directly or indirectly responsible for the suffering of the recipients. In contrast, compassion requires a willingness to acknowledge responsibility for conditions of structural violence (e.g., corporate and state policies of one's nation) and to express solidarity with the marginalized through personal and social actions for local/global justice.

In many North societies, a whole spectrum of aid and development NGOs has grown over the decades to promote links of solidarity with South peoples, NGOs and POs engaged in grassroots development~ to advocate for alternative aid, trade and other foreign policies of their Governments that would reverse North South inequities~ And to challenge those activities of global organizations and globalization that further marginalize poor and vulnerable majorities. Hence, there is a great need for education which develops a spirit of compassion and justice among the affluent peoples and sectors in both North and South nations.

Promoting Human Rights and Responsibilities

For over fifty years, much effort has been undertaken to realize the vision embodied in the Universal Declaration on Human Rights and numerous successive covenants, conventions, treaties and other international instruments. Whether civil, political, economic, social or cultural in focus and application, human rights legislation, policies and practices have reminded us that all people have inalienable rights that must be promoted at individual, community, national and international levels of life. While acknowledging the progress that has been made in promoting human rights, still it is essential to be reminded that a wide gap still exists between theory and practice. In so many societies, human rights violations continue to cause great suffering, pain and indignities to countless men, women and children.

The enormous challenges of promoting and respecting human rights can be likened to trying to keep alight candles in the midst of a storm, where the candles refer to the inherent dignities that all human beings deserve in the spirit of the Universal Declaration and successive covenants, conventions and charters. However, the power entrenched in structures of state, private interests, sociocultural systems and global agencies still blow strong winds trying to snuff out the light of human rights and dignities. The risk taking and dedicated work of human rights campaigners to educate and mobilize citizens and institutions to resist violations and to assert rights in all spheres and levels of life is surely another vital pathway towards building a culture of peace.

Our human rights will be better protected and promoted when ordinary peoples educate and empower ourselves to build a strong civil society to which agencies of state and private power must be accountable in the spirit of authentic democracy. The field of human rights is complex, so we must try to understand fully its complexity if we are to embark on this pathway. For example, we must uphold the universality of all human rights, although we need to be sensitive to cultural diversity. But as human rights advocates and the numerous international conventions and instruments emphasize, cultural beliefs and practices cannot be used as a rationale to violate human rights. For example, in some cultures and communities, women can be subject to physical or other violence in their homes. Such domestic violence cannot be justified as a cultural norm or practice.

We must recognize the indivisibility and interrelatedness of all rights, thereby avoiding the earlier emphasis on individual civil and political rights to the neglect of social, economic, cultural, group, peoples and solidarity rights. We must legitimize the role of NGOs and peoples' organizations in promoting human rights, and to address root causes rather than symptoms of human rights violations. Finally, in promoting human rights, we must also equally promote human responsibilities. More specifically, a culture of peace is very attentive to the vital realm of women's and children's human rights. Women's contribution not only to their own peace but to their entire communities and societies is acknowledged as indispensable hitherto gender biased development models are reshaped to equitably benefit women.

Mobilizing around the historic Convention on the Rights of the Child, NGOs have engaged in critical education and to defend children against exploitation, marginalization and violence (economic, sexual, cultural, social, and domestic). In formal educational institutions, advocates have worked hard to integrate human rights education into teaching and learning. Teachers, parents, students and human rights NGOs like Amnesty International and the People's Decade for Human Rights Education have designed various curricula for promoting student awareness of local, national and global realities of human rights, and empowered action to protect and respect human rights in their societies or abroad. From the role modelling of human rights in their own school institution to advocating for release of political prisoners, abolition of the death penalty and improved rights of marginalized sectors, students will hopefully embrace a culture of human rights which in turn positively contributes to a culture of peace.

In this regard, it needs to be emphasized that educating for human rights also entails developing a sense and practice of responsibilities. At international and global levels, there is emerging a critical mass of human rights workers and organizations that are collaborating in public education across regions and continents for a fuller implementation of human rights provisions that many Governments have formally ratified, and demanding the human rights accountability of international development and global economic agencies. The recent positive steps forward in establishing the International Criminal Court, and tribunals for war crimes and other crimes against humanity, reflect the possibilities for peacefully bringing to justice those guilty of committing human rights violations. In connecting this theme of promoting human rights and responsibilities with interfaith dialogue, it is hopeful to see an increasing engagement of faith leaders with human rights advocates.

While the concept of "human rights' is not necessarily explicitly found in faith doctrines, the spirit underlying human rights norms is reflected in the principle of dignity and in values and norms of good conduct and human relationships taught by faith prophets and founders. As faith institutions join the human rights community to clarify the meaning of human rights embedded in all civilizations, this will help to overcome resistances to a universal conception of human rights achieved through participatory and equitable consensus rather than be determined by only one group or civilization. The relationships between human rights and faith are clearly very complex, and at times understandably controversial. In the field of human rights, the principle of the universality of rights is upheld, although as noted in the Vienna Convention, we need to be mindful of cultural and social differences.

Nevertheless, as human rights advocates and the numerous international conventions and instruments emphasize cultural beliefs and practices cannot be used as a rationale to violate human rights (e.g. the rights of women or children). Most importantly, the dialogue between faiths and human rights needs to be open to clarifying faith values, norms and practices that may be barriers to the full realization of human rights and dignities (e.g. on issues of gender, children, sexuality, conscience, individual visàvis group rights etc).

Reconciliation and Solidarity

Conflicts between peoples of different cultures, ethnic/ "racial" identities, while not new in human history, are posing major problems of peacelessness and tragic violence in the context of a militarized and structurally violent world. Often, it is not the cultural differences alone that result in conflict. Rather we have to look at a broad range of root causes and factors such as the contest for resources and territories. There are also often historical injustices which are the underlying causes of such conflicts, as in the colonization of Indigenous or aboriginal peoples. As earlier noted, the dominant modernization paradigm is further marginalizing Indigenous or aboriginal peoples who are portrayed as standing in the way of "progress" as forests are logged, energy infrastructures constructed, mining proliferate to meet industrialization and consumerism, and agribusinesses expand into the hinterlands.

In societies which have traditionally been culturally diverse, or have become more multicultural through immigration, such as Canada and Australia, there is a need to promote values and attitudes as well as cultural policies based on mutual respect, understanding, nondiscrimination, and no racism on the basis of ethnicity, faith, and other cultural characteristics., In recent decades, the growth of ethnic and religious intolerance and prejudices have led to tragic conflict including physical violence in different parts of the Asia Pacific region. Since 9/11 and the subsequent "war on terrorism", peoples of Arab and/or Muslim heritage have also suffered racist attacks and profiling, which need to be challenged and overcome. Another pathway towards building a culture of peace is therefore promoting active harmony between cultural groups within nations and between nations.

A peaceful world is not feasible without the ability and willingness of all groups to live nonviolently in unity amidst diversity. In this regard, the thesis being promulgated by some thinkers and political leaders that world security is being threatened by a "clash of civilizations" urgently needs demystification. This simplistic argument overlooks the complexities of "civilizations", and also dangerously pits one civilization or culture against another despite the historical evidence of cooperation and solidarity even when conflicts or even wars have occurred. In many multicultural societies, formal school curricula and institutional environments have been integrating principles, values and strategies of intercultural and multicultural education. It means that when we look at the history of a nation, it must be inclusive of the histories of all groups and cultures.

We need to raise our consciousness and sensitivity of different cultures. All groups deserve to receive equitable respect and nondiscrimination. We need skills training to reconcile existing intercultural conflicts nonviolently. However, peace educators are also critical of versions of multicultural education that merely "celebrate" cultural differences in superficial ways without promoting critical understanding of and solidarity in resolving root causes of intercultural disharmony (e.g. racism, discrimination, structural injustices, and historical oppression). In this regard, Indigenous peoples would not view intercultural education as valid if it does not actively promote their identity and wisdom traditions so crucial to their cultural survival.

The current forces of globalization are also resulting in "cultural homogenization". There is strong psychological pressure on more and more peoples regardless of civilization to consuming the same fast food, wearing the same jeans, shirts, cosmetics~ talking and texting into the same cell phones~ Watching the same TV programmes~ singing the same popular songs and emulating the movie stars. Hence in the pathway of active harmony between cultures, we must also encourage a healthy pride in one's cultural identity and roots. On the pathway of active harmony between cultures, representatives of diverse faiths, religions and spiritual traditions are meeting to promote interfaith, interreligious or ecumenical dialogue deemed crucial to developing greater active harmony of peoples within and across societies. From dialogue and respect comes a process of reconciliation and healing of bitterness, enmity and distrust?

At local, national and international levels, faith and interfaith organizations and networks such as the World Conference on Religions and Peace or the World Parliament of Religions are providing educational and empowering spaces for diverse faith leaders and followers to work for nonviolent and just interfaith and intercultural relationships. Through dialogue, members of diverse faiths are recognizing that they all have many common values and ethical principles for guiding relationships among all peoples and cultures. In turn, this sense of common humanity will hopefully lead to collaborative action among all faiths to resolve common societal and global problems (e.g., injustice, violence, human rights violations, discrimination, racism, and ecological destruction).

Importantly, peace educators focusing on intercultural harmony are also acknowledging the vital role of Indigenous or traditional social cultural ways of resolving conflicts. Furthermore, in educating toward a culture of peace, building cultural respect and reconciliation, will not suffice. Also urgently needed is cultural solidarity. This is because in situations of unequal power relations and injustices, cultural groups that are already economically and politically advantaged have a social responsibility to be in solidarity with marginalized groups and communities.

This is especially clear in the struggles of Indigenous peoples for their right to self determination and to challenge globalization from above. No Indigenous peoples need to express solidarity with their Indigenous sisters and brothers and with other minority groups to challenge and dismantle prejudices, discrimination, and racism. Hence, in promoting interfaith dialogue for peace through the Griffith University Multifaith Centre, we have focused on themes such as reconciliation with Indigenous peoples, compassion for refugees, and social justice for the marginalized worldwide.

Living in Harmony with the Earth

In every region and corner of the world, the effects of environmental destruction are being increasingly felt, whether it be pollution of land, air, and water~ soil degradation, depletion of nonrenewable resources~ exhaustion of fisheries~ deforestation~ and global warming. This deepening ecological crisis reflects the violence that humanity is inflicting on the earth, which demands a truly determined effort to protect the environment from further destruction and to design alternative relationships between human beings and planets based on principles of sustainability. Clearly a root cause of environmental destruction stems from an unsustainable paradigm of development based on unlimited economic growth that prioritizes profit maximization and aggressive competition for resources.

As Wackernagel and Rees and other environmentalists have estimated, the ecological footprint of industrialized North societies is many times heavier than that of South countries. Each person, country, and society has a responsibility to lighten their ecological footprint by, among other remedies, rejecting over consumerism and shifting towards renewable sources of energy (e.g., solar, wind, hydrogen, etc.). Even before the Rio Conference on Environment and Development, the impact of the environmental movement on individual citizens, institutions and governments was clearly noticeable. The world has been inspired by grassroots initiatives such as the famous Chipko campaign among tribal Indians to save their forests and hence their social, economic and cultural survival, as well as nonviolent actions taken by global environmental NGOs against environmentally destruction (e.g. nuclear testing, deforestation, toxic waste dumping, reduction of biodiversity).

Citizens and communities in virtually all regions and countries have been empowered to speak out and act to live in peace with mother earth. In many countries, women and Indigenous peoples who have borne the brunt of environmental degradation, have organized to act as "stewards" to save their local environment in order to better and sustainably meet the basic needs of their families and communities. Increasingly, religious institutions and leaders have spoken out for "green theology" and inspired their communities to practice their faith inclusive with reverence for the earth. A growing number of governments and even corporations are also adding their voices on behalf of environmental protection in response to the deepening problems of global warming, ozone layer destruction, and other symptoms of the ecological crisis. Yet, as the Rio Conference outcomes and the recent World Summit on Sustainable Development in South Africa indicated, determined action by governments and private sector agencies to promote ecologically sustainable "development" remain limited by the overriding principles of growth centred globalization.

While encouraging some efforts by business to contribute to sustainability in policies and practices, there is regrettably growing evidence of a kind of corporate 'green washing" that is being challenged by civil society groups worldwide. A fourth crucial pathway towards building a culture of peace is therefore, educating for saving the environment. But "sustainable development" needs to go beyond individual and state action to recycle, limit greenhouse gas emissions, efficient energy use, or save species from extinction. Unless human beings relate to the natural environment according to the ethic of intergenerational responsibility, future generations will not be able to survive. Hence, peace oriented environmental education raises basic questions of over materialist and over consumerist lifestyles. Secondly, it must talk about green justice, so that environmentalist agendas and North South relationships simultaneously enable peoples to meet their basic needs and rights free from structural violence.

If "sustainable development" is conditioned to serve the unchanged goals of growth centred globalization, the roots of the ecological crisis will remain unshaken. In formal educational systems, environmental education has become a regular theme in school curricula and pedagogy. While initial emphasis has been placed on educating children to be personally and socially green and for schools to be environmentally friendly (e.g. recycle, reuse, reduce, save animal and plant species), there is a recognition that a holistic perspective to environmental education must dig deep into the roots of the crisis. Hence, personal earth caring must integrate principles of structural justice and rights between groups and nations, challenge modernization ideals of growth and consumerism, advocate voluntary simplicity in lifestyle and promote the concept of earth rights. Turning to interfaith dialogue, there is clearly a growth of awareness and commitment among many faith leaders, believers and institutions on the theme of living in harmony with the earth.

The values and principles of ecospirituality or "green theology" can be found or discerned in the holy texts and doctrines of diverse faiths. Christian environmentalists like Thomas Berry and Sean McDonagh emphasize that "stewardship" is a more authentic expression of Christ's message than "dominion". The Holy Qur'an teaches us to care for all creatures, not just humanity. In Buddhism, all parts of the universe are interdependent, and hence loving kindness and compassion needs to be extended to all beings and the earth. Many other faiths, including Indigenous spirituality, call on their communities to practice their faith inclusive with reverence for the earth. It is also in the link between the themes of "living with justice and compassion" and "living in harmony with the earth" where interfaith dialogue can be an integrating force. The values and principles of faiths should motivate people to consume more moderately and live simpler lifestyles, which in turn create conditions for a just world where everyone can meet their basic needs in dignity and sustainably.

Cultivating Inner Peace

The five previous themes of education for a culture of peace have focused mainly on visible relationships and structures of human life. But there is a growing consensus that the inner dimensions and sources of peaceful values and practices should not be ignored. As the prophets, saints, and sages of diverse faiths and spirituality traditions have counselled, each human being has a need and responsibility to cultivate a deep sense of inner peace. For thousands of years, many methods of meditation and contemplation have been shown to help develop inner equilibrium and tranquility. The patient growing of spirituality that accompanies this deepening of inner peace is seen as an intrinsic goal of living. There is also a basic assumption here that core values and root principles of diverse cultures and/or faiths provide guidance and inspiration for developing a culture of inner peace.

This is especially relevant in today's frantic pace of life, as more and more people find less and less time for quiet contemplation and equilibrium surrounded by excessive competition and consumerism. Serious symptoms of inner peacelessness are evident such as increasing diseases of addictions, depression and alienation, for which chemicals are prescribed as "cures". At the same time, peace education cautions us against cultivating inner peace in a selfcentered way. Can we, for example, be contented with a sense of inner peace while ignoring the multiple and pervasive realities of peacelessness in our societies and our world, or even more importantly, avoiding a self critical assessment of our potential or actual complicity in generating outer conflict and violence?

It is vital therefore for educators to link cultivation of inner peace with a strong responsibility to the building of outer peace. Furthermore, there are many voices arguing that in cultivating inner peace, peoples from diverse traditions, faiths and cultures are better prepared ethically, emotionally, and spiritually to work for outer or society have emerged largely in South contexts under the inspiration of ''liberation theology'', members are motivated to deeply embrace Christian values and principles so as to experience authentic inner transformation. At the same time, such interiorization goes hand in hand with critical social analysis that challenges members to work for more peaceful, just communities and the larger society. In Buddhist societies, there is also a growing reinterpretation of the role of the clergy as well as Buddhist practices of inner peace or the search for personal "enlightenment". Thus while the central principles and purposes of prayer and meditation practices towards self enlightenment remain vital, Social Buddhism does not remain alienated from societal events, especially those promoting peacelessness.

A search for inner peace is guided by Buddhist principles of nonattachment to things and power, moderation in lifestyle, and compassion for all beings. In Islam, the greater "jihad" is to struggle for inner purification. But at the same time, a Muslim is expected to strongly promote the principle of social justice and to care for the wellbeing of all other members of society and by extension, the whole world. In some programs of holistic peace education, the theme of inner peace is explored through exercises that challenge learners to examine meanings and implications of inner peace development across various levels of life: the very personal and interpersonal~ One's work and institutional environment place citizens in the society and world. This approach reminds learners that the "inner" and the "personal" are infused with the social and structural and vice versa so that social action for peace draws deeply on inner peace values and spiritualities.

Education, Empowerment and Transformation

The journey along the six possible themes will not be easy, short or smooth. It will demand commitment, courage and above all patience. It calls for a process of education, which then empowers, and hopefully leads to transformation. Education and acting for a culture of peace, no matter which pathway you are walking on, is also not a simplistic process. There are four principles that are essential guides in educating for a culture of peace. First, we have the principle of holism. We need to be holistic. A holistic framework always tries to clarify possible interrelationships between and among different problems of peacelessness, conflict and violence in terms of root causes and resolutions. Holism also applies in not isolating various levels and modes of peace education (e.g. formal, nonformal, children to adults, social, economic and cultural groups) since they need to complement, sustain and support each other as being more superior or inferior.

Secondly, educating for a culture of peace emphasizes the role of values. The peace educator constantly encourages learners to surface innermost values that shape their understanding of realities and their actions in the world. Clearly, peace education needs to be very explicit about its preferred values, such as compassion, justice, equity~ gender fairness, caring for life, sharing, reconciliation, integrity, hope and active nonviolence. Commitment to nonviolence needs to be active, not passive, so that we are indeed moved to transform a culture of violence. Hope is vital to avoid being overwhelmed by the massive problems of conflicts into helplessness or powerlessness. A third pedagogical principle of peace education rests on the value and strategy of dialogue. It would be a contradiction if educating for peace becomes an exercise in "banking", as teachers assumes the role of authoritarian "experts" and learners become passive recipients of peace knowledge. A dialogical strategy, however, cultivates a more horizontal teacher learner relationship in which both educate and learn from each other.

The realities and voices of learners yield essential inputs into the learning process and learners have opportunities for critical reflection leading to transformation. A fourth principle for practicing peace education is critical empowerment or what the Brazilian adult educator Paulo Freire has called concretization. While dialogical, participatory and non banking pedagogies and methodologies are crucial, they are not sufficient. Peace education must move not just our minds but also our hearts and spirits into personal and social action for peace building. In short, educating for peace is educating for critical empowerment through which we develop a critical consciousness that actively seeks to transform the realities of a culture of war and violence into a culture of peace and nonviolence.

General Information on Religion

The word religion is one that has been at the centre of total unity and peace, and yet has also been the cause of war, death, and destruction. Religion is a very diverse subject and has had a profound impact upon the world for thousands of years. There are many different religions in the world, and within each religion there can also be different variations, so religions can be a complex and very detailed topic. A religion is a set of beliefs and the belief in one or several supreme beings. Some religions worship and believe in one God, whereas others, such as Hinduism, believe in several Gods. The largest religion in the world is Christianity, and even this is split into a number of variations, such as Roman Catholics and Protestants.

Religion is subject than can spawn both love and hate, and is one of the most controversial subjects in history. Those that practise their religions have a set of certain beliefs, a set of traditions that are followed, and a variety of holy days that are celebrated. Devout religious people and families live their lives in a certain way, as is required by their religion. This site aims to provide some basic details about some of the different and more wellknown religions from around the world. You can find out more about the background of these religions, as well as look into the beliefs, variations, traditions, and holy days of each of the religions. You will notice that some of the religions are very similar in their beliefs and traditions, such as Judaism and Christianity.

Judaism

Judaism is one of three Abrahmic religions, along with Islam and Christianity. The Jewish influence on the world throughout history has been prominent. The religion, which is about 3500 years old, began in the Middle East. Known as the parent faith of Christianity, it is based on a founding by Moses and Abraham. There are currently around twelve millions followers of Judaism, and they are mainly situated in Israel and the United States. One of the tragedies in which Jews will always be remembered for their suffering is the holocaust, where six millions Jews lost their lives in an attempt to wipe out Judaism.

The religion and culture of the Jewish people includes historical, social, and political dimensions in addition to the religious. The word "Judaism" derives from the Greek Ioudaismos, a term first used in the intertestamental period by Greek speaking Jews to distinguish their religion from hellenism. In the NT the word appears twice in reference to Paul's prior consuming devotion to Jewish faith and life. Hebrew religion began to give rise to Judaism after the destruction of the temple and the exile of Judah in 586 BC. The term "Jew," in its biblical use, is almost exclusively postexilic.

The Jewish religion of the biblical period evolved through such historical stages as the intertestamental, rabbinic, and medieval to the modern period of the nineteenth century with Orthodox, Conservative, and Reform Judaism. Along the way Jewish religion took on new teachings and practices. But with the lengthy development of Judaism and its many changes it is incorrect to posit, as some have done, that Jewish history produced two separate religions: an OT religion of Israel and the postexilic religion of Judaism. Despite the shifting phases of its history, the essence of the religious teaching of Judaism has remained remarkably constant, firmly rooted in the Hebrew Scriptures (OT). Judaism is a religion of ethical monotheism. For centuries many Jews have sought to distill its essential features from one biblical verse that calls Israel "to act justly, to love mercy and to walk humbly with your God".

The Babylonian exile brought certain modifications in Jewish religious life. Deprived of land, temple, and cultic priestly ministrations, Judaism began to adopt a no sacrificial religion. Jews began to gather in homes for the reading of Scripture, for prayer and instruction. Here may be traced the earliest roots of the synagogue. Now "lip sacrifice" (prayer and penitence) rather than "blood sacrifice" (sheep and goats) became central to the life of piety. There was one thing Israel carried to Babylon and clung to dearly. It was the law, the Torah, for by it Israel was assured of its divine calling and mission. In the fifth century the "father of Judaism," Ezra the scribe enacted religious reforms by appealing to the Torah.

The priesthood was purified and mixed marriages dealt with as the principles of the law became applied to every detail of life. Gradually many Jews came to believe that here lay the only real proof of who was a true Jew: vigorous, unflinching obedience to the teachings of Torah. Scribes became the priestly interpreters of the Torah, setting forth their own authoritative teachings. By the second century BC the Pharisees taught that the oral law carried the same authority as the Law of Moses. Later Jesus denied that the traditions of men were equal in authority to the written law (Mark 7:1 23); in addition, Paul denied that man could be justified before God by perfect obedience to that law.

The destruction of the temple in 70 AD and the scattering of thousands of Jews from the land brought a sudden demise to the priesthood. Johanan ben Zakkai, a Pharisee, was soon permitted by the Romans to open an academy at Jabneh. He took it upon himself to install rabbis as the keepers and legislators of Torah. By word of mouth the rabbis passed their teachings from generation to generation until the oral law (Mishnah) was written down about 200 AD, Rabbi Judah ha Nasi its chief editor. By 500 AD the Talmud was completed with the issuing of the Gemara, a rabbinical commentary on the Mishnah. The Talmud contains more than 6,000 folio pages and references to more than 2,000 scholar teachers. It became the basic document of rabbinic Judaism, and still holds a major place in shaping Jewish thought.

Basic Doctrines and Beliefs

According to the teaching of Judaism there is no set of beliefs upon the acceptance of which the Jew may find salvation. Even Maimonides' thirteen articles of faith, as close as Judaism ever came to a catechism, is not binding on the conscience of Jews. Judaism has historically put more stress upon the deed (miswa) than the creed ('ani ma 'amin, "I believe"). Nevertheless, from Talmudic times, as a way of life Judaism has been distinguished by giving special emphasis to certain beliefs and ethical values.

In the Mishnah (Abot 1:2) one sees the broad philosophy that governed the minds of the early rabbis:

"By three things is the world sustained:

- By the law,
- By the (temple) service,
- And by deeds of lovingkindness."

This basic teaching is further underscored by the threefold function of the synagogue as a "house of study" (for learning of Torah), "house of prayer" (for worship of God), and "house of assembly" (for the care of community needs). Contemporary Judaism often speaks of four foundational pillars of the Jewish faith, each interacting as a major force as part of the covenant: (1) The Torah, always a living law as the written Torah is understood in light of the oral Torah; (2) God, a unity (one), spiritual (not a body), and eternal; (3) The people (Israelites

Jews), called into being by God as members of one family, a corporate personality, a community of faith; and (4) The land (known today as Eretz Yisrael), a bond going back to Abraham, the "father of the Hebrew people".

In its modern expression Judaism is also shaped by the following traditional beliefs:

1. Man is pivotal in the universe. He sees himself as partner with God in the unending process of creation. In rabbinic thought, "God needs man as much as man needs God."
2. Man is a responsible moral agent, fully accountable for his acts. He is free to shape his own destiny.
3. Human progress is possible as man realizes the great potential within him. The nature of man is basically good, or neutral, free from the encumbrance of original sin. Thus man may be optimistic and hopeful about his future.
4. "This worldliness" is a distinguishing mark of Judaism. The Hebrew Scriptures focus more on earth and man than upon heaven and God. Hence, lengthy speculation about the afterlife and otherworldly realities has never occupied a major position in Jewish thought.
5. All of life must be regarded as sacred. Man is to seek to imitate God in sanctifying his every action. Time must be imbued with the seeds of eternity.
6. Man is to pursue peace, justice, and righteousness. Salvation is dependent upon the betterment of society through good deeds. Historically, Jews have seen the Messiah as God's anointed human representative (not a God man) who would usher in a golden age of societal and spiritual redemption. Today, however, Reform Judaism teaches that the Messianic Age will appear when humankind collectively, by its acts, reaches a level of true enlightenment, peace, and justice.

Some Basic Jewish Beliefs

Judaism is based around a single God who created the Universe and continues to affect people and everything they do. Jewish people abide by God's laws and attempt to live holy lives, as they believe that they were chosen by God to set an example of holiness to the world. This is not to say that they see themselves as superior to others, but simply as chosen to set an example to others. Jews also believe strongly in a community life, and this is strongly affected by the way they live their lives and in everything that they do. This religion and the events and activities tied to Judaism is strongly based around home and family life.

The Jewish also believe that all people are created equal, because all people are created in the image of God. The Jewish also believe that this likeness extends to peoples' intellect, and therefore people are responsible for their choices and actions because they have free will. Unlike Christians, the Jewish religion does not recognize Jesus as the Messiah, which is the major difference between Christianity and Judaism, as both religions are very similar in many other ways. The topic of Jewish beliefs is a complex and detailed one, but the most widely accepted listing of beliefs is Rambam's thirteen principles of faith.

Practices in Judaism

There are a number of Jewish practices that are part of normal life as part of this faith. They include:

- Observing the day of rest, Sabbath, and ensuring that all chores are finished by sundown each Friday. This lasts until sundown on Saturday.
- The celebration of Bar Mitzvah and Bat Mitzvah, which signify the Jewish coming of age of a boy (at age thirteen) or a girl (at age twelve)
- Attending a synagogue regularly
- The celebration of Passover, which is each spring, where it is customary to eat a special, ritual meal at home.

Jewish Holy Days

There are a number of Holy days in Judaism, and the holiest time of the year is in the autumn. Some of the holy days and festivals celebrated as part of Judaism include:

- Sabbath (also known in Hebrew as Shabbat) This runs from sunset Friday to sunset Saturday, and is the day of rest as required by God.
- Rosh Hashanah A commemoration of the creation of the world, and a celebration of the New Year.
- Passover: This is a celebration to remember the escape from captivity in Egypt.
- Days of Repentance This is a tenday period, which allows people to repent.
- Yom Kipper This comes at the end of the Days of Repentance and is a very sacred day in the Jewish calendar.
- Sukkot This is to celebrate God taking special care of the Jewish when traveling through the desert to reach the Promised Land. It is also in remembrance of the time spent traveling through the desert.

Christianity

Christianity has over one thousand millions followers, making it the most popular religion in the world. This faith is based on the teaching of Jesus Christ, who was believed to be the Son of God. Over 2000 years old, this religion began in the Middle East, and was founded by Jesus Christ's followers. The holy book studied by Christians is the old and new testament of the Bible.

Some Basic Christian Beliefs

Christianity is a hugely popular religion, and beliefs can vary amongst practising Christians. However, some Christian beliefs include:

- There is only one God, and Christians refer to God as 'Father'.
- Jesus Christ was the Son of God, sent as a Saviour to mankind, and that he was crucified and resurrected.
- God is the Trinity–the Father, the Son, and the Holy Spirit.
- There is life after death and eternal life.
- God created the universe and all that is in it.

- Jesus Christ was born from an immaculate conception to the Virgin Mary.
- Jesus will one day return to judge both the living and the deceased.
- Repenting your sins and confirming your belief in Jesus means you will be forgiven.
- Anyone can have salvation in the name of Jesus.

Practices in Christianity

There are a number of Christian practices that are part of normal life as part of this faith. They include:

- Sharing of bread and drinking wine in commemoration of the last supper. This is known as Eucharist.
- Confessing in order to gain forgiveness, which is known as penance.
- Baptism, which is immersion in or anointment with holy water, as a representation of being born again and the belief in Christ.
- Sunday worship – attending church in order to worship.

Christian Holy Days

- Annunciation : This is to signify the announcement of Mary's pregnancy by the angel Gabriel. The Feast of Annunciation is on 25 th March.
- Christmas : A celebration of the birth of Jesus Christ
- Lent : This is a forty day period of repenting, where Christians fast and deny themselves of something that they enjoy. This signifies Jesus' time in the desert, when he fasted for forty days.
- Palm Sunday : This is the Sunday before Easter, and is a commemoration of Jesus' entry into Jerusalem.
- Maundy/Holy Thursday : This is on commemoration of the Last Upper, and is on the Thursday prior to Easter Sunday.
- Good Friday : This is in commemoration of Jesus' crucifixion, and is signified by prayer and penance.

- Holy Saturday : This is in commemoration of Jesus' burial.
- Easter Sunday : This is in commemoration of the resurrection of Jesus.

Hinduism

Hinduism is the major religion of the people of Southeast Asia, but there are followers of Hinduism in every country of the world. Beginning in India about 30,000 years ago, it is based on ancient writings known as the "Vedas". This religion embraces an entire way of life. It includes a set of rules that has traditionally organized the people into the caste system. Hindis (people who follow Hinduism) maintain there are many ways to believe in God and there is very little set doctrine that they must believe.

There are many temples that are supervised by priests, but the followers can worship in any way they choose. Hinduism contains a belief in nature gods, village gods, spirits and sacred objects. Some Hindis have organized these gods into a trinity of Brahma the Creator, Vishnu the Preserver and Shiva the Destroyer combined in one single Supreme Being.

Some of the Beliefs and Practices of Hinduism

Views of God:

- Impersonal God : Some Hindis regard God as an impersonal spirit called Brahman. They call the physical world maya or appearance because they believe that physical appearance is a distorted view of reality.
- Personal God : Many Hindis believe the Supreme Being is a God of Love who created the universe, preserves it for billions of years and then destroys it to start the cycle all over again. This God is often shown in statues of Vishna with several heads or many arms and legs. Worshippers of Vishnu are called Vaishnavas and believe that God hears their prayers and comes to earth to help men. Some Hindis believe this personal God to be Shiva and are called Shivas. They believe God to be the personification of many forces of nature and represent him

as dancing, symbolizing the cosmic creation of creation and destruction.

Views of Man:

- Man and the Universe : All objects in the universe have souls related to God and these are ranked in accordance of the level on which they are aware of their spiritual nature. Man is the highest level, but as long as he remains at the mercy of the demands of his body he remains ignorant of his spiritual nature. He is condemned to be reborn and his morality determines the level at which he will be reborn.
- Man and Society *:* Souls are born into varying levels of economic and social groups. There are four broad classifications of the economic divisions called varnas. Priests, teachers and government officials are the highest level with rulers, officials and soldiers on the next level. Farmers, bankers and other who control the economy are on the third level and craftsmen and labourers make up the fourth level of the caste system.

Stages of Salvation

Hinduism includes three margas, or paths to salvation. They are also called yogas and each path requires a different kind of discipline. The first stresses active participation in society, the second stresses devotion to God and the third stresses study and mystical contemplation. The first path of duty must be mastered before the others. Those who follow this must fulfill the social, economic and ritual obligations of his caste. The second marga is the most popular as it involves devotion to a personal God through worship.

Five sacrifices or offerings are made in homes every day – to the gods, to the ancestors, to the holy men of Hinduism, to all men who come as guests and to animals. Pious Hindis will not eat meat or kill any creatures and cows are regarded as scared. They fast at certain times of the year hold family religious celebrations and worship at temples. The third path to salvation is the path of knowledge. It is considered an effective, but hard method because it requires years of selfdiscipline, study and meditation.

Holy Days of Hinduism

Hindi celebrations vary widely according to location, but they generally include:

- Maha Shivrathri : A festival dedicated to Shiva in midFebruary.
- Holi : A carnival like festival held in early March dedicated to Krishna, the God of Pleasure.
- Ramnavami : The anniversary of the birth of Rami, who was believed to be an incarnation of Vishnu. This is held in late March.
- Wesak : The birthday of Buddha held in early April.
- Dusserah : A festival celebrating the triumph of good over evil celebrated in early November.
- Diwali : The Indian Festival of Lights held in mid November. This is mainly dedicated to Laskshmi, the Goddess of Wealth and is the Hindu New Year.

Buddhism

Buddhism Related Information:

Buddhism is a world religion based on the teachings and writings of Gautama Buddha – the Enlightened One. It has spread throughout Asia and has about 500 million people worldwide, but the heaviest concentration of followers is in Asia. It began as a reform movement within the Brahmin religion as opposition to the caste system. Buddha rejected the belief that the priests were at the top of this caste and that it was only after a lifetime of good conduct and rebirth could one attain salvation.

He taught that every man in his lifetime should strive to save himself from suffering by understanding that it was caused by egotistical desires. He believed that these desires were only a temporary bond holding together all the elements that composed the individual and it was only when man realized this truth about himself that he could overcome his desires.

Basic Beliefs of Buddhism

The basic Buddha belief is called the Four Noble Truths called the Middle Path a middle way between man's worldly physical indulgence and the religious ideal of extreme asceticism.

- First Noble Truth : Suffering pervades all life
- *Second Noble Truth:* The cause of suffering is desire for worldly things and this leads to future rebirths into future suffering.
- Third Noble Truth : To conquer what is desired is to attain Nirvana – a blissful state without desire.
- Fourth Noble Truth : The outline of a practical program for conquering desire, called the Noble Eightfold Path. This requires a correct orientation of mind and will with the right knowledge and resolve. There are three moral requirements*:* Right speech, right conduct and right occupation. There are also three mystical requirements*:* Right effort, right mindfulness and right concentration.

Divisions of Buddhism

There are two basic divisions within Buddhism – Thervada and Mahayana. Thervada holds to the strict interpretation of Buddha. The term means "doctrine of the elders" and demands extreme selfreliance. Each follower believes that there are no gods or men to help him achieve Nirvana. The goal is to become a saint who has attained Nirvana. The usual way to achieve this is to enter a monastic order in order to spend his life preparing for Nirvana. A monk refrains from violence, intoxicating substances, women, and unethical acts. His only possessions are his yellow robe, a begging bowl, a needle, prayer beads, a razor to shave his head and a filter to remove insects from drinking water so that he will not harm them. Buddhist laymen follow the ethics of Buddha and can gain merit by fasting, giving food to the monks and by building temples and monasteries.

Mahayana is a more liberal form of Buddhism emphasizing mercy, both in ethics and the view of the superhuman world. Its followers believe that they are not alone in their search for Nirvana and that there is one Supreme Being manifested through lesser Buddhas, such as Buddha and Amitabha. They pray to many men who have attained Nirvana. Monks are prevalent in this division, but they may marry and own property. Laymen worship at household shrines and public temples.

Buddhist Holy Days:

- Nirvana Day : Commemorates the death of Siddhartha Guatana Buddha and is held in mid February.
- New Year Day *:* Celebrated in mid February in China, Korea and Vietnam.
- Wesak : Buddha's birthday celebrated in April or May.
- Khao Pansa *:* The beginning of Lent and is the day most Buddhists are ordained as monks. It is celebrated in the full moon of the eighth month, typically July.
- Boun Ok Pansa *:* The end of Lent coming at the end of October in the rainy season.
- Bodhi Day *:* Buddha's enlightenment in 596 BC, celebrated in early December.

Islam

Islam is one of the world religions that is practiced by over one billion people, with about 20% of these in the Middle East. The term "Islam" means surrender and the followers of Islam are called Muslims who surrender to the will of Allah, the Arabic word for God. In this religion, Allah is seen as the creator, sustainer and restorer of life. The will of God was transmitted to Mohammed in the Qur'an. He was persecuted for his teachings and fled to Mecca. Here his teachings were accepted and the Islamic religion emerged.

The date of the flight of Mohammed, called the hijrah, in

622 AD, is the date Muslims attribute to the beginnings of their calendar. Islam has acquired a characteristic of uniting the spiritual and temporal and aspects of life. It seeks to regulate an individual's relationship with God, as well as the relationship with people in social setting. There is an Islamic private institution and an Islamic code governing society as a whole. To the followers, Islam is a religious community committed to bringing its own value systems to the world through the jihad - holy war.

The Religion of Islam

Introduction

A. "Islam" means "submission". A follower of the religion of Islam is called a "Muslim" which means "one who is in submission to the divine will."

B. Islam is the youngest of the 5 major religions of the world. According to the best estimates, there are 800,000,000 to 1 billion Muslims worldwide. At present, over 20 million Muslims reside in Europe. There are now over 2000 mosques in England! The U.S.S.R., the 4th largest Muslim nation in the world, has 53 million adherents representing 1/5th of the total population. After ethnic Russians, Muslims are the largest population group but are growing 4 times as fast, and may outnumber them in less than 20 years. Currently, there are 48 nations where adherents of Islam are in the majority.

C. The current resurgence of Islam began with the oil cartel following the Yom Kippur War of 1973. Millions of dollars from enormous foundations are being spent to fuel the worldwide expansion of Islam. There are now more adherents of Islam in the U.S. than Episcopalians!

D. Nota bene: The greatest threat to world peace and stability in the next decade or two may be the result of the religion of Islam. Almost every controversy in the Middle East can be traced to this religion, either through intraparty squabbles, or Islam verses nonIslam.

The religion was founded by Muhammad who was born in 570 A.D. in a small village (Mecca) along a caravan route in what is today known as Saudi Arabia. The young Muhammad, an orphan at an early age, had an inquiring mind and an intense interest in religion. The prevailing religion at this time in Arabia was one of polytheism and animism. He inquired of both Judaism and Christianity. The Christianity that he came into contact was of a very heretical sort. Christianity at this time was losing its vitality and was about to enter the Dark Ages.

At about 25 years of age Muhammad married a wealthy widow 15 years his senior. Due to the ensuing economic security, Muhammad turned the more to religious contemplation often retiring to caves in the wilderness for long periods of time. He practiced fasting and was prone to dreams. He had a profound dissatisfaction with the polytheism and superstition of his day. He received his first of many "revelations" at 40 years of age, and thought at first he was possessed of a demon. Later he claims he was visited by the angel Gabriel who informed him to warn the people. This marked the beginning of his prophetic office.

The response in Mecca to his claims was small and limited mainly to family members. Soon he and his followers (around 200) were forced to flee. This flight to Medina occurred in 622 A.D. and is known as "The Hegira". In Medina, Muhammad became a leader and theocratic head of the town. Muslims reckon time from the Hegira. 622 A.D. = the year 1 A.H. In less than a 100 years Islam spread from the Atlantic Ocean across central Asia deep into India. This empire lasted over 1000 years. Only a handful of countries have ever reversed themselves after becoming an Islamic nation in 14 centuries of history!

Some Basic Beliefs of Islam

The most basic belief is the shahadah, the Muslim confession of faith There is no god but God; Muhammad is the prophet of God. They believe that God is merciful and is always willing to forgive if the person is genuinely repentant. The fundamental beliefs of Islam also include believing in angels, both good and bad, the books and Scriptures revealed to Mohammed, a series of prophets and the Last Day of Judgement. The foundation of Islam is the Five Pillars:

- Iman (Faith) – Faith or belief in the Oneness of God and the finality of the prophet.
- Salah (Prayer) – Prayers have to be preformed five times a day – dawn, middau, late afternoon, sunset and nightfall. There are no priests and a learned person from the congregation leads the prayers. The usual place for prayers is in a Mosque, but they can be said anywhere.
- Zakah (Financial obligation of Muslims) – Everything belongs to God and is only held by humans in trust for him. Usually Muslims are expected to give a fortieth of their capital, but each one calculates his/her own zakah. An individual can give much more in secret if he/she desires.
- Sawm (Fasting) – Every year in the month of Ramadan, all Muslims fast from dawn until sunset. They refrain from food, drink and sexual relations with their spouses. This is a method of selfpurification to cut oneself off from worldly comforts and focus upon the purpose of life.
- Hajj (Pilgrimage) – Muslims who are financially able to do so are expected to make one pilgrimage to Mecca during their lifetime. The annual pilgrimage begins in the twelfth month of the year. The pilgrims wear simple clothes and no distinction is made between rich and poor. At Mecca, the pilgrims make seven trips between the hills of Safa and Marwa. Then they stand together on the plains of Arafat and join in prayers of forgiveness.

Holy Days of Islam

There are two main Islamic festivals:

- EidulFitr – This is a celebration at the end of Ramadan. Muslims go to the Mosque to pray and then special celebration meals are served. Many families get together to celebrate.

- Eid-ul-Adha - This is the end of the pilgrimage. Muslims sacrifice a goat to symbolize the time when the Prophet Abraham was about to sacrifice his son to God and replaced him with an animal.

Other Holy days:

- The Islamic New Year - The first day of the first Islamic onth - Muharram.
- Ashura - The tenth day of Muharram and is a time of fasting and inner thoughts.
- Mawlid an-Nabi - Mohammed's birthday
- Isra Mer'Aj - Celebrated on the 27 th day of Rajab, the seventh month of the calendar. It is a very special night in the Islamic faith meaning "the night journey and ascension" of Mohammed.
- Ramadan - A holy month dominated by prayer and fasting.

Sunni Muslim

Sunni Muslims make up a division within the religion of Islam. The division was created after the death of the Prophet Mohammed in the 7th century. The division occurred over a dispute about who should succeed him. The largest group of Muslims elected Abu Bakr, a close companion of Mohammed, as the next Caliph, while another group wanted his soninlaw, Ali, to be the leader. This caused a rift in the religion, with the followers of Abu Bakr becoming known as the Sunni. In spite of the belief over who should be leader, the Sunni Muslims still follow the traditional Islam beliefs that Mohammed received the Five Pillars of truth from Mohammed. The followers of Sunni follow the Islamic traditions of the first several centuries espousing the beliefs of the first century scholars - Hanbali, Hanafi, Maliki and Shaafii.

Some Beliefs of Sunni Muslims

Sunni Muslims share the Islamic belief in the Oneness of God, rather than a Trinity of three persons in one God, the revelations of Mohammed and the belief in resurrection on the Last Day of Judgement. The most basic belief is the shahadah, the Muslim confession of faith There is no god but God; Muhammad is the prophet of God. They believe that God is merciful and is always willing to forgive if the person is genuinely repentant.

The fundamental beliefs of Sunni Muslims also include believing in angels, both good and bad, the books and Scriptures revealed to Mohammed, a series of prophets and the Last Day of Judgement. The foundation of Islam is the Five Pillars as delivered to Mohammed from God:

- Iman (Faith) - faith or belief in the Oneness of God and the finality of the prophet.
- Salah (Prayer) - prayers have to be preformed five times a day - dawn, middau, late afternoon, sunset and nightfall. There are no priests and a learned person from the congregation leads the prayers. The usual place for prayers is in a Mosque, but they can be said anywhere.
- Zakah (Financial obligation of Muslims) - everything belongs to God and is only held by humans in trust for him. Usually Muslims are expected to give a fortieth of their capital, but each one calculates his/her own zakah. An individual can give much more in secret if he/she desires.
- Sawm (Fasting) - Every year in the month of Ramadan, all Muslims fast from dawn until sunset. They refrain from food, drink and sexual relations with their spouses. This is a method of selfpurification to cut oneself off from worldly comforts and focus upon the purpose of life.
- Hajj (Pilgrimage) - Muslims who are financially able to do so are expected to make one pilgrimage to Mecca during their lifetime. The annual pilgrimage begins in the twelfth month of the year. The pilgrims wear simple clothes and no distinction is made between rich and poor. At Mecca, the pilgrims make seven trips between the hills of Safa and Marwa. Then they stand together on the plains

of Arafat and join in prayers of forgiveness. Sunni Muslims put more emphasis on completing this pilgrimage as being an important demonstration of their faith.

Holy Days of Sunni Muslims

There are two main Islamic festivals:

- Eid-ul-Fitr - This is a celebration at the end of Ramadan. Muslims go to the Mosque to pray and then special celebration meals are served. Many families get together to celebrate.
- Eid–ul–Adha - This is the end of the pilgrimage. Muslims sacrifice a goat to symbolize the time when the Prophet Abraham was about to sacrifice his son to God and replaced him with an animal.

Other Holy days:

- The Islamic New Year - the first day of the first Islamic month - Muharram
- Ashura - The tenth day of Muharram and is a time of fasting and inner thoughts.
- Mawlid anNabi - Mohammed's birthday
- Isra Mer'Aj - Celebrated on the 27 th day of Rajab, the seventh month of the calendar. It is a very special night in the Islamic faith meaning "the night journey and ascension" of Mohammed.
- Ramadan - A holy month dominated by prayer and fasting.

Shiite

The Shiite Muslims are one of the divisions that exist within the religion of Islam. There are fewer followers of this division than in the Sunni division. The basic difference between the two developed over a dispute about who should be the leader after the death of Mohammed in the 7 th century. The Shiites believed that the Prophet's soninlaw Ali should succeed him, but the larger Sunni group elected Abu Bakr, a close friend of Mohammed. The Shiite Muslims believe that

Mohammed was the Prophet, but claim that the Qu'ran explicitly showed that Ali was to succeed Mohammed.

The term "Shiite" or "Shia" means partisans of Ali. The largest sect of Shiite Muslims is called the Twelvers. They believe that Muhammad alMuntazar alMahdi, the twelfth imman in line from the Prophets family, was hidden in a cave below a mosque in Samarra when he was a young boy. He disappeared and the Shiite Muslims still await his return.

Some Basic Beliefs of Shiite Muslims

The Shiite Muslims differ from the Sunni in their interpretation of the Hadith. The Shiite prefers to use the Hadith as narrated by Ali and Fatima and their associates. They do not approve of honouring scholars who lived centuries ago, but believe that only living scholars should be followed. In all other ways, the Shiite Muslims follow the basic beliefs of Islam. Their holy book is the Qu'ran that they believe was dictated to Mohammed by God through the Angel Gabriel. They are told in the Qu'ran to read three other holy books – the Torah (the first five books of the Old Testament), the Zabur (the psalms of David) and the Injeel (the Gospel of Christ).

Islam has seven fundamental beliefs that all Shiite Muslims must accept as part of their religion:

- Belief in God
- Belief in the angels
- Belief in the revealed Books of God
- Belief in the many prophets
- The Last Judgement Day
- Belief in the divine measurement of human affairs
- Belief in life after death

Shiite Muslims believe in Satan. They also believe that Ishmael was the son that Abraham was willing to sacrifice on an altar for God. He used an animal instead and this is why Muslims use goats when they offer sacrifices to Allah. They believe that their land was given to them by God and this is why they feel they have a God given right to the land.

There are five ways by which Muslims believe they will be saved:

- Say the confession of faith – There is no God but Allah and Mohammed is the prophet of Allah.
- Pray five times a day just before sunrise, mid morning, noon, mid afternoon and after sunset.
- Give alms to the poor – at least 2.5 % of their wealth.
- Fast during Ramadan – no food or drink from sunrise to sunset for thirty days.
- Make a pilgrimage to Mecca, the birthplace of Islam.

Muslims pray at a mosque every Friday and during the time of prayer they face Mecca. Both men and women pray together, but the men are at the front and the women as at the back.

Holy Days of Islam

There are two main Islamic festivals:

- Eid-ul-Fitr – This is a celebration at the end of Ramadan. Ramadan begins and ends on a Friday because this is the Muslim holy day of the week. Muslims go to the Mosque to pray and then special celebration meals are served. Many families get together to celebrate.
- Eid–ul–Adha – This is the end of the pilgrimage to Mecca. Muslims sacrifice a goat to symbolize the time when the Prophet Abraham was about to sacrifice his son to God and replaced him with an animal.

The Belief System of Islam:

A. Islam is a religion of rigid monotheism and an allencompassing law. It is a belief system, i.e a world and life view. Everything is seen from an Islamic perspective.

B. Islam's five fundamental articles of faith:

1. There is no God but God. "Allah" is the Arabic word for "God". This god is the sovereign Lord of the universe. Everything that occurs is according to his will. He is also the source of both good and

evil. The Qur'an assigns 99 names to Allah. The 100th name is secret and is known only to the camel!

2. God gave prophets (the Qur'an mentions 28) to every age from Adam to Muhammad. Muhammad, the last and greatest prophet, was sinless as were all the other prophets. Jesus was the prophet of the previous age. They affirm that Jesus was born of a virgin and performed many miracles, but they vehemently deny that he was
3. Islam believes that each age was given a book through its prophet, but all have been lost except portions of the Old Testament and the Gospel of Jesus which was corrupted by Christians. The Qur'an was given to Muhammad and supersedes all other revelations. The Qur'an is divided into 114 Suras (chapters) and was given directly to Muhammad. To the Muslim, every word of the Qur'an is the Word of God and is of an eternal nature. In other words, it existed in heaven prior to being dictated by the angel Gabriel. The Qur'an governs every area of the life of a Muslim, from how to prevent crime to the proper use of a toothpick! It is often the only constitution of some Muslim countries.
4. There are good and bad angels. The chief good angel is Gabriel. The chief fallen angel is Shaitan (Satan).
5. There will be a day of judgment in which all the dead will be resurrected. Allah will be the judge and each person will be sent either to heaven, a place of sensual pleasure, or hell, a place of torment. Hell is for those who opposed Allah and his prophet, Muhammad. Salvation is attained by the quality of a person's obedience to the law as determined by Allah. Muhammad is seen as a

mediator who helps a person attain salvation. The bridge to paradise is likened to a razorsharp sword; Muhammad waits to assist in crossing.

C. Each Muslim has six obligatory duties:
   1. Reciting the creed. "There is no God but Allah". The word "Quran" in Arabic means "to recite".
   2. Pray five times a day facing Mecca.
   3. Tithe to the poor and for the furtherance of Islam. It varies from 2 to 10 per cent.
   4. Fast for one month each year during the 9th month, the lunar month of Ramadan. This month of fasting is during the day only. Feasting takes place after sundown.
   5. Make a pilgrimage to Mecca a least once during a lifetime. A male who makes a pilgrimage to Mecca is called a "Hajj" a title of honor similar to the English "Sir".

D. The concept of "Jihad" ("holy war") is sometimes referred to as a 6th pillar. Jihad is also a religious duty of all adult males who must commit to any summons of war against infidels. Any who die in such a war are assured paradise. Today there is controversy as to who in the Arab world can legally declare a Jihad. In the past, this has been a most successful form of "evangelism". Polytheistic cultures have been given the option of submission or death. Historically, Jews and Christians, since they were considered "people of the Book" were given a choice of submission or paying tribute (taxes).

Other Muslim Beliefs:

A. The unforgivable sin to a Muslim is to attribute deity to anything other that God himself. To claim that Jesus is God or the Son of God is blasphemy to a Muslim. They believe that God is unbegotten and begets not.

B. Most Muslims believe Jesus predicted the coming of Muhammad when He said that He would send "another

Comforter" in John 14:16. Muslims even refer to Muhammad as the "Holy Spirit".

C. Muslims are very antitrinitarian. The Qur'an teaches that Christians believe in a Trinity of God, the Father, Jesus, the Son, and Mary the Mother!

D. Most Muslims believe Judas died on the cross, not Jesus. God caused Jesus to be ascended into heaven.

E. Most Muslims do not separate church and state, i.e. politics and religion. There is no such thing as secular and sacred. This is a cause of some of their intramural conflicts. Occasionally a ruler attempts to secularize the state. For this Sadat was assassinated. Turkey gets away with it, but it is resented in much of the Muslim world.

F. The Qur'an allows a man to have up to four wives if he believes he can treat them equally!

G. The Qur'an teaches that if a Muslim soldier kills another Muslim soldier in an unjust war he will go to hell! In the recent war, many Iraqi soldiers did not believe it was just war, hence they deserted in large numbers (and probably for other reasons as well!).

H. Muslim soldiers can declare a victory in battle even though they were stomped by the enemy, because to a Muslim, win or lose, it is the will of Allah. So if you lose, you win, because it is the will of Allah.

I. The Qur'an teaches that Muslims should take up arms against infidels. The following quote from the Qur'an should give insight into Saddam's behaviour:

- "When ye encounter unbelievers, strike off their heads until ye have made a great slaughter among them, and bind them in bonds; and either give them free remission afterwards or exact a ransom...Verily if God please he could take vengeance on them, without your assistance, but he commands you to fight his battles...And to those who fight in defense of God's true religion, God...will lead them into paradise..."

Other Holy Days:

- The Islamic New Year – The first day of the first Islamic month – Muharram

- Ashura – The tenth day of Muharram and is a time of fasting and inner thoughts.
- Mawlid an-Nabi – Mohammed's birthday
- Isra Mer'Aj – Celebrated on the 27 th day of Rajab, the seventh month of the calendar. It is a very special night in the Islamic faith meaning "the night journey and ascension" of Mohammed.
- Ramadan – A holy month dominated by prayer and fasting.

Impacts of Religious Doubt

Religious doubt has been defined as: "... a feeling of uncertainty toward, and a questioning of, religious teachings and beliefs." Various groups promote different beliefs about doubt:

Secularism and liberal religious faiths, like progressive Christianity, Unitarian Universalism, cherish doubt. They value the search for truth as more important than the acceptance of what others have already defined as truth. A humorist once commented on a Unitarian Universalist who arrived in Heaven only to find a signpost pointing in one direction to God, and in the other direction towards a discussion of God. He took the latter path. Most conservative faiths regard doubt as something to be battled against because it is dangerous to one's faith. It can lead to heresy, doubting the existence of God, and, according to their belief, perhaps loss of salvation and eternal torture in the fires of Hell. Scientific progress is fuelled by doubt, as researchers exhibit scepticism towards current beliefs, and seek a better understanding of nature.

Religious doubt may hasten positive cultural change:

A case can be made that doubt has a critical and positive role to play in the effect of religion on social evils. In the past, some faith groups and devout individuals have been responsible for:

- Restrictions on religious freedom — Both beliefs and practice, The burning and hanging of heretics, The preservation of slavery, Massive loss of life in faithbased wars, Sexual repression, Religiouslybased genocides, etc.

A dose of healthy doubt might have alleviated or avoided such atrocities. In recent decades, faith groups have been divided over equal rights for women, abortion access, equal rights for gays, lesbians and bisexuals, samesex marriage, etc. On the horizon is a conflict over equal rights for transgender and transsexual persons. All of these conflicts will undoubtedly be resolved in one direction or the other during upcoming decades.

Lack of doubt causes people to hold tenaciously to a specific set of beliefs which may or may not be on the winning side. Honest doubt would greatly facilitate the resolution of conflicts more quickly, to the benefit of all. Doubt forms a part of every attempt at dialogue where people holding conflicting viewpoints freely explore each other's beliefs in a search for truth. It is debatable whether the 19 radical fundamentalist Muslim terrorists would have crashed airplanes into buildings on 9/11 if they had even a small shred of doubt about the wishes of Allah or the rewards that they believe awaited them as martyrs in the Muslim paradise.

4

Understanding Terrorism

The events of 9/11 have already generated a huge number of publications, but readers looking to go beyond exploitative instant journalism, political exposés or first person humaninterest accounts are often frustrated. For serious scholarly analysis usually requires a long gestation period. However, this volume of essays written by members of the American Psychology Association (APA) – and dedicated to the victims of 9/11 – provides a valuable context for academics, students and laypersons to engage in a discussion of international terrorism shaped by the ongoing research of psychologists. The topic, of course, has been extensively studied well before 9/11. Indeed, the long and very helpful list of references included in Understanding Terrorism suggests the history and broad scope of existing research.

Nevertheless, this timely approach responds to an intellectual need that deserves to be satisfied. It succeeds partly because the contributors respect crosscultural perspectives and recognize that if psychologists are to understand terrorism they require substantial help from researchers in other fields. The editors, moreover, are consciously motivated by an admirable sense of social responsibility. For the goal of the collection as a whole, according to Moghaddam and Marsella is to promote not just "peace" but a worldview "that can accommodate and tolerate diversity, uncertainty and trust". Understanding Terrorism is divided into three sections: the first concentrates on the conceptual difficulties involved in the definition of terrorism, the second delineates the psychosocial conditions that help us understand the formation of terrorists or terrorist groups, and the third explores how psychologists can best respond to the consequences of terrorism.

This division generally works well although definitional issues predictably overrun the boundaries of section one. Several essays explicitly recognize questions standing in the way of a consensus regarding the meaning of terrorism – for example, are the terms "state terrorism" or "war on terrorism" incoherent? Yet most stipulate a definition and proceed to develop a particular thesis. "Psychology's Response to Terrorism," the book's concluding essay by Levant, Barbanel and DeLeon, seems best able to avoid such questions because it is largely a descriptive account of how the APA mobilized its members to respond to the attack on New York, an event that surely meets all the relevant criteria of terrorism.

More specifically, although the authors mention efforts made to study the consequences of the attack (conferences and research publications, etc.) the heart of the essay is a firsthand story of an APA member trying to assist those who needed help on the ground. In concert with the American Red Cross, that is, Laura Barbanel helped relatives of victims and other emergency workers such as firemen by acting as listener for those who wanted to talk, or sympathetic companion for shocked and vulnerable people trying to cope with limited information and physical resources. Ironically enough, however, this least conceptual essay in Understanding Terrorism ends up raising a most intriguing question regarding psychology's selfunderstanding.

After all, Barbanel notes that providing "emotional firstaid as it came to be named" is not the work for which professional psychologists are trained, and she sharpens the edge on this point by saying that such intervention "was not therapy" but "it was certainly therapeutic". This apt statement implies that "therapy," in the strict sense of the word, might be appropriately offered only to a very small subset of the large numbers of people who benefited greatly from the "therapeutic" assistance of the diverse group of volunteer works during the immediate aftereffects of the terrorist attack. If so, then psychologists do not, on the face of it, have a special professional responsibility to intervene directly since they have no "therapeutic" expertise, in the colloquial sense of the word. Another essay in section three, "The Psychosocial Aftermath of Terrorism" by Danieli, Engdahl and Schlenger also deals with the traumatic experiences of witnesses, relatives and emergency workers in New York.

However, when these authors claim that psychologists must "match appropriate therapeutic interventions to particular forms of reaction" to trauma on the basis of an individual's distinctive history, personality and circumstances, "therapeutic intervention" clearly means the sort of therapy that only psychologists are qualified to offer. The essay explicitly discusses promising psychotherapeutic and pharmacological treatments. This sharp contrast is entailed by methodology. For the primary concern of Danieli et al is to study the empirical literature on the consequences of the New York attack, and this literature is shaped by the conceptualization of trauma as a biomedical phenomenon. Consider that post traumatic stress disorder (PTSD) is defined in both the International Classification of Diseases (ICD10) and the Diagnostic and Statistical Manual of Mental Diseases (DSMIV) in terms of a cluster of symptoms that provide a focus for epidemiological researchers gathering data on New Yorkers.

According to the conclusion of one representative study, approximately 75,000 New York public schoolchildren in grades 412 could be said to be suffering from PTSD after 9/11. Given the scientific data, therefore, massive numbers of people would have benefited only from specialized treatment after 9/11. Is this plausible? In "Terrorism and the Mental Health and WellBeing of Refugees and Displaced Persons," Michael G. Wessells sidesteps the possibility of methodological circularity. He acknowledges high rates of PTSD amongst nonWestern victims of violence and never suggests that this category of Western psychiatry and psychology simply manufactures a problem. Still, as someone with extensive experience assisting refugees and displaced persons, Wessells warns against a "narrow focus on mental illness" and utilizes a holistic concept of well-being in his own work.

Hence trauma might best be understood in the context of spiritual beliefs and social fragmentation. And effective intervention might depend upon an "ecological approach" that does not privilege treatment but rather job training, language acquisition, social networking, and the like. Wessells aims to empower victims of political violence. However, he concludes that the practical measures required to achieve this goal also constitute the only way for psychologists to help prevent the formation of terrorists. For it is futile to seek a pathological "terrorist personality" type. Mental illness is no more the root cause of terrorism than it is the prime consequence. This essay, then, reflects back nicely upon the second section of Understanding Terrorism. "Terrorism From A Peace Psychology Perspective" by Wagner and Long, for example, points to life conditions – "hunger, sickness and shelter for oneself or one's family" as one structural cause of terrorism; lack of security, self-determination and social respect are additional causes that must be alleviated by civic education and strategies for reconciling groups with a history of ethnic or religious conflict. Since terrorism is not a necessary consequence of harsh socioeconomic conditions, most contributors probe special cultural conditions.

In "Understanding and Responding to Group Violence: Genocide, Mass Killing and Terrorism" Ervin Staub discerns values and beliefs – strong respect for authority, unhealed wounds of past victimization, etc. – that magnify a dangerous sense of impotence. And "Terrorism and the Quest for Identity" by Taylor and Louis contains an excellent discussion of how a matrix of social, ideological and religious norms rooted in the lack of a "clearly defined collective self" favour the emergence of terrorist groups (along with their distinctive organizational ethos). Fathali M. Moghaddam's "Cultural Preconditions For Potential Terrorist Groups: Terrorism and Societal Change" gives a comprehensive overview of terrorism's "enabling conditions" and highlights a theoretical assumption underlying other essays: the diverse "preconditions" of terrorism do not operate consistent with a hierarchical psychological model, but rather "reinforce one another and work as a Gestalt".

As section two delves into specifically cultural beliefs, another question about psychology's selfunderstanding appears. It can be glimpsed in the very title of an essay on the purposeful rationality of terrorists: "Malevolent Minds: The Teleology of Terrorism" by U.S. Defense Department psychologist Thomas Ditzler (emphasis added). However, the best context in which to consider this question is perhaps Albert Bandura's insightful account, in "The Role of Selective Moral Disengagement in Terrorism and Counterterrorism," of how terrorists justify to themselves acts that horrify many people In one crucial passage, Bandura sharply contrasts the "bad things" performed by terrorists and "good things" performed by a helicopter pilot during the My Lai massacre and Nelson Mandela during the fight against apartheid. This moral judgment is plausible. Nevertheless, in making it Bandura steps into the territory of normative ethics. At one point he suggests that he is only acknowledging "experimental research" but in making such judgments he is actually embracing an exceedingly metaphysical claim. Bandura repeatedly insists that decent people have the capacity to discern a "common humanity" underlying any of our differences, whereas terrorists suffer from moral blindness.

Rom Harré's "The Social Construction of Terrorism," by contrast, argues that social psychology has no business answering substantive questions of good or evil. He himself uses "that branch of discursive psychology called positioning theory" to delineate the complex manner in which George W. Bush and Osama Bin Laden construct their moral identities out of mutually interacting and "competing story lines".

Unlike a politician, citizen or philosopher, however, he conceives his job as a psychologist to be that of understanding the process not defending particular protagonists.

Harré's Bush and Bin Laden example draws attention to the fact that many persons identified by mainstream Western media as terrorists justify their actions in the name of Islam. Anthony J. Marsella's "Reflections on International Terrorism: Issues, Concepts, and Directions" and, in more detail, Naji AbiHashem's "Peace and War in the Middle East: A Psychopolitical and Sociocultural Perspective" respond by trying to do justice to the spiritual, ethical, and social values of Islam. To a great degree, contributors such as Marsella and AbiHashem are successful in deepening our understanding. Consider, though, that nonMuslims are urged to recognize that jihad "has a personal as well as communal dimension" that resists appropriation as a rallying cry for war against America by "demagogues who pander to simplistic solutions for complex problems".

In passages such as these, Understanding Terrorism is not just pointing to the diversity of Islam but defending a specific version of it (in the face of an "extremist" or "fundamentalist" theological interpretation). It needs to do so, moreover, precisely because promoting peace is the book's goal. At the same time, however, by implying that "terrorists" are to be criticized partly because they distort Islam, these passages reflect a tendency to repress this normative dimension. This could be a matter of recognizing Harré's disciplinary proscription against embracing substantive moral or religious ideals. Or it might be due to the fact that standard psychological categories and methods of classification are simply not designed to grapple effectively with evaluative issues.

Nevertheless, the essays in section one never adequately resolve the root conceptual ambiguity, namely, that the word terrorist is used both to identify and morally condemn a person. Perhaps the most satisfying attempt to do so is Brian Hallett's "Dishonest Crimes, Dishonest Language: An Argument About Terrorism." Hallett launches a withering attack on conventional wisdom, according to which terrorism is "the 'weapon of the weak' needed to wage an asymmetric war' against" the powerful. For he claims that a terrorist act can be distinguished from a common crime by only two characteristics: the "theatrical aspect" of the crime and the "delusional selfinterest ... masquerading as selfsacrifice" by which the terrorist justifies it.

Hallett supports these claims with a brilliantly conceived and wellexecuted argument that contrasts a terrorist unfavourably with Ghandi's satyargahi. He does this from the point of view of political strategy as well as substantive values. He argues, for example, that Ghandi is more practical than Machiavelli and his discussion of the relationship between terrorism and guerrilla warfare would be valuable as a Defense Department backgrounder. It should be read in conjunction with Ditzler's "Malevolent Minds." Hallett's essay accepts the necessity of making value judgments but adjusts the character of his argument appropriately. Harré might say that it is, therefore, a work of moral or political philosophy not psychology. Nevertheless, it is a fine addition to an excellent collection.

Sociology of Terrorism

Sociologists had until September 11, 2001, shown little interest in terrorism. Although conflict analysis, in one form or another, is a long established approach in the field, researchers have focused mostly on class and labour struggles, race relations, criminalization and other deviancelabeling, and the collective violence of riots and revolutions.

Nonetheless, sociological concepts and methods have been fruitfully applied (albeit mostly by non sociologists) in efforts to understand and counter terrorism. The aim of this review is to note what has been learned in order to suggest agendas for future research on the dynamics through which terrorism becomes a social phenomenon.

The Social Construction of Terrorism

Probably the most significant contribution of sociological

thinking to our understanding of terrorism is the realization that it is a social construction. Contrary to the impression fostered by official incidence counts and media reports, terrorism is not a given in the real world but is instead an interpretation of events and their presumed causes. And these interpretations are not unbiased attempts to depict truth but rather conscious efforts to manipulate perceptions to promote certain interests at the expense of others. When people and events come to be regularly described in public as terrorists and terrorism, some governmental or other entity is succeeding in a war of words in which the opponent is promoting alternative designations such as "martyr" and "liberation struggle."

More powerful conflict parties, especially governments, generally succeed in labeling their more threatening (i.e., violent) opponents as terrorists, whereas attempts by opponents to label officially sanctioned violence as "state terrorism" have little chance of success unless supported by powerful third parties (e.g., the United Nations). Superpowers such as the United States, of course, are highly selective and influential in determining which parties and their activities in violent struggles will be labeled. Lists of terrorist organizations and individuals, supporters, and sponsors are the results of policy decisions regarding the potential costs and benefits of including or excluding specific parties on such lists. Pronouncements by the U.S. State Department, for example, reflect assessments not only of objective threat but also of the political, economic, and military implications of naming particular entities as terrorist.

During the last decade of the cold war, the concept of "statesponsored terrorism" was given full credence. Bulgaria, East Germany, Libya, North Korea, and Syria were named as Sovietcontrolled sponsors of antiAmerican terrorism. However, adequate evidence was never presented to support the listing of these nations as sponsors, much less under Soviet direction. That the Soviet KGB often encouraged antiAmerican violence is clear, but there were many terrorist groups and incidents having no direct involvement in the U.S.Soviet conflict. Most terrorists were in nongovernmental organizations that set their own ideological, ethnic, nationalist, or religious agendas. Without presuming to know why the five nations (and not equally plausible others such as Cuba or Iran) were listed, one may speculate that American policymakers found it useful to label the Soviets as the font of terrorism and to associate especially troublesome regional threats (to Israel, Western Europe, and South Korea) with the putative Soviet terrorist network. The United States has a long history of violence associated with political, labour, racial, religious, and other social and cultural conflicts. Assassinations, bombings, massacres, and other secretive deadly attacks have caused many thousands of casualties. Yet, few incidents have been defined as terrorism or the perpetrators as terrorists. Instead, authorities have typically ignored or downplayed the political significance of such violence, opting to portray and treat the violence as apolitical criminal acts by deranged or evil individuals, outlaws or gangsters, or "imported" agitators such as the radical Molly Maguires of Pennsylvania's coal miners' struggles.

Although violent acts believed to be politically motivated are assigned the highest investigative priority, those accused are rarely charged with terrorism. In official public usage, terrorism is far more likely to refer to incidents associated with agents and supporters of presumably foreignbased terrorist organizations such as al Qaeda than with the violence of homegrown militants acting in the name of such groups as the Animal Liberation Front, Earth First!, or the American Coalition for Life Activists (one of whose founders, Paul Hill, was executed in Florida on September 3, 2003, for murder, not terrorism).In sum, to study terrorism presupposes investigating the ways in which parties in conflict are trying to stigmatize one another. The construction and selective application of definitions of terrorism are embedded in the dynamics of political conflicts, where ideological warfare to cast the enemy as an evildoer is a dimension of the struggle to win support for one's own cause.

Terrorism as Political Violence

Differing sociological perspectives encourage contrasting views of political violence. Insofar as functionalism assumes that order and peace are normal, violence is an aberration, a presumably temporary deviation from the normal state of human social life. Even archaic versions of functionalism (e.g., Germanic "combat theories") arguing that war is necessary to sustain national identity and strength do not imply acceptance of nongovernmental violence, especially assaults on public order and authority, as other than deviant behaviour. More liberal and critical theories tend to posit that violence is an understandable response to oppression and exploitation, the last resort of the deprived and desperate. Whether reflecting anarchist objections to regimentation, communist or socialist critiques of capitalism, or simply liberal objections to excessive "possessive individualism," critical theories presume that political and/or economic inequalities are the sources of collective violence.

While acknowledging that social inequities may be causally involved, particularly in originating conflicts, analytical or "structural" conflict theories attend more to the possibility that violence may be a product of strategic and tactical decisions in a process of ongoing conflict. That interests or values may not be reconcilable is accepted, as is the proposition that various forms of violent action may be political options within the perceptual range of parties in conflict. It is increasingly clear that terrorism is most usefully defined, for empirical research purposes, as the deliberate targeting of more or less randomly selected victims whose deaths and injuries are expected to weaken the opponent's will to persist in a political conflict.

Terrorist acts are political, rarely involving psychopathology or material deprivation. Indeed, the evidence is mounting that terrorism is associated with relative affluence and social advantage rather than poverty, lack of education, or other indicators of deprivation. The typical terrorist comes from a relatively welloff part of the world, and appears to be motivated by politicalideological resentments rather than economic distress. Suicide bombers, for instance, appear increasingly likely to be respected individuals from advantaged classes, with stable family and community ties. Although their violent deaths may surprise relatives and friends, they are far more likely to be honoured than to be condemned or stigmatized as somehow deviant.

Arguments for censorship:

1. Terrorists use the media for propaganda, which helps recruit new supporters.
2. Publicity is a major goal of terrorism.
3. Detailed reporting of incidents gives potential terrorists suggestions and models for action.
4. Information broadcast during an incident can be useful to the terrorists involved.
5. Media presence can endanger hostages.
6. Reporting terrorist acts can lead to imitation.
7. Media reports may panic kidnappers into killing their victims.
8. People without respect for others' lives should not be enabled to command public attention by using violence.
9. Describing terrorist acts might promote sadism in some members of the public.
10. Reporting terrorist outrages might provoke vigilantism and revenge attacks on the group for whom the terrorists claim to be acting.
11. Negative news is demoralizing.

Arguments against censorship:

1. Not reporting terrorist atrocities might lead people to less negative judgments of terrorists.
2. Publicity can be a substitute for violence.
3. Censorship might force terrorists to raise the level of violence.
4. Not reporting terrorist events would encourage rumours, which might be worse.

5. Media presence can help prevent police actions that cause unnecessary casualties among both terrorists and victims.
6. Censorship enables officials to label any dissidents as terrorists, thus undermining legal safeguards.
7. Media credibility would decline.
8. Lack of news might result in a false sense of security, leaving the public unprepared to deal with terrorist attacks.
9. Lack of awareness would keep the public from understanding the political situation.
10. Feeling deprived of information might increase public distrust of the authorities.
11. Terrorists' claims that democracies are not really free would gain credibility.

Socializing Terrorists

High on the research agenda understands why and how individuals become terrorists. Although some earlier commentators argued that political criminals were either deranged or lacking proper "moral socialization," it is now well established that opposition to authority or a particular social order is more likely to stem from a reasoned position than from pathology or deficient socialization. As indicated above, reasoning in cosmological, religious terms is increasingly characteristic of the rationales by which terrorists justify their acts to themselves and others.

People learn to accept terrorism as a political option when their experiences lead them to see truth in messages that defending their way and kind cannot be accomplished by nonviolent means. In democratic societies political radicals usually come from relatively advantaged sectors and go through a sequence beginning with conventional political activism. The more educated and affluent their backgrounds, the more impatient they are likely to be with the inevitable disappointments of political life—where one rarely gets all that is envisioned. Socialized to be knowledgeable about the gaps between ideals and realities and to see themselves as significant participants in political struggles, higher class young people (especially from liberal or otherwise contrarian families and communities) are more likely than their less advantaged counterparts to become involved in a process of radicalization moving toward violence.

Although social banditry and peasant uprisings may challenge social orders, organized terrorism is by far most likely to originate in the alienation and analytics of higher status younger people. Whether the Weather Underground of Vietnamera America or the Al Qaeda network of today, initiating and committing terrorist acts is nearly always the work of radicalized younger persons with the intellectual and financial resources, and the ideological drive, to justify (at least to themselves) and enable adopting the violence option. However, although liberal family and educational backgrounds may encourage openness to violence as a political option, few even of the most militant radicals become terrorists. Those who do appear to have undergone something of a conversion experience in making the transition from a willingness to "trash" public property and fight riot police, to a readiness to murder specific politically significant persons (e.g., governmental or corporate leaders, police officers, or soldiers), and then to the random targeting of populations including noncombatants as well as combatants.

Exposure to ideologies justifying terrorism appears to be a crucial ingredient in the mix of personal and vicarious learning experiences leading to a commitment to terrorism. Before bombing the Murrah federal office building in Oklahoma City (killing 168 men, women, and children), Timothy McVeigh immersed himself in the writings of William Pierce (author of Hunter and The Turner Diaries). Pierce detailed his vision of how brave heroes resist the imminent threat to the white race and America posed by Jews, blacks, and other minorities. McVeigh, encouraged by his coterrorist Terry McNichols and probably others, was so impressed that he visited Elohim City, a white supremacist bastion, and sold or gave away copies of The Turner Diaries at gun shows.

McVeigh's military background, including distinguished service in the Gulf War, undoubtedly played a role in his selfdefinition as a soldier who had merely inflicted "collateral damage" in performing his duty.

One may hypothesize that selfeducation to terrorism is less likely in societies where personal mobility and access to intellectual resources are more limited. Islamist fundamentalism, in particular, seems to depend on radicalization through formal education consisting mostly of religious indoctrination. In madrassas throughout the world, potential recruits to organized terrorism are drilled in the most extreme interpretations of Sunni theology, emphasizing the duty to engage in holy war (jihad) against all enemies of the true Islam. The most spectacular product of the madrassas so far is the Taliban ("students of religion") of Afghanistan, who until overthrown by the United States and allied troops in 2001 provided a base for al Qaeda, and who still threaten all who do not accept their archaic and rigid version of an Islamic society. Once underway, campaigns of terrorism and related political violence tend to gain momentum. Inspired by the ideological messages, the charisma of leaders, the potential for material or status gains, or whatever else attracts them, others are likely to join.

Particularly in nondemocratic societies, conflicts are likely to proceed along fault lines reflecting class, ethnic, racial, or religious divisions. If such conflicts persist, years of reciprocal violence tend to result in its institutionalization, so that individuals caught up in the conflict may have no real comprehension of why they go on attacking one another – the classic feud. The bloody yearslong slaughter of whole villages of "conservatives" by "liberals," and vice versa, in Colombia's la violencia is a chilling historic example. In such contexts, explaining why people become terrorists is relatively straightforward: They see themselves as having to fight for "us" against "them." The key to explaining the socialization of terrorists understands how specific individuals are brought to the point where they see themselves as bearers of the responsibility for violent actions. Education, training, socialization—deliberate or not—may encourage the development of a selfconcept as one who must fight against the threat to "us."

However, little has been learned so far about how eventual terrorists are selected in the course of their political socialization. It is woefully unhelpful merely to point to religious schools as "factories" producing terrorists, or to assume that only the foolish or aberrant become terrorists, or to blame terrorists as evil souls or acclaim them as heroic fighters. Researchers have to be much more aware of the impact of media and politicalideological influences on the definition and characterization of terrorists if their life courses are to be understood.

Theorizing Terrorism

Developing a sociological explanation of terrorism is a politically and intellectually formidable task. Political obstacles abound: Officials are inclined to be wary of outsiders with independent agendas and resources. Policymakers and control agencies prefer operational findings clearly applicable to targeting and neutralizing. Funding priorities are affected by rivalries within and among intelligence and enforcement agencies, as well as competition for budgetary influence among politicians, lobbyists, and other interested parties such as grant applicants, whose concerns seldom include basic research. The organizational penchant for keeping records confidential is heightened in agencies charged with controlling terrorism. Such political constraints exacerbate the intellectual problems encountered in terrorism research.

Gurr is one of the first to have explicated methodological options in studying terrorism and indicated which kinds of research questions are appropriate to each method. Theoretically significant levels of analysis are posited: global, national, group, incident, and individual. Gurr argues cogently for "question first" (i.e., theorydriven) research that treats terrorist groups and incidents, for example, as "independent" rather than "dependent" variables, focusing on their causation rather than their traits and consequences. The crucial need for relevant datasets is emphasized, as is the necessity for their availability to researchers "insulated from direct involvement in policymaking or operations". Regardless of whether official or independent datasets are constructed, transforming information about terrorism into measures of conceptually meaningful variables is clearly a daunting task. For instance, decisions have to be made about what level of modelling is most appropriate for sorting out information about temporal and organizational processes in the formation of terrorist networks.

The intellectually ambitious and stimulating research on terrorism from a world systems perspective begins with the premise that the passage of time makes structural analysis more applicable than participant analysis. As time passes, the appropriate level of analysis moves from (a) the individual to (b) group and social movement, (c) nation and state, (d) the present historical period, (e) a past historical analogy, and finally (f) longer historical cycles. At this ultimate level of analysis, terrorism is to be explained in terms of cyclical rhythms in which waves of terrorist activity are associated with cycles of political economic deterioration and replacement by new forms of political order. As the previous global order breaks down, semiperipheral areas are drawn into a process of modernization characterized by conflict in the absence of a unifying hegemonic power (core).

Perforce, once peripheral areas are caught up in the dynamics of political (re)organization, "the first signs of strain in the semi peripheral zones are those of terrorism and panreligious/ethnic ideological movements". Bergesen & Lizardo raise the question of whether the current wave of terrorism signals the beginning of a global restructuring that will end the hegemony of the United States. Most terrorism specialists may find the world systems approach too abstractly conceptualized and too remote from specific political conflicts to generate much theoretical payoff. A research strategy more closely attuned to limited political contexts may be more fruitful, or at least popular (e.g., as in the American Terrorism Study, a project recently initiated by Brent Smith, Kelly Damphousse, and their associates, and the studies produced by the Center for the Study of Terrorism and Political Violence at St. Andrews University). In any case, the appropriate level of analysis and explanation will depend on what kinds of questions are being asked. At this very early stage in the sociological study of terrorism, it would certainly be premature to declare one level or approach to be preferable to another.

Complementing Gurr's assessment of methodological problems and strategies, Gibbs (1989a) provides a characteristically rigorous analysis of issues and problems in conceptualizing terrorism. Rejecting Laqueur's view that terrorism can be studied without defining it, Gibbs argues that productive research necessitates defining the research object to include elements of both theoretical significance and empirical applicability—which involves some regard for the essentially a theoretical definitions used in the nonscientific sources on which researchers frequently rely: the reports of government officials, journalists, and historians. He identifies five questions reflecting the issues that must be dealt with in defining terrorism. Is terrorism necessarily criminal? Is it necessarily undertaken to achieve a particular kind of goal? How does terrorism differ from conventional, civil, or guerrilla war? Can only opponents of government engage in terrorism? Is terrorism a distinctive strategy in the use of violence?

His finely crafted (complex and lengthy) definition of terrorism constitutes his answers and may be paraphrased in summary form as follows: Terrorism is threatening, perhaps illegal, clandestine (avoiding conventional warfare) violence against human or nonhuman objects that is intended to change or maintain some belief, law, institution, or other social "norm" by inculcating fear in persons other than the immediate targets. To facilitate the recognition of logical connections and possible empirical associations among the components of the definition, an integrating and causally impressive notion is needed. He argues strongly that "attempted social control" is the most promising base on which to build an explanatory theory. Amore recent attempt by Ross to provide a framework for research offers a model integrating structural and psychological causes of terrorism suggested by commentaries, case studies and analyses, research critiques, and literature reviews.

The primary goal is to help researchers "test the relative importance of previously identified factors and their interactions that determine the scope, intensity, and amount of terrorism". He posits "five interconnected processes that this model explains: joining, forming, staying in, and leading a terrorist organization and engaging in terrorist activities". It is assumed that some independent variables lead to low levels of terrorism and others to higher levels. Interactions among structural factors (including historical factors as well the political and economic system) create an environment permitting terrorism by constituting a range of options including terrorism available to individuals and organizations. Ross then presents an array of hypotheses drawn from seven psychological theories advanced to explain why individuals choose the terrorist option. Adding to the complexities of theorizing and researching terrorism, Black has proposed looking at terrorism as social control.

Instead of delimiting the research object to resistance to political authority, or expanding it to include state terrorism, he defines terrorism "in its purest form" as "unilateral selfhelp by organized civilians who covertly inflict mass violence on other civilians". Although more akin to guerrilla warfare than to conventional military operations, terrorism is distinctive in that it targets civilians—although guerrillas may engage in terrorism and terrorists may engage in guerrilla war, depending on the nature of the target. Terrorism differs from ordinary crime in that it targets a population, applying a standard of collective liability for perceived violations of normative expectations. Efforts to control terrorism are made particularly difficult because the social distance between adversaries is extreme, precluding the shared normative understandings assumed in law, and because the quasiwarfare of terrorism tends to attract quasiwarfare in return. Insofar as the demands of terrorists are impossibly beyond negotiation (e.g., that Americans radically change their way of life), and the quasiwarfare of each side persists, successful control (short of extermination) is improbable.

Even though the casualties from terrorist violence may be shocking for a while, Black's prognosis is that the technological advances lessening social distance among peoples and cultures will ultimately destroy the polarities and collectivization of violence that generate and sustain terrorism. "Its inevitable fate is sociological death". However one approaches the sociological study of terrorism, the distinctive objective is to develop an explanation of its causation, the dynamics of its escalation and deescalation in relation to other forms of political violence, and its impact on the stability and change of social orders. Turk has outlined a scheme for analyzing the social dynamics involved in the progression from coercive, to injurious, to destructive violence—the most extreme of which is terrorism.

The main hypothesis is that terrorism is the culmination of a conflict process that predictably, having reached this extreme, ends in either the annihilation of one party or mutual exhaustion. Assuming that they must somehow continue to live in proximity and interdependence, survivors have to begin anew the search for a viable relationship. Whether "cosmic wars" can stop short of the extermination of one or both sides, and be ended by acceptance of the need to recognize one another's right to exist, has still to be determined.

Terrorism as a Military Weapon

Terrorism is a disease of modern society. It is a virus growing in an ill body. The effects of the virus can sometimes be ameliorated, but there is no certain cure. The causes of terrorism are diverse; often one cause overlaps another or several causes. There is the social cause: Uruguayan young people denied their rightful place in a society that was stagnating. There is the racial cause: black and Indian militant groups in the United States. And, of course, there is the political cause: Israelis seeking independence from Great Britain; Cubans seeking freedom from Dictator Batista and then from Dictator Castro; Algerians seek independence from France; northern Irish Catholics seeking to destroy British rule, and, conversely, Irish Protestants seeking to neutralize the Catholics.

Each instance was or is one of armed conflictin a word, of war. Whether the cause be. social discontent or national aspirations, a larger or smaller segment of a population wars on another segment or on a foreign adversary. The feasible weapon is terrorism. A military observer, Colonel William D. Neale, noted, "Terror, it is obvious, is a legitimate instrument of national policy." The complexities of causes of terrorism, the diverse ideologies that have employed terrorism, the multitudinous arms and tactics available to terrorists all these factors have made terrorism one of the most complicated problems of the times. Certainly the scope of the problem defies understanding by any single discipline. Terrorism is a tangled skein of varied human motivations, actions, hopes, emotions, and goals.

Terrorism cannot be explained by psychologists who construct facile theories. It cannot be countered by police who view terrorism as simply one more type of criminal activity: identify the criminals, arrest them, throw them in prison or perhaps shoot them, and the problem is solved. Terrorism cannot be handled by conventional military men who scoff at it as being beneath their notice. The academician who wishes to study terrorism with academic dispassionateness finds theories, explanations, and chronological statistics but little else. Penetrating interviews with genuine terrorists, for example, are of minimal availability.

Terrorism is a tangled skein, and any observer attempting to unravel and separate one thread leaves himself open to criticism, justified criticism. "You say terrorism is a military weapon. What about the kidnappings solely for financial gain in Italy and the brigandage in Argentina motivated by monetary profit?" Precisely the skein is a mess of threads; it may not be possible to separate anyone of them cleanly. Nevertheless, the effort is worth attempting if it contributes a pinpoint of light in what is certainly a long, dark tunnel. This chapter will attempt to focus on one thread: terrorism as a military weapon. Basically, terrorism is a form of psychological warfare (frighten your enemy; publicize your cause). Seen within this context, the Olympic attack achieved its purpose.

Kidnapping the Israeli athletes did no military harm to Israel. As a psychological blow, however, it probably boosted Palestinian morale, and it certainly spotlighted worldwide the Palestinian cause. It encouraged future moves by Palestinian terroriststhe historical record attests to this. As a psychological blow the Olympic attack demonstrated that wherever Israeli figures of prominence went abroad, whether they are diplomats or athletes or whatever, they were susceptible to terrorist attack.

War is armed conflict, and armed conflict is the province of the military. Terrorism is a form of armed conflict; it is therefore within the military sphere. When diplomats fail, soldiers take over. When soldiers fail, terrorists take over. The political terrorist, however, is a soldier, too. He wears no uniform, he may have received little or no training, he may accept minimal discipline, his organization may be ephemeralbut he is a soldier. Terrorism is sometimes believed to be synonymous with urban guerrilla warfare. Urban guerrilla warfare, however, is a broader term: it encompasses urban terrorism but other actions as well, i.e., ambushes, street skirmishes, assaults on official installations, and other types of hitandrun urban combat. Also, it may be noted that terrorism is not confined to urban zones: it can be conducted in rural areas as well, as was notably the case in South Vietnam.

Terrorism as a military arm is a weapon of psychological warfare. The purpose, as the very word indicates, is to engender terror in the foe. The terror thrust encompasses the following ingredients:

- Terrorism publicizes the terrorists' political cause.
- Terrorism demonstrates the capability of the terrorists to strike blows. Terrorism heartens sympathizers of the terrorists' cause.
- Terrorism disconcerts the enemy.
- Terrorism eventuallythe ultimate goaldemoralizes the enemy and paralyzes him.
- Conceivably, in certain circumstances, terrorism could deter potential allies of the terrorists' target country from assisting that country. ("If you provide aid to our enemy, we will unleash our terror tactics against you, too."
- Sabotage causes material damage to an enemy's vital installations; the damage, in turn, has a psychological effect on the foe and on the populace. It frightens the foe and emboldens the ally. Terrorists function within an area controlled by the enemy whether it be a metropolis or an airliner in flight. The terrorists either:
    - Represent a significant portion of the population (as in the case of a struggle against an unpopular dictator), and their actions are applauded, even when they cause discomfort to the population (as when rebels knocked out a substantial portion of Havana's electric and water systems during the Cuban civil war).
    - Do not receive any significant amount of popular support and are generally condemned as outlaws (the minuscule ethnic militant groups in the United States are an example).
    - Or, are foreign or foreignsupported and are seeking to destroy the enemy's control structure or to achieve some other political result (as in the

case of the IRA bombs in restaurants and other public places in London).

Whereas in Case one the terrorist may try to minimize civilian casualties in order not to turn the population against him, in Case three the more casualties there are the better the terrorist feels his goals are served: he is applying ruthless pressure against his enemy, and the number of casualties is a measure of his success. In Case Two, whether the terrorist concerns himself over civilian casualties is largely determined by whether his fanaticism is tempered by mercy. AT WHAT point does terrorism become the concern of the "regular" military? For a military establishment that is attacking, terrorism can be used as a substitute for conventional warfare or in conjunction with conventional warfare and/ or rural guerrilla warfare.

For a military establishment that is responsible for defending an area or a country, the military role in the handling of a terrorist problem is determined by local circumstances: Is the government of the country under attack run by civilians or by the military? What constitutional and other legal responsibilities and restrictions are placed on the military? What useful capabilities do the military have that the police do not have? The level of intensity of terrorist activity appears to be a determinant of military response more than any other factor. In most national cases military activity has been largely limited to guard and military intelligence duties in support of the police authorities. In other cases, howevernotably in preIsrael Palestine, Cyprus., Algeria, Uruguay, Argentina, and Northern Irelandthe military took over primary responsibility for combating terrorists because the police were overwhelmed. In those cases cited where the military sought to maintain foreign control over populations, it is significant that the independence struggles were nevertheless successful (except in Ireland, where the conflict continues).

In the two countries where indigenous military have sought to suppress major terrorist movements, the military were successful in one instance (Uruguay), and the outcome is as yet inconclusive in the other (Argentina). One may reasonably gather from this that terrorism is an effective weapon when used by a substantial portion of a population against foreign occupation troops. As a weapon against indigenous authorities supported by a military establishment, its efficacy is open to question. Terrorism appears to have succeeded only in such cases wherein it was used in conjunction with other military tactics (Cuba, South Vietnam).

There appear to be three fundamental functions of terrorism as a military weapon:

- Psychological warfare : Demoralize the enemy (his government, armed forces, police, even the civilian population) through assassinations, bomb explosions, agitation, and so on. The Viet Cong utilized the entire arsenal of violence in their campaign in' South Vietnam.
- Material destruction : Destroy or damage the enemy's utilities, communications, and industries. Destruction by sabotage, particularly against specific targets limited in size, can be as effective as destruction by air raid.
- Economic damage : Engender a state of psychological unease and uncertainty in a city or a country and commerce dries up, investment funds vanish. The deterioration of the Cuban economy during the 1956-58 revolution was a major factor in the downfall of the Batista regime.

Terrorism utilized as a military weapon, whether by a foreign power or by domestic insurgents, is somewhat akin to air raids: it is warfare conducted in the enemy's rear. In both cases the tactic aims at destroying the foe's installations, killing his officials, and battering his morale. Lamentably, in both cases the deaths of civilians are an additional result, unacknowledged as a goal but nevertheless often deliberately sought. If, then, terrorism is a military weapona weapon to be used for a military goal: the defeat of an enemy how much recognition of this weapon has been extended by "regular" military establishments? Traditionally the regular military have looked askance at any type of unconventional warfare.

This remains true today even though the line of differentiation between conventional and unconventional warfare grows increasingly blurred. In the cases of the British, Israeli, Argentine, and Uruguayan armies, the military have been forced by circumstances to recognize their responsibility in dealing with terrorism. Reality has legitimatized' the bastard, military terrorism, in fact if not in name. The daring Israeli commando rescue of 102 airlinehijack hostages at Entebbe, Uganda, in July 1976 was a dramatic example of the utilization of military power in a counter terror endeavour.

5

Religion and Terrorism

Religion has nothing to do with terrorism - and everything. Distortions of the teachings of various organized religions have always been used to justify everything under the sun. Similarly, great wrongs have been committed in the name of the family and the State. It should then come as no surprise that activities by terrorist or insurgent groups in the name of various religions over the past several centuries have succeeded in giving all organized religion, and ultimately all forms of religious belief, a very black allseeing eye. If suchandsuch can be done in the name of religion, the reasoning goes, then religion must be a very bad thing indeed. Such reasoning, while plausible, is not well thought out. It is a form of the logical fallacy called "hasty generalization."

That is, because we see instances of the misuse of organized religion, we generalize on insufficient knowledge and data, and assume that all organized religion (and ultimately all religion) constitutes misuse of what Aristotle called the "virtue of religion." That is, by engaging in terrorism, individuals and groups are acting contrary to the habit of rendering to that which you believe to be God or gods His or their due as Supreme Being or beings. Such hypocrisy - so we assume - invalidates the very real beliefs and motivations behind the actions. Human society is divided into three principal parts. These are domestic society (the family), civil society (the State), and religious society (organized religion). Demagogues have always used the natural affinity that normal people have for all three parts of human society to distort and pervert people's beliefs in order to achieve their private ends, particularly when they make the Machiavellian assumption that the end justifies the means.

The visceral reaction that normal people feel when they are persuaded that their family, faith, or country are in danger can very easily be manipulated by unscrupulous individuals or groups all in a good cause, of course. This is in large measure how other people can be persuaded that, because religion is used to justify terrorism, religion is bad. Similarly, because "patriotism is the last refuge of the scoundrel," we fall into the error that patriotism isn't the first refuge of the patriot. Family, faith, and country, because of the distortions and violations we see in the name of all three, become viewed by the cynical and suspicious as phonies, ploys used to trap and control the gullible. The only solution to this problem is to reorient people and help them to understand that organized religion, as well as family, and the State, have specific and necessary roles to play.

We cannot allow such critical social props to be hijacked by any individual or group bent on using them in support of "brief and transient causes" - or anything that is not ordered for the benefit of everyone within the common good and in a manner consistent with that essential human nature on which society is based. The social order must be restructured to comply with basic principles of natural law, which human reason helps us discern, and which organized religion helps us learn and understand. The natural law being consistent with human nature and based on it, this will maximize the delivery of justice within the social order, thereby removing the chief cause of terrorism: people convinced that they are being treated unjustly by others (whether or not this is true).

Once the structures of injustice have been removed or reformed into structures of justice, the family, the State, and, yes, organized religion can take their proper places in a wellorganized social order. This will not be achieved overnight, but removing the causes of terrorism will ultimately eliminate terrorism. One possible program that would in large measure remove the causes of terrorism in the Middle East is called the "Abraham Federation," which (while based on principles found in the three great Abrahamic faiths of Judaism, Christianity, and Islam) can be adapted for use in virtually any set of circumstances. This is because the essential principles of the Abraham Federation (an application of a proposal called "capital homesteading for every citizen") are consistent with the natural law discerned in and derived from human nature.

Any terrorist action, no matter who does it and for what purpose, is the greatest threat to democracy, peace and humanity. For this reason, no one and certainly Islam and other religions don't allow any terrorist action. Terrorism has no place in one's quest to achieve freedom or salvation. It costs the lives of many innocent people. The world must be assured that, although there might always be some who use any religion just for their interests, Islam does not support terrorism in any form. Terrorism cannot be used to achieve any Islamic or personal goal, in fact no terrorist can be a true Muslim, and no true Muslim can be a terrorist. Islam orders only peace and the Holy Quran demands from each true Muslim that he or she should be a symbol of peace and support the maintenance of essential human rights.

If a boat is carrying ten criminals and one innocent person, Islam does not allow the ship to be sunk just to punish the criminals, for doing so would violate the rights of innocent person. Islam respects all rights of individual person and states clearly that none of them can be violated or changed, even if doing so would be in the community's favour. The Quran says that one who takes a life of innocent person has, in effect, taken the lives of humanity, and that one who saves a life has, in effect, saved the lives of humanity. Also Prophet Muhammad (PBUH) says that a Muslim is one who does no harm with either her or his hand or tongue. The term 'Muslim terrorist' is used to consider Islam as a terrorist and dangerous religion.

This is completely wrong, some people and terrorist groups are trying to damage the image of Islamic religion by teaching wrong concepts. It should be noted that the violent actions of a small group or an individual do not necessarily represent the values of any religion, nor is that religion responsible for such brutal actions. Therefore, the media's labeling of those who are responsible for these actions as 'Muslim Terrorist' and relating such actions to Islam or the Holy Quran, is totally incorrect. Muslims are even supposed to be kind to animals and are prohibited to hurt them. Once the Prophet Muhammad (PBUH) said:

"A woman was punished because she imprisoned a cat until it died. On account of this, she was doomed to Hell. While she imprisoned it, she did not give the cat food or drink, nor did she free it to eat the insects of the earth."

Islam never supports criminal activities like High jacking planes, bombing building, kidnapping and killing innocent people. Some people are arguing that if the terrorist have the knowledge to fly a plane; it means they have a good level of intelligence, then why they don't understand the concept of Islam or other religion. The main reason behind is they are not thinking in the right direction, they are capable of thinking and learning, but they are not using there intelligence in right direction. Other reason is wrong concepts, they are taught by big terrorists' gangs that these acts are not violent, but you are doing these acts to save your religion and you will be rewarded after death, in the form of heaven.

In reality, Islam not only condemns terrorist actions and suicide bombing missions, but also prohibits them completely. Religion Islam commands love, peace and mercy. Terror, on the other hand, is the opposite of religion; it is unkind, merciless and demands killing and misery. Islam is a religion which provides freedom of ideas, thought and life. It has issued commands to avoid and prohibit tension, disputes and even negative thinking among people. In the same way that it is determinedly opposed to terrorism acts, terrorist and all acts of violence. Islam allows war only for defensive purposes. Muslims are strictly warned against the use of unnecessary provocation and violence. Islam is a religion of mercy, peace, and forgiveness, and the majority of Muslims have nothing to do with the brutal events. If any Muslim is committing any act of terrorism or violence, this person would be guilty of breaching the laws of Islamic religion.

The Jews in Israel and in other places are both the perpetrators and victims and of terrorism. I can understand where Jews are not happy over violent acts committed against them. But I have also looked and I know what is going on in the middle east and in Palestine, it's pretty clear to me that there is an attitude of organized ethnic cleansing against the Palestinians and other Muslims and this is not only wrong but it also makes me ashamed. Jews and Catholics are also prohibited from any terrorist acts, they are not allowed to kill anyone or hurt anyone. People who are committing these acts and pretend to be Muslims, Jews or Catholics, are just terrorists, they don't belong to any religion. Their aim is to destroy the image of all religions and to hide the actual beliefs and values of religion.

Religion and terrorism are incompatible, if a Muslim is fighting with a Hindu or a Hindu is fighting with a Sikh, they are fighting for their own reasons, religion is not involved at all, they lack complete information about their religion and they just think we right and all other religions are wrong. Sometimes religion is not the only reason for fighting or violence, there might be some personal and family or land disputes, and in India it is the major cause of all fighting between Muslims, Sikhs and Hindus. Take Kashmir as an example, Muslims and Hindus there are just fighting over land disputes, religion is not the main reason, they are not even concerned about their religion, and their aim is just occupy the land. Same case is in Palestine, where Jews are fighting and killing Muslims for land dispute, although religion is also involved but is not main reason, so people all over the world take it as religion terrorism.

Research on Terrorism

Terrorism is not new, and even though it has been used since the beginning of recorded history it can be relatively hard to define. Terrorism has been described variously as both a tactic and strategy; a crime and a holy duty; a justified reaction to oppression and an inexcusable abomination. Obviously, a lot depends on whose point of view is being represented. Terrorism has often been an effective tactic for the weaker side in a conflict. As an asymmetric form of conflict, it confers coercive power with many of the advantages of military force at a fraction of the cost. Due to the secretive nature and small size of terrorist organizations, they often offer opponents no clear organization to defend against or to deter. That is why preemption is being considered to be so important. In some cases, terrorism has been a means to carry on a conflict without the adversary realizing the nature of the threat, mistaking terrorism for criminal activity.

Because of these characteristics, terrorism has become increasingly common among those pursuing extreme goals throughout the world. But despite its popularity, terrorism can be a nebulous concept. Even within the U.S. Government, agencies responsible for different functions in the ongoing fight against terrorism use different definitions. The United States Department of Defense defines terrorism as "the calculated use of unlawful violence or threat of unlawful violence to inculcate fear; intended to coerce or to intimidate governments or societies in the pursuit of goals that are generally political, religious, or ideological." Within this definition, there are three key elements—violence, fear, and intimidation—and each element produce terror in its victims. The FBI uses this: "Terrorism is the unlawful use of force and violence against persons or property to intimidate or coerce a government, the civilian population, or any segment thereof, in furtherance of political or social objectives."

The U.S. Department of State defines "terrorism" to be "premeditated politicallymotivated violence perpetrated against noncombatant targets by subnational groups or clandestine agents, usually intended to influence an audience. Outside the United States Government, there are greater variations in what features of terrorism are emphasized in definitions. The United Nations produced this definition in 1992; "An anxietyinspiring method of repeated violent action, employed by (semi) clandestine individual, group or state actors, for idiosyncratic, criminal or political reasons, whereby in contrast to assassination the direct targets of violence are not the main targets." The most commonly accepted academic definition starts with the U.N. definition quoted above, and adds two sentences totalling another 77 words on the end; containing such verbose concepts as "message generators" and 'violence based communication processes." Less specific and considerably less verbose, the British Government definition of 1974 is"...the use of violence for political ends, and includes any use of violence for the purpose of putting the public, or any section of the public, in fear." Terrorism is a criminal act that influences an audience beyond the immediate victim.

The strategy of terrorists is to commit acts of violence that draws the attention of the local populace, the government, and the world to their cause. The terrorists plan their attack to obtain the greatest publicity, choosing targets that symbolize what they oppose. The effectiveness of the terrorist act lies not in the act itself, but in the public's or government's reaction to the act. For example, in 1972 at the Munich Olympics, the Black September Organization killed 11 Israelis. The Israelis were the immediate victims. But the true target was the estimated 1 billion people watching the televised event. The Black September Organization used the high visibility of the Olympics to publicize its views on the plight of the Palestinian refugees. Similarly, in October 1983, Middle Eastern terrorists bombed the Marine Battalion Landing Team Headquarters at Beirut International Airport. Their immediate victims were the 241 U.S. military personnel who were killed and over 100 others who were wounded. Their true target was the American people and the U.S. Congress. Their one act of violence influenced the United States' decision to withdraw the Marines from Beirut and was therefore considered a terrorist success. There are three perspectives of terrorism: the terrorist's, the victim's, and the general publics.

The phrase "one man's terrorist is another man's freedom fighter" is a view terrorists themselves would accept. Terrorists do not see themselves as evil. They believe they are legitimate combatants, fighting for what they believe in, by whatever means possible. A victim of a terrorist act sees the terrorist as a criminal with no regard for human life. The general public's view is the most unstable. The terrorists take great pains to foster a "Robin Hood" image in hope of swaying the general public's point of view toward their cause. This sympathetic view of terrorism has become an integral part of their psychological warfare and needs to be countered vigorously. Terrorist acts or the threat of such action have been in existence for millennia.

Despite having a history longer than the modern nationstate, the use of terror by governments and those that contest their power remains poorly understood. While the meaning of the word terror itself is clear, when it is applied to acts and actors in the real world it becomes confused. Part of this is due to the use of terror tactics by actors at all levels in the social and political environment. Is the Unabomber, with his solo campaign of terror, a criminal, terrorist, or revolutionary? Can he be compared to the French revolutionary governments who coined the word terrorism by instituting systematic state terror against the population of France in the 1790s, killing thousands? Are either the same as revolutionary terrorist groups such as the Baader-Mienhof Gang of West Germany or the Weather Underground in the United States? So we see that distinctions of size and political legitimacy of the actors using terror raise questions as to what is and is not terrorism. The concept of moral equivalency is frequently used as an argument to broaden and blur the definition of terrorism as well.

This concept argues that the outcome of an action is what matters, not the intent. Collateral or unintended damage to civilians from an attack by uniformed military forces on a legitimate military target is the same as a terrorist bomb directed deliberately at the civilian target with the intent of creating that damage. Simply put, a car bomb on a city street and a jet fighter dropping a bomb on a tank are both acts of violence that produce death and terror. Therefore (at the extreme end of this argument) any military action is simply terrorism by a different name. This is the reasoning behind the famous phrase "One man's terrorist is another man's freedom fighter". It is also a legacy of legitimizing the use of terror by successful revolutionary movements after the fact. The very flexibility and adaptability of terror throughout the years has contributed to the confusion. Those seeking to disrupt, reorder or destroy the status quo have continuously sought new and creative ways to achieve their goals. Changes in the tactics and techniques of terrorists have been significant, but even more significant are the growth in the number of causes and social contexts where terrorism is used.

Over the past 20 years, terrorists have committed extremely violent acts for alleged political or religious reasons. Political ideology ranges from the far left to the far right. For example, the far left can consist of groups such as Marxists and Leninists who propose a revolution of workers led by a revolutionary elite. On the far right, we find dictatorships that typically believe in a merging of state and business leadership. Nationalism is the devotion to the interests or culture of a group of people or a nation. Typically, nationalists share a common ethnic background and wish to establish or regain a homeland. Religious extremists often reject the authority of secular governments and view legal systems that are not based on their religious beliefs as illegitimate. They often view modernization efforts as corrupting influences on traditional culture. Special interest groups include people on the radical fringe of many legitimate causes; e.g., people who use terrorism to uphold antiabortion views, animal rights, radical environmentalism. These groups believe that violence is morally justifiable to achieve their goals.

Terror in Antiquity

The earliest known organization that exhibited aspects of a modern terrorist organization was the Zealots of Judea.

Known to the Romans as sicarii, or daggermen, they carried on an underground campaign of assassination of Roman occupation forces, as well as any Jews they felt had collaborated with the Romans. Their motive was an uncompromising belief that they could not remain faithful to the dictates of Judaism while living as Roman subjects. Eventually, the Zealot revolt became open, and they were finally besieged and committed mass suicide at the fortification of Masada. The Assassins were the next group to show recognizable characteristics of terrorism, as we know it today. A breakaway faction of Shia Islam called the Nizari Ismalis adopted the tactic of assassination of enemy leaders because the cult's limited manpower prevented open combat. Their leader, HassamI Sabbah, based the cult in the mountains of Northern Iran.

Their tactic of sending a lone assassin to successfully kill a key enemy leader at the certain sacrifice of his own life (the killers waited next to their victims to be killed or captured) inspired fearful awe in their enemies. Even though both the Zealots and the Assassins operated in antiquity, they are relevant today: First as forerunners of modern terrorists in aspects of motivation, organization, targeting, and goals. Secondly, although both were ultimate failures, the fact that they are remembered hundreds of years later, demonstrates the deep psychological impact they caused.

Early Origins of Terrorism

From the time of the Assassins (late 13th century) to the1700s, terror and barbarism were widely used in warfare and conflict, but key ingredients for terrorism were lacking. Until the rise of the modern nation state after the Treaty of Westphalia in 1648, the sort of central authority and cohesive society that terrorism attempts to influence barely existed. Communications were inadequate and controlled, and the causes that might inspire terrorism (religious schism, insurrection, ethnic strife) typically led to open warfare. By the time kingdoms and principalities became nations, they had sufficient means to enforce their authority and suppress activities such as terrorism. The French Revolution provided the first uses of the words "Terrorist" and "Terrorism".

Use of the word "terrorism" began in 1795 in reference to the Reign of Terror initiated by the Revolutionary government. The agents of the Committee of Public Safety and the National Convention that enforced the policies of "The Terror" were referred to as 'Terrorists". The French Revolution provided an example to future states in oppressing their populations. It also inspired a reaction by royalists and other opponents of the Revolution who employed terrorist tactics such as assassination and intimidation in resistance to the Revolutionary agents. The Parisian mobs played a critical role at key points before, during, and after the Revolution. Such extralegal activities as killing prominent officials and aristocrats in gruesome spectacles started long before the guillotine was first used.

Entering the Modern Era: The 19th Century

During the late 19th century, radical political theories and improvements in weapons technology spurred the formation of small groups of revolutionaries who effectively attacked nationstates. Anarchists espousing belief in the "propaganda of the deed" produced some striking successes, assassinating heads of state from Russia, France, Spain, Italy, and the United States. However, their lack of organization and refusal to cooperate with other social movements in political efforts rendered anarchists ineffective as a political movement. In contrast, Communism's role as an ideological basis for political terrorism was just beginning, and would become much more significant in the 20th century. Another trend in the late 19th century was the increasing tide of nationalism throughout the world, in which the nation (the identity of a people) and the political state were combined.

As states began to emphasize national identities, peoples that had been conquered or colonized could, like the Jews at the times of the Zealots, opt for assimilation or struggle. The bestknown nationalist conflict from this time is still unresolved - the multi-century struggle of Irish nationalism. Nationalism, like communism, became a much greater ideological force in the 20th century. The terrorist group from this period that serves as a model in many ways for what was to come was the Russian Narodnya Volya (Peoples Will). They differed in some ways from modern terrorists, especially in that they would sometimes call off attacks that might endanger individuals other than their intended target. Other than this quirk, we see many of the traits of terrorism here for the first time; clandestine, cellular organization; impatience and inability for the task of organizing the constituents they claim to represent; and a tendency to increase the level of violence as pressures on the group mount.

Terrorism in the 20th and 21st Century

The Early 20th Century

The first half of the 20th century saw two events that influenced the nature of conflict to the present day. The effects of two World Wars inflamed passions and hopes of nationalists throughout the world, and severely damaged the legitimacy of the international order and governments.

Nationalism on the Rise

Nationalism intensified during the early 20th century throughout the world. It became an especially powerful force in the subject peoples of various colonial empires. Although dissent and resistance were common in many colonial possessions, and sometimes resulted in open warfare, nationalist identities became a focal point for these actions. Gradually, as nations became closely tied to concepts of race and ethnicity, international political developments began to support such concepts.

Members of ethnic groups whose states had been absorbed by others or had ceased to exist as separate nations saw opportunities to realize nationalist ambitions. Several of these groups chose terror as a method to conduct their struggle and make their situation known to world powers they hoped would be sympathetic. In Europe, both the Irish and the Macedonians had existing terrorist campaigns as part of their ongoing struggle for independence, but had to initiate bloody uprisings to further their cause. The Irish were partially successful, the Macedonians failed.

Damaged Legitimacy

The "total war" practices of all combatants of WWII provided further justification for the "everybody does it" view of the use of terror and violations of the law of war. The desensitization of people and communities to violence that started in World War I accelerated during World War II. The intensity of the conflict between starkly opposed ideologies led to excesses on the part of all participants. New weapons and strategies that targeted the enemies' civilian population to destroy their economic capacity for conflict exposed virtually every civilian to the hazards of combatants. The major powers' support of partisan and resistance organizations using terrorist tactics was viewed as an acceptance of their legitimacy. It seemed that civilians had become legitimate targets, despite any rules forbidding it.

Cold War Developments

The bipolar world of the Cold War changed perception of conflicts the world over. Relatively minor confrontations took on significance as arenas where the superpowers could compete without risking escalation to full nuclear war. Warfare between the East and the West took place on the peripheries, and was limited in scope to prevent escalation. During the immediate postwar period, terrorism was more of a tactical choice by leaders of nationalist insurgencies and revolutions. Successful campaigns for independence from colonial rule occurred throughout the world, and many employed terrorism as a supporting tactic. When terrorism was used, it was used within the framework of larger movements, and coordinated with political, social, and military action.

Even when terrorism came to dominate the other aspects of a nationalist struggle, such as the Palestinian campaign against Israel, it was (and is) combined with other activities. Throughout the Cold War, the Soviet Union provided direct and indirect assistance to revolutionary movements around the world. Many anticolonial movements found the revolutionary extremism of communism attractive.

Leaders of these "wars of national liberation" saw the advantage of free weapons and training. They also realized that the assistance and patronage of the Eastern Bloc meant increased international legitimacy. Many of these organizations and individuals utilized terrorism in support of their political and military objectives. The policy of the Soviet Union to support revolutionary struggles everywhere, and to export revolution to noncommunist countries, provided extremists willing to employ violence and terror as the means to realize their ambitions.

The Internationalization of Terror

The age of modern terrorism might be said to have begun in 1968 when the Popular Front for the Liberation of Palestine (PFLP) hijacked an El Al airliner en route from Tel Aviv to Rome. While hijackings of airliners had occurred before, this was the first time that the nationality of the carrier (Israeli) and its symbolic value was a specific operational aim. Also a first was the deliberate use of the passengers as hostages for demands made publicly against the Israeli government. The combination of these unique events, added to the international scope of the operation, gained significant media attention. The founder of PFLP, Dr. George Habash observed that the level of coverage was tremendously greater than battles with Israeli soldiers in their previous area of operations. "At least the world is talking about us now."

Another aspect of this internationalization is the cooperation between extremist organizations in conducting terrorist operations. Cooperative training between Palestinian groups and European radicals started as early as 1970, and joint operations between the PFLP and the Japanese Red Army (JRA) began in 1974. Since then international terrorist cooperation in training, operations, and support has continued to grow, and continues to this day. Motives range from the ideological, such as the 1980s alliance of the Western European Marxist-oriented groups, to financial, as when the IRA exported its expertise in bomb making as far afield as Colombia.

Current State of Terrorism

The largest act of international terrorism occurred on September 11, 2001 in a set of co-ordinate attacks on the United States of America where Islamic terrorists hijacked civilian airliners and used them to attack the World Trade Center towers in New York City and the Pentagon in Washington, DC. Other major terrorist attacks have also occurred in New Delhi (Indian Parliament attacked); Bali car bomb attack; London subway bombings; Madrid train bombings and the most recent attacks in Mumbai (hotels, train station and a Jewish outreach center). The operational and strategic epicenter of Islamic terrorism is now mostly centered in Pakistan and Afghanistan.

Jewish Justification

Jewish Religious Terrorism

Jewish religious terrorism is religious terrorism committed by Jews who interpret Judaism to justify violence.

Extremist Religious Organizations

The following groups were all started or branched off from those started by Meir Kahane in the 1970s. Kahanist groups are banned in Israel:

The Jewish Defense League (JDL, 1969 to present) was founded in 1969 by Rabbi Meir Kahane in New York City, with its declared purpose the protection of Jews from harassment and antiSemitism. FBI statistics show that, from 1980 to 1985, 15 terrorist attacks were attempted in the U.S. by members of the JDL. The FBI's Mary Doran described the JDL in 2004 Congressional testimony as "a proscribed terrorist group". The National Consortium for the Study of Terror and Responses to Terrorism states that, during the JDL's first two decades of activity, it was an "active terrorist organization."

- Kach and Kahane Chai: (defunct) Israel and the United States.
- Gush Emunim Underground: (defunct) Sometimes called the (Jewish Terror Organization), formed by prominent members of Gush Emunim.

A new 'Jewish underground' is thought by Ehud Olmert to be behind the 25 September 2008 pipe bombing of Zeev Sternhell, a political scientist at Jerusalem's Hebrew University. The attack has been likened to the grenade attack that killed Emil Grunzweig.[10] In a hearing following the attack, Knesset's Committee for Internal Affairs, Chairman Ophir PinesPaz stated: "we are calling this an act of terror because that is precisely what it is, especially when it pertains to an ideological debate on the direction Israel is going.. . . We have to take very firm action. These are terroristsJewish, but terrorists just the same."

Christian Justification

Christian terrorism is religious terrorism by groups or individuals, the motivation of which is typically rooted in an idiosyncratic interpretation of the Bible and other Christian tenets of faith. From the viewpoint of the terrorist, Christian scripture and theology provide justification for violent political activities. In the beginning, Christianity was terrorized ruthlessly, with members losing their property, citizenship, privileges, tortured and often killed horribly by Roman authorities. When Emperor Constantine became a Christian, it was declared the state religion and the scales had reversed. The pagans were persecuted brutally and forced to convert.

A wave of conversions backed up with force spread Christianity across Europe, until Lithuania fell as the last pagan nation. The Crusades pitted Christians against Muslims, who had used the same methods. As recounted by many sources, when Jerusalem fell the first time, every Muslim and Jew in the city was killed, except perhaps for a few spared by less ruthless Crusaders. On the way, dissident monks and Eastern Christians had also been attacked, even slaughtered. Heretical Christian sects were stamped out by force, often with followers massacred or forced to give up their beliefs. When the Reformation occurred, religious wars began that killed millions in the struggled between Catholics and Protestants. Ian Gilmour has cited the historical case of the St. Bartholomew's Day massacre as an instance of Christian terrorism on par with modern day terrorism, and goes on to write, "That massacre, said Pope Gregory XIII, gave him more pleasure than fifty Battles of Lepanto, and he commissioned Vasari to paint frescoes of it in the Vatican". It is estimated that ten thousand to possibly onehundred thousand Huguenots (French Protestants) were killed by Catholic mobs, and it has been called "the worst of the century's religious massacres".

The massacre led to the start of the fourth war of the French Wars of Religion. Peter Steinfels has cited the historical case of the Gunpowder Plot, when Guy Fawkes and other Catholic revolutionaries attempted to overthrow the Protestant aristocracy of England by blowing up the Houses of Parliament, as a notable case of Christian terrorism. Meanwhile, the Christian and Muslim worlds often clashed with great bloodshed. The Inquisition tortured and put to death thousands of heretics. In the New World and other regions of the globe, converts were often made by force, with massacres of entire villages. The Portuguese colony Goa, part of India, was forcibly converted by their Inquisition with dissident Hindus and Muslims burned at the stake.

Christianity motivated conquering the Americas' natives and converting them. Black Africans were enslaved with the justification of Christianizing them, and the excuse they were Children of Ham, condemned to servitude. Islam used the same conversion excuse for slavery. These arguments were used into the 1860s, until civil war in the U.S. freed the slaves. AntiSemitism has been justified from preMedieval times because "Jews killed the Lord Jesus," of course forgetting that Christ and the first disciples were also Jews, while he was killed by the Roman under Pharisees sect demands, according to scripture. Even so late as 1914, British troops were extorted by the Church of England to kill the "Huns" of Germany, who they claimed were crucifying Belgians on the church doors, while most Germans were of course also Christian. Terrorist groups and crimes occur even today, as discussed below.

Islamic Justification

The Religious Sources of Islamic Terrorism

While terrorism—even in the form of suicide attacks — is not an Islamic phenomenon by definition, it cannot be ignored that the lion's share of terrorist acts and the most devastating of them in recent years have been perpetrated in the name of Islam. This fact has sparked a fundamental debate both in the West and within the Muslim world regarding the link between these acts and the teachings of Islam. Most Western analysts are hesitant to identify such acts with the bona fide teachings of one of the world's great religions and prefer to view them as a perversion of a religion that is essentially peaceloving and tolerant. Western leaders such as George W. Bush and Tony Blair have reiterated time and again that the war against terrorism has nothing to do with Islam. It is a war against evil.

The nonIslamic etiologies of this phenomenon include political causes (the Israeli-Arab conflict); cultural causes (rebellion against Western cultural colonialism); and social causes (alienation, poverty). While no public figure in the West would deny the imperative of fighting the war against terrorism, it is equally politically correct to add the codicil that, for the war to be won, these (justified) grievances pertaining to the root causes of terrorism should be addressed. A skeptic may note that many societies can put claim to similar grievances but have not given birth to religious-based ideologies that justify no-hold-sbarred terrorism. Nevertheless an interpretation which places the blame for terrorism on religious and cultural traits runs the risk of being branded as bigoted and Islamophobic.

The political motivation of the leaders of Islamist jihadisttype movements is not in doubt. A glance at the theatres where such movements flourished shows that most fed off their political – and usually military – encounter with the West. This was the case in India and in the Sudan in the nineteenth century and in Egypt and Palestine in the twentieth. The moral justification and levers of power for these movements, however, were for the most part not couched in political terms, but based on Islamic religious sources of authority and religious principles. By using these levers and appealing to deeply ingrained religious beliefs, the radical leaders succeed in motivating the Islamist terrorist, creating for him a social environment that provides approbation and a religious environment that provides moral and legal sanction for his actions.

The success of radical Islamic organizations in the recruitment, posting, and ideological maintenance of sleeper activists (the 911 terrorists are a prime example) without their defecting or succumbing to the lure of Western civilization proves the deep ideological nature of the phenomenon. Therefore, to treat Islamic terrorism as the consequence of political and socioeconomic factors alone would not do justice to the significance of the religious culture in which this phenomenon is rooted and nurtured. In order to comprehend the motivation for these acts and to draw up an effective strategy for a war against terrorism, it is necessary to understand the religiousideological factors – which are deeply embedded in Islam.

The Weltanschauung of Radical Islam

Modern international Islamist terrorism is a natural offshoot of twentiethcentury Islamic fundamentalism. The "Islamic Movement" emerged in the Arab world and Britishruled India as a response to the dismal state of Muslim society in those countries: social injustice, rejection of traditional mores, acceptance of foreign domination and culture. It perceives the malaise of modern Muslim societies as having strayed from the "straight path" and the solution to all ills in a return to the original mores of Islam. The problems addressed may be social or political: inequality, corruption, and oppression. But in traditional Islam – and certainly in the worldview of the Islamic fundamentalist – there is no separation between the political and the religious. Islam is, in essence, both religion and regime and no area of human activity is outside its remit. Be the nature of the problem as it may, "Islam is the solution."

The underlying element in the radical Islamist worldview is ahistoric and dichotomist: Perfection lies in the ways of the Prophet and the events of his time; therefore, religious innovations, philosophical relativism, and intellectual or political pluralism are anathema. In such a worldview, there can exist only two camps – Dar alIslam ("The House of Islam" – i.e., the Muslim countries) and Dar alHarb ("The House of War" – i.e., countries ruled by any regime but Islam) – which are pitted against each other until the final victory of Islam. These concepts are carried to their extreme conclusion by the radicals; however, they have deep roots in mainstream Islam. While the trigger for "Islamic awakening" was frequently the meeting with the West, Islamicmotivated rebellions against colonial powers rarely involved individuals from other Muslim countries or broke out of the confines of the territories over which they were fighting.

Until the 1980s, most fundamentalist movements such as the Muslim Brotherhood were inwardlooking; Western superiority was viewed as the result of Muslims having forsaken the teachings of the Prophet. Therefore, the remedy was, first, "reIslamization" of Muslim society and restoration of an Islamic government, based on Islamic law. In this context, jihad was aimed mainly against "apostate" Muslim governments and societies, while the historic offensive jihad of the Muslim world against the infidels was put in abeyance (at least until the restoration of the caliphate). Until the 1980s, attempts to mobilize Muslims all over the world for a jihad in one area of the world (Palestine, Kashmir) were unsuccessful. The Soviet invasion of Afghanistan was a watershed event, as it revived the concept of participation in jihad to evict an "infidel" occupier from a Muslim country as a "personal duty" for every capable Muslim.

The basis of this duty derives from the "irreversibility" of Islamic identity both for individual Muslims (thus, capital punishment for "apostates"—e.g., Salman Rushdie) and for Muslim territories. Therefore, any land (Afghanistan, Palestine, Kashmir, Chechnya, Spain) that had once been under the sway of Islamic law may not revert to control by any other law. In such a case, it becomes the "personal duty" of all Muslims in the land to fight a jihad to liberate it. If they do not succeed, it becomes incumbent on any Muslim in a certain perimeter from that land to join the jihad and so forth. Accordingly, given the number of Muslim lands under "infidel occupation" and the length of time of those occupations, it is argued that it has become a personal duty for all Muslims to join the jihad. This duty — if taken seriously — is no less a religious imperative than the other five pillars of Islam (the statement of belief or shahadah, prayer, fasting, charity, and haj). It becomes a de facto (and in the eyes of some a de jure) sixth pillar; a Muslim who does not perform it will inherit hell.

Such a philosophy attributing centrality to the duty of jihad is not an innovation of modern radical Islam. The seventhcentury Kharijite sect, infamous in Islamic history as a cause of Muslim civil war, took this position and implemented it. But the Kharijite doctrine was rejected as a heresy by medieval Islam. The novelty is the tacit acceptance by mainstream Islam of the basic building blocks of this "neoKharijite" school. The Soviet defeat in Afghanistan and the subsequent fall of the Soviet Union were perceived as an eschatological sign, adumbrating the renewal of the jihad against the infidel world at large and the apocalyptical war between Islam and heresy which will result in the rule of Islam in the world. Along with the renewal of the jihad, the Islamist Weltanschauung, which emerged from the Afghani crucible, developed a Thanatophile ideology in which death is idealized as a desired goal and not a necessary evil in war.

An offshoot of this philosophy poses a dilemma for theories of deterrence. The Islamic traditions of war allow the Muslim forces to retreat if their numerical strength is less than half that of the enemy. Other traditions go further and allow retreat only in the face of a tenfold superiority of the enemy. The reasoning is that the act of jihad is, by definition, an act of faith in Allah. By fighting a weaker or equal enemy, the Muslim is relying on his own strength and not on Allah; by entering the fray against all odds, the *mujahidin* is proving his utter faith in Allah and will be rewarded accordingly. The politics of Islamist radicalism has also bred a mentality of bello ergo sum (I fight, therefore I exist) – Islamic leaders are in constant need of popular jihads to boost their leadership status. Nothing succeeds like success:

The attacks in the United States gave birth to a second wave of *mujahidin* who want to emulate their heroes. The perception of resolve on the part of the West is a critical factor in shaping the mood of the Muslim population toward radical ideas. Therefore, the manner by which the United States deals with the present crisis in Iraq is not unconnected to the future of the radical Islamic movement. In these circles, the American occupation of Iraq is likened to the Soviet invasion of Afghanistan; a sense of American failure would feed the apocalyptical ideology of jihad.

The Legality of Jihad

These beliefs are commonly viewed as typical of radical Islamic ideology, but few orthodox Islamic scholars would deny that they are deeply rooted in orthodox Islam or would dismiss the very ideology of jihad as a military struggle as foreign to the basic tenets of Islam. Hence, much of the debate between radicals and non radicals is not over the religious principles themselves, but over their implication for actual behaviour as based on the detailed legal interpretation of those principles. This legal interpretation is the soul of the debate. Even among moderate Islamic scholars who condemn acts of terrorism (albeit with reservation so as not to include acts perpetrated against Israel in such a category), there is no agreement on why they should be condemned: Many modernists acknowledge the existence of a duty of jihad in Islam but call for an "Islamic Protestantism" that would divest Islam of vestiges of anachronistic beliefs; conservative moderates find in traditional Islamic jurisprudence legal justification to put the imperative of jihad in abeyance; others use linguistic analysis to point out that the etymology of the word jihad actually means "to strive," does not mean "holy war," and does not necessarily have a military connotation.

The legalistic approach is not a barren preoccupation of scholars. The ideal Islamic regime is a monocracy: The law is given and immutable, and it remains for the leaders of the (the Islamic nation) to apply it on a daytoday basis. Islam is not indifferent to any facet of human behaviour; all possible acts potentially have a religious standing, ranging between "duty" (fard, pl. fara'id); "recommended" (mandub); "optional" (jaiz); "permitted" (mubah); "reprehensible" (makruh); and "forbidden" (haram). This taxonomy of human behaviour has farreaching importance for the believer: By performing all his religious duties, he will inherit paradise; by failing to do so ("sins of omission") or doing that which is forbidden ("sins of commission"), he will be condemned to hell. Therefore, such issues as the legitimacy of jihad—ostensibly deriving from the roots of Islam— cannot be decided by abstract morality or by politics, but by meticulous legal analysis and ruling (fatwa) according to the shari'ah, performed by an authoritative Islamic scholar ('alem, pl. 'ulama).

The use of fatwa to call for violent action first known in the West as a result of Ayatollah Khomeini's fatwa against Salman Rushdie, and again after Osama bin Laden's 1998 fatwa against the United States and Israel. But as a genuine instrument of religious deliberation, it has not received the attention it deserves. Analysts have frequently interpreted fatwa as no more than the cynical use of religious terminology in political propaganda. This interpretation does not do justice to the painstaking process of legal reasoning invested in these documents and the importance that their authors and their target audience genuinely accord to the religious truthfulness of their rulings.

The political strength of these fatwa has been timetested in Muslim political society by rebels and insurgents from the Arabian Peninsula to Sudan, India, and Indonesia. At the same time, they have been used by Muslim regimes to bolster their Islamic credentials against external and domestic enemies and to legitimize their policies. This was done by the Sudanese mahdi in his rebellion against the British (188185); by the Ottoman caliphate (December 1914) in World War i; by the Syrian regime against the rebellion in northern Syria (1981); and, mutatis mutandis, by Egyptian President Anwar Sadat to legitimize his peace policies toward Israel. The fatwas promulgated by sheikhs and 'ulama who stipulate that jihad is a "personal duty" play, therefore, a pivotal role in encouraging radicalism and in building the support infrastructure for radicals within the traditional Islamic community. While one may find many fatwas which advocate various manifestations of terrorism, fatwas which rule that those who perform these acts do not go to paradise but inherit hell are few and far between.

The questions relating to jihad which are referred to the religious scholars relate to a number of issues: The very definition, current existence, and area of application of the state of jihad. Is jihad one of the "pillars" (arkan) or "roots" (usul) of Islam? Does it necessarily imply military war, or can it be perceived as a duty to spread Islam through preaching or even the moral struggle between one's soul and Satan? If the former, then what are the necessary conditions for jihad? Does a state of jihad currently exist between Dar alIslam and Dar alHarb? And how can one define Dar alIslam today, in the absence of a caliphate? Is the rest of the world automatically defined as Dar alHarb with which a state of jihad exists, or do the treaties and diplomatic relations which exist between Muslim countries and "infidel" countries (including the charter of the United Nations) change this?

Who must participate in jihad, and how? Is jihad a personal duty (fard 'ein) for each and every Muslim under all circumstances or a collective duty (fard kiffaya) that can be performed only under the leadership of a leader of all Muslims (imam, khalifa, amir almu'aminin)? Is it incumbent on women? On minors? (According to Islamic law, in the case of a defensive jihad for the liberation of Islamic territory from infidel occupation, a woman need not ask permission of her husband or a child of his parents nor a slave of his master".) May a Muslim refrain from supporting his attacked brethren or obey a nonMuslim secular law which prohibits him from supporting other Muslims in their struggle?

How should the jihad be fought (jus in bellum)? The questions in this area relate, inter alia, to: (a) Is jihad by definition an act of conflict against the actual "infidels" or can it be defined as a spiritual struggle against the "evil inclination"? If it is the former, must it take the form of war (jihad fisabil Allah) or can it be performed by way of preaching and proselytization (da'awah)? (b) Who is a legitimate target? Is it permissible to kill noncombatant civilians – women, children, elderly, and clerics; "protected" nonMuslims in Muslim countries – local nonMuslims or tourists whose visas may be interpreted as Islamic guarantees of passage (aman); Muslim bystanders? (c) The legitimacy of suicide attacks (istishhad) as a form of jihad in the light of the severe prohibition on a Muslim taking his own life, on one hand, and the promise of rewards in the afterlife for the shahid who falls in a jihad on the other hand. (d) The weapons which may be used. For example, may a hijacked plane be used as a weapon as in the attacks of September 11 in the light of Islamic prohibitions on killing prisoners? (e) The status of a Muslim who aids the "infidels" against other Muslims. (f) The authority to implement capital punishment in the absence of a caliph.

How should jihad be funded? "Pocketbook jihad" is deeply entrenched in Islamic tradition. It is based on the injunction that one must fight jihad with his soul or with his tongue (jihad allissan or da'awah) or with his money (jihad fimal). Therefore, financial support of jihad is politically correct and even good for business for the wealthy supporter. The transfer of zakat (almsgiving) raised in a community for jihad fisabil Allah (i.e., jihad on Allah's path or military jihad) has wide religious and social legitimacy. The precepts of "war booty" (ghaneema or fay') call for a fifth (khoms) to be rendered to the *mujahidin*. Acts that would otherwise be considered religiously prohibited are thus legitimized by the payment of such a "tax" for the sake of jihad. While there have been attempts to bring Muslim clerics to denounce acts of terrorism, none, to date, have condemned the donation of money for jihad.

The Dilemma of the Moderate Muslim

It can be safely assumed that the great majority of Muslims in the world have no desire to join a jihad or to politicize their religion. However, it is also true that insofar as religious establishments in most of the Arabian Peninsula, in Iran, and in much of Egypt and North Africa are concerned, the radical ideology does not represent a marginal and extremist perversion of Islam but rather a genuine and increasingly mainstream interpretation. Even after 911, the sermons broadcast from Mecca cannot be easily distinguished from those of al Qaeda. Facing the radical Weltanschauung, the moderate but orthodox Muslim has to grapple with two main dilemmas: the difficulty of refuting the legalreligious arguments of the radical interpretation and the aversion to — or even prohibition of — inciting an Islamic Kulturkampf which would split the ranks of the ummah.

The first dilemma is not uniquely Islamic. It is characteristic of revelationbased religions that the less observant or less orthodox will hesitate to challenge fundamental dogmas out of fear of being branded slack or lapsed in their faith. They will prefer to pay their dues to the religious establishment, hoping that by doing so they are also buying their own freedom from coercion. On a deeper level, many believers who are not strict in observance may see their own lifestyle as a matter of convenience and not principle, while the extreme orthodox is the true believer to whom they defer. This phenomenon is compounded in Islam by the fact that "Arab" Sunni Islam never went though a reform. Since the tenth century, Islam has lacked an accepted mechanism for relegating a tenet or text to ideological obsolescence.

Until that time, such a mechanism – ijtihad – existed; ijtihad is the authorization of scholars to reach conclusions not only from existing interpretations and legal precedents, but from their own perusal of the texts. In the tenth century, the "gates of ijtihad" were closed for most of the Sunni world. It is still practiced in Shiite Islam and in Southeast Asia. Reformist traditions did appear in nonArab Middle Eastern Muslim societies (Turkey, Iran) and in Southeast Asian Islam. Many Sufi (mystical) schools also have traditions of syncretism, reformism, and moderation. These traditions, however, have always suffered from a lack of wide legitimacy due to their nonArab origins and have never been able to offer themselves as an acceptable alternative to ideologies born in the heartland of Islam and expressed in the tongue of the Prophet.

In recent years, these societies have undergone a transformation and have adopted much of the Middle Eastern brand of Islamic orthodoxy and have become, therefore, more susceptible to radical ideologies under the influence of Wahhabi missionaries, Iranian export of Islam, and the crosspollination resulting from the globalization of ideas in the information age. The second dilemma – the disinclination of moderates to confront the radicals – has frequently been attributed to violent intimidation (which, no doubt, exists), but it has an additional religious dimension. While the radicals are not averse to branding their adversaries as apostates, orthodox and moderate Muslims rarely resort to this weapon. Such an act (takfir – accusing another Muslim of heresy [kufr] by falsifying the roots of Islam, allowing that which is prohibited or forbidding that which is allowed) is not to be taken lightly; it contradicts the deeprooted value that Islam places on unity among the believers and its aversion to fitna (communal discord).

It is ironic that a religious mechanism which seems to have been created as a tool to preserve pluralism and prevent internal debates from deteriorating into civil war and mutual accusations of heresy (as occurred in Christian Europe) has become a tool in the hands of the radicals to drown out any criticism of them. Consequently, even when pressure is put on Muslim communities, there exists a political asymmetry in favour of the radicals. Moderates are reluctant to come forward and to risk being accused of apostasy. For this very reason, many Muslim regimes in the Middle East and Asia are reluctant to crack down on the religious aspects of radical Islam and satisfy themselves with dealing with the political violence alone. By way of appeasement politics, they trade tolerance of jihad elsewhere for local calm. Thus, they lose ground to radicals in their societies.

The Western Dilemma

It is a tendency in politically oriented Western society to assume that there is a rational pragmatic cause for acts of terrorism and that if the political grievance is addressed properly, the phenomenon will fade. However, when the roots are not political, it is naïve to expect political gestures to change the hearts of radicals. Attempts to deal with the terrorist threat as if it were divorced from its intellectual, cultural, and religious fountainheads are doomed to failure. Counterterrorism begins on the religiousideological level and must adopt appropriate methods. The cultural and religious sources of radical Islamic ideology must be addressed in order to develop a longrange strategy for coping with the terrorist threat to which they give birth. However, in addressing this phenomenon, the West is at a severe disadvantage.

Western concepts of civil rights along with legal, political, and cultural constraints preclude government intervention in the internal matters of organized religions; they make it difficult to prohibit or punish inflammatory sermons of imams in mosques (as Muslim regimes used to do on a regular basis) or to punish clerics for fatwas justifying terrorism. Furthermore, the legacy of colonialism deters Western governments from taking steps that may be construed as antiMuslim or as signs of lingering colonialist ideology. This exposes the Western country combating the terrorist threat to criticism from within. Even most of the new and stringent terrorism prevention legislation that has been enacted in some counties leans mainly on investigatory powers (such as allowing for unlimited administrative arrests, etc.) and does not deal with prohibition of religionbased "ideological crimes" (as opposed to antiNazi and antiracism laws, which are in force in many countries in Europe).

The regimes of the Middle East have proven their mettle in coercing religious establishments and even radical sheikhs to rule in a way commensurate with their interests. However, most of them show no inclination to join a global (i.e., "infidel") war against radical Islamic ideology. Hence, the prospect of enlisting Middle Eastern allies in the struggle against Islamic radicalism is bleak. Under these conditions, it will be difficult to curb the conversion of young Muslims in the West to the ideas of radicalism emanating from the safe houses of the Middle East. Even those who are not in direct contact with Middle Eastern sources of inspiration may absorb the ideology secondhand through interaction of Muslims from various origins in schools and on the internet.

Fighting Hellfire with Hellfire

Taking into account the above, is it possible — within the bounds of Western democratic values — to implement a comprehensive strategy to combat Islamic terrorism at its ideological roots? First, such a strategy must be based on an acceptance of the fact that for the first time since the Crusades, Western civilization finds itself involved in a religious war; the conflict has been defined by the attacking side as such with the eschatological goal of the destruction of Western civilization. The goal of the West cannot be defense alone or military offense or democratization of the Middle East as a panacea. It must include a religiousideological dimension: active pressure for religious reform in the Muslim world and pressure on the orthodox Islamic establishment in the West and the Middle East not only to disengage itself clearly from any justification of violence, but also to pit itself against the radical camp in a clear demarcation of boundaries.

Such disengagement cannot be accomplished by Westernstyle declarations of condemnation. It must include clear and binding legal rulings by religious authorities which contradict the axioms of the radical worldview and virtually "excommunicate" the radicals. In essence, the radical narrative, which promises paradise to those who perpetrate acts of terrorism, must be met by an equally legitimate religious force which guarantees hellfire for the same acts. Some elements of such rulings should be, inter alia:

- A call for renewal of jihad as the basis to reform Islamic dogmas and to relegate old dogmas to historic contexts.
- That there exists no state of jihad between Islam and the rest of the world (hence, jihad is not a personal duty).
- That the violation of the physical safety of a non-Muslim in a Muslim country is prohibited (haram).
- That suicide bombings are clear acts of suicide, and therefore, their perpetrators are condemned to eternal hellfire.
- That moral or financial support of acts of terrorism is also haram.
- That a legal ruling claiming jihad is a duty derived from the roots of Islam is a falsification of the roots of Islam, and therefore, those who make such statements have performed acts of heresy.

Only by setting up a clear demarcation between orthodox and radical Islam can the radical elements be exorcized. The priority of solidarity within the Islamic world plays into the hands of the radicals. Only an Islamic Kulturkampf can redraw the boundaries between radical and moderate in favour of the latter. Such a struggle must be based on an indepth understanding of the religious sources for justification of Islamist terrorism and a plan for the creation of a legitimate moderate counterbalance to the radical narrative in Islam. Such an alternative narrative should have a sound base in Islamic teachings, and its proponents should be Islamic scholars and leaders with wide legitimacy and accepted credentials. The "Middle-Easternization" of Asian Muslim communities should also be checked.

A strategy to cope with radical Islamic ideology cannot take shape without a reinterpretation of Western concepts of the boundaries of the freedoms of religion and speech, definitions of religious incitement, and criminal culpability of religious leaders for the acts of their flock as a result of their spiritual influence. Such a reinterpretation impinges on basic principles of Western civilization and law. Under the circumstances, it is the lesser evil.

Justifications for Terrorism

Terrorism in democracies can be justified on four general grounds, to force changes in policy on specific issues. They are

- The scale of the problem, and the number of people affected.
- The degree of suffering involved.
- The democratic process itself as cause, or partial cause.
- The democratic process as obstruction, to action or solution.

The example gave earlier - of terrorism to force western governments to give food and medical treatment to the starving illustrates all four aspects. Hundreds of millions of people are threatened by famine at some time in their lives, and the individual suffering during famines is acute (it generates a trauma comparable to those of concentration camp survivors). The cause of starvation is the refusal of rich western countries to share their wealth, primarily from racist and selfish motives. Democratic majorities block all attempts to increase aid to the required level, which would imply income tax rates of 80% to 90%. Because the democratic process, by definition, does not allow any override (or alternative decision-making process), terrorism is the only way to save millions of lives.

European spatial planning and transport issues as typical areas where terrorism is necessary. They are not usually considered in connection with terrorism, but they meet three of the criteria: the problems are very large in scale, they are the result of cumulated democratic decisions, and democracy usually obstructs any improvement. Vehicle particulate pollution is a good example. It results from the democratic decisions of European governments to promote roads and road traffic, since the 1920's, and it affects perhaps 200 million people in Europe. Yet the draconian transport and planning measures which would now be required to reduce it substantially are totally unacceptable for the electorate. The pollution will probably get worse, although it is now a serious health problem.

There are many other policy issues, not seen as related to political violence, where violence is in fact the only option. That in itself is a historical phenomenon, related to the inability of democratic systems to take unpopular decisions, and their inherent conservative bias. The longer democracies exist, the bigger the backlog of 'democratically impossible' policy changes. As a general rule, if a democratic government can choose between a good policy and an evil policy, and chooses the evil policy as a result of the democratic process, then undemocratic means may be used to reverse the policy. Respect for the democratic decision, in such circumstances, would imply that 'democracy' is a higher value than the priority of Good over Evil. It would imply that any policy no matter how evil, unjust or cruel was morally right, simply because it was democratic.

Although that suggestion is implicit in much prodemocracy theory, democracy is not the supreme moral value. Beside these four general grounds for terrorism in democracies, there are other specific justifications. Political violence is inherent in geopolitics. It is a historical reality that state formation and boundary changes are violent processes, and that war is the normal geopolitical ordering process. The fact that some (or all) states are democracies is irrelevant here. Inherently, the democratic order is internal to the demos-democracy does not determine which democracies exist, or how many, or what their borders are. More specifically, most democracies provide no peaceful means of secession. No democracy ever provided a means for simply establishing a new state, and neither does international law.

A specifically egalitarian state, then you will have to fight for it. That is the historical, legal and political reality, which is unaffected by pious denunciations of violence. Selfdefence is a general justification for violence, and this is particularly relevant in countries with ethnic and religious tensions, where the risk of overt violence against minorities is always present. That is now the case in Dutch and British cities; it is not simply a 'Balkan issue'. Where the appropriate organs of the state fail to protect the minority, then they are entitled to defend themselves. That failure usually results from domination of the state by the majority ethnic or religious group Protestants in Northern Ireland in the 1970's, for instance. The Dutch Ministry of Justice has an official policy not to prosecute incitements to kill minorities, especially Muslims.

As a result, there has been open incitement to kill all Muslims in the Netherlands, including a call to reopen the Auschwitz death camp for that purpose. As tensions with Islamic immigrants increase, and xenophobic movements become more aggressive, the issue of defensive armed force will reappear on the political agenda of European democracies, as it did in Northern Ireland. Many of these justifications also apply to violence by individuals, although it is not usually classified as terrorism. The politics of Tony Blair, that if he is assassinated, then probably by someone who suffered under the intense meritocracy in Blairite Britain, rather than at the hands of Al-Qaeda.

For instance by someone from a deprived background who was refused entry into the elite university of Oxford, for 'lack of talent'. Under a democratic system and the rule of law, there is indeed nothing an individual can do to alter this, and a revenge assassination is understandable. It can be no more than revenge: it will not change policy, or bring an egalitarian state, and it would not fall under the EU terrorism definition. But remember, Tony Blair has no moral justification himself, for submitting individuals to a meritocracy, if they object to that. He could have offered an escape route - for instance a 'non-meritocratic zone' in Scotland or Wales, or parallel nonmeritocratic institutions. He did not, because he sees meritocracy as a universal truth. The ethics of forced meritocracy are related to those of forced conversion.

Terrorism, Religion and Global Politics

The suspects of the Bali bombings may indeed just be "dummy agents" sacrificed to protect greater powers, yet further investigation has reportedly led to an extreme religious group planning ruthless attacks on foreign targets in Indonesia. No matter how quick the completion of the investigation, the debates on whether terrorism in Indonesia derives from Islamic militants or "American conspiracy" will continue. Two things have emerged from the debate. First, a belief that terrorism is connected to religion especially the radical followers of a particular religion. Secondly, a growing antiAmerican sentiment especially among Muslims following the war in Afghanistan and the growing tension in the Middle East. The U.S. policies in the Middle East, Afghanistan and Iraq are seen as part of "a Jewish-Christian" conspiracy against the Muslim world.

If terrorism is related to religion, what seems to have served as the root causes of radicalism that leads to terrorist attacks deserves more serious attention. In the early 1990s at least 20 percent of 50 known active terrorist groups throughout the world can be described as having a dominant religious motivation. Religion and terrorism share a history. Indeed, the main references to terrorist acts are derived from the names of religious sects committing assaults to cause public disorder many centuries ago. The word "zealot" can be traced back to a millenarian religious sect who fought against the Roman occupation of what is now Israel between 66 AD and 73 AD. The zealots waged a ruthless campaign employing a primitive form of chemical warfare, poisoning wells and granaries used by the Romans going so far to even sabotaging water supply.

Terrorism assumes a transcendental dimension and its perpetrators are thus unconstrained by moral, ethical and normative constraints. The religious or "holy" terrors compared to purely "secular" terror have radically different value systems in terms of mechanisms of legitimization, justification, and the world view that they embrace. Whereas secular terrorists generally consider indiscriminate violence immoral and counter-productive for their struggle, religious terrorists regard such violence not only as morally justified, but as a necessary means to achieve their goals. Here religion serves as a legitimizing force. Consequently, religious terrorism faces no moral constraints. Although terrorist groups emerge within particular religious context such as The Real IRA (of the Irish Catholic republicans), no religion has ever taught their followers to commit terrorist acts. "To blame Islam for what happened in New York on Sept. 11, 2001 is like blaming Christianity for the troubles in Northern Ireland!" wrote the British scientist Richard Dawkins (The Guardian, Sept. 15, 2001).

The problem is not with the religion itself but within radicalism growing in a religion. The most common resort to violence occurs when a religious group feels threatened and thinks of itself as chosen. In extreme cases, militant leaders of groups can demand their members to slaughter others in the name of deity. Here religion often provides a cloak of respectability of terrorism. There are at least two dangerous signs of religious radicalism. These include the charismatic leaders who dominate followers spiritually and emotionally and paranoia and demonization of outsiders, accompanied by intentional isolation within a cloistered community. Sociologist Gustav Le Bon once argued that in every radical movement, there are always the "men of words" and "the men of actions".

Using their charisma, the former convinces followers that their religion mandates acts of terror as sacred duty in an endless, cosmic struggle for the best way to please God. Nobody seems to care who or how many get killed in spiritual warfare.

Terrorist acts may also emerge from alienation that generates paranoia, often leading to demonization of outsiders or enemies. This occurs when conflicts come to be seen as "holy" wars where one side is upholding the forces of light (goodness) against the forces of darkness (evil). One of most prominent regional conflict is probably the war between the Israelis and the Palestinians in the Middle Eastern region. To many Muslims the superpower and its allies do too little to pressure Israel to end its atrocities against Yasser Arafat and the Palestinian settlers. They believe that the Western world has largely been unwilling to restore justice in the Middle East. It is this political setting which seems to have give birth to the JewishChristian conspiracy theory, to which many radical Muslims subscribe. Abu Bakar Ba'asyir, a Muslim cleric under police detention for his alleged involvement in a radical organization, argued: "Muslim clerics have agreed that both Jews and Christians are promoting a new Crusade".

The growing antiAmerican sentiment in most terrorist acts is also generated by the growing fear that the U.S. will lead the world into a scene of onrushing economic, technological and ecological forces that demand uniformity of values. This uniformity seems to mesmerize people everywhere with fast music, trendy fashions, and fast food. This "McWorld" trend, Benjamin Barber writes is a product of popular culture driven by expansionist commerce. Its template is American, and is quickly copied all over the world. It is about culture as commodity and apparel as ideology. The imposing of this highly secular way of life has unfortunately taken religious norms and values to its toll. In being reduced to a choice between the market-driven universalism and a set of politics and particularistic identities, people around the world are threatened with an atavistic return to medieval politics, where local tribes or religious groups stood up to defend their identities.

In extreme cases many people resort to religious identity to wage a total war against this universalism in order to amplify their appeal and to obtain spiritual justification. Here, McWorld appears to recreate and reinforce jihad. In its mildest form, jihad refers to religious (Islamic) struggles on behalf of faith. In its most extreme form it could mean militant acts that make the slaughter of the "other" a higher duty. While the disclosure of those behind the Bali bombing will bring much relief, it remains unclear whether terrorist acts motivated by religious reasons will cease to exist in Indonesia and elsewhere. As long as the "men of words" exist, terrorism with religious motives will continue to survive. One or two perpetrators may be captured and severely punished, but new players sharing the same ideology and hatred against infidels soon take their place.

Violence in the Bible and the Qur'an

After the events of September 11th, the issue of violence and religion has once again come into intense discussions and debate. As soon as Christians and others of good will condemn the Islamic justification and foundation for resorting to violence in the name of God—justifications found both in the Qur'an and the life of prophet Muhammad—we are quickly told that the Bible (especially the Old Testament scriptures) and Christian history are also filled with violence and that we should not single out Islam or the Qur'an in this regard.

The roots of Islamic rage—and what we can do about it" writes, "The historian Paul Johnson has argued that Islam is intrinsically an intolerant and violent religion. Other scholars have disagreed; pointing out that Islam condemns the slaughter of innocents and prohibits suicide. Nothing will be solved by searching for 'true Islam' or quoting the Qur'an. The Qur'an is a vast, vague book, filled with poetry and contradictions (much like the Bible) condemnations of war and incitements to struggle, beautiful expressions of tolerance and stern pictures against unbelievers. Quotations from it usually tell us more about the person who selected the passages than about Islam. Every religion is compatible with the best and the worst of humankind. Through its long history, Christianity has supported inquisitions and antiSemitism, but also human rights and social welfare." How can Christians respond to such countercharges?

Are Christians and their scriptures no different than Muslim terrorists and others who use violence in the name of God to destroy their enemies? What can we say in light of our own dark Church history and also graphic passages found in portions of the Old Testament that do not seem to cast any better light on the roots and actions of our own faith tradition? The following are some of my reflections on these questions. Time does not allow me to develop each point fully, but that they can be of some help and bring some clarification to these issues. As Christians we must be very emphatic that Christians have and continue to do many shameful things in the name of Christ, BUT the issue is this: Christians who use violence in the name of God to destroy their enemies have no justification for their actions from Jesus Christ, his life and teachings as found in the New Testament. Whereas, Muslims who are engaged in violence and destruction of anyone who opposes Islam, have ample justification for their actions from the Qur'an and the life and sayings of prophet Muhammad. It is beyond the scope of this chapter to quote verses and passages from the Qur'an, the Hadith and biographies of prophet Muhammad (the reader can refer to other articles on this web site, e.g. in the sections Muhammad and his enemies or Islam & Terrorism), but suffice it to say that it is beyond doubt that the prophet of Islam did encourage the killing and intimidation of his enemies, not just in self defense as it is commonly reported by Muslims, but in the promotion of the cause of God and the spread of Islam.

Needless to say, the actions of the prophet were in direct contradiction to the teachings and actions of Jesus Christ and his disciples. So the point is not that Christians have never resorted to violence and other horrible atrocities. They have indeed committed many horrible acts, but when they have done this, they have betrayed the very person that they claim to follow. But when Muslims commit such acts, they can in fact claim that they are following the example of their prophet and thus fulfilling the will of God and promoting His cause. That, certainly, is a big difference! When we turn our attention to the Old Testament and look at passages that are found in the book of Joshua regarding the extermination of the Canaanites living in the land, we can still notice a dramatic difference in those passages and the events in the early history of Islam. The primary theme in those accounts is the issue of God's holiness. Even hundreds of years before the invasion of Canaan, God had told Abraham that the sins of the people living in the land had not reached its limit, but when the inhabitants had defiled the land to its limit, the land was going to "throw them up."

In fact, God later warned the nation of Israel to be careful in not repeating the sins of the previous people; otherwise the land was going to throw them up too. So we see that God is using Israel as an instrument of His justice to purge the land of its sinfulness and later in history God used other nations like the Assyrians and the Babylonians as His instruments to cleanse the land by destroying the people of Israel for their sinfulness. However, when one reads the early accounts of prophet Muhammad's raids and wars, not only one sees no mention of the theme of divine holiness and its opposition to sin, but the primary motivations that one constantly encounters are the looting of the enemies and the obtaining of booty and the spoils of war or the relief and pleasures of Paradise or conquering the enemies and spreading the rule of the prophet. Another important point that we need to keep in mind is the fact that the divine command for the destruction of the few cities of Canaan, was for a specific people, a specific time and place and a specific purpose. Nowhere in the later Old Testament period do we see God commanding the nation of Israel to go and attack other pagan nations, either as selfdefense or as a way to promote faith in the true God of heaven and earth.

However, in the Qur'an, we encounter general commands to kill and destroy the enemies of Islam that are applicable for all times and places and people groups. It is beyond dispute that from the earliest times, right after the death of the prophet, Muslim splinter groups began fighting, killing and assassinating even each other, in the name of God. The history of Islam, down to the present day is filled with the appeals of various Muslims to everapplicable Qur'anic passages to destroy and kill their enemies. Muslims generally believe that since Islam is the final great monotheistic religion, it is superior in every respect to Judaism and Christianity. Living in the Middle East and growing up in a Muslim country, we were always told that Judaism was like elementary school, Christianity was like high school and Islam is like university.

Each religion was from God, but each one became progressively higher and better. Now the question that we must ask is this, how can Islam claim to have a superior ethics to the New Testament, and yet resort back to the use and justification of violence, elements that were supposedly part of the early Jewish tradition? It seems that Islam not only has not improved on the teachings of Jesus and the New Testament in regard to the use of force, but that in fact Islam has gone back many steps in this regard.

The Limits of Freedom

In some respects fundamentalism may be understood in terms of whatever it is "against. The term is often used as "a pejorative description for anyone who is regarded as having a closed mind with regard to a particular issue" observes that the history and identity of fundamentalism is, indeed, quite complex. "It is sometimes said that moral panic explains the appeal of Fundamentalism. Certainly the issues which stimulate political action involve a crisis mood that Christian civilization is at risk. Fundamentalism is after all a popular movement which flourishes by interpreting current issues in simplified and distorted ways". Furthermore, in response to the criticism that religion, and in particular fundamentalist religion, is but an epiphenomenon riding on what are really political ideas and actions, or that fundamentalism is really just a passing fad, such studies have only served to highlight what subsequent history and recent events underscore: that religious fundamentalism is a deeply rooted phenomenon that can give rise to, rather than itself relies upon, political acts.

Religious fundamentalism can imply a narrow, strict and limited metaphysics and set of doctrines, which to a greater or lesser degree hardly impinge on the wider life of a society; it can mean a worldview perspective that engenders, if not demands, the advocacy of a sociopolitical ordering and action to achieve an intended outcome. Religious fundamentalism denotes a worldviewtype that can be found across different religions in the world today. Specifically, the term connotes a paradigm that paves the way for a shift in mentality from the relative harmlessness of an otherwise quaint, ultraconservative religious belief system; to a religiously motivated and fanatically followed engagement in aggressively impositional, even terrorizing, activity. Understanding the structure, logic, and implementation of this paradigm is of vital importance in today's world.

Religious Extremism

Another dimension to exploring the relationship of religion to terrorism is that of a consideration of extremism as such, for it is extreme forms or expressions of religion and religious ideology which, under the guise of fundamentalism, is arguably the point of connectivity between religion and terrorism. The ordinarily religious person or community does not engage in violence as a matter of course: religions normatively espouse values of peace and harmony, even in contexts of challenge and contestation. So, the first step in considering religious extremism is to ask an obvious question: what is the meaning of extremism as such? And a second step will be to discern and describe an ideological template of religious extremism.

'Extremism' Mean

The term extremism evokes a sense of being at the margins, of existing on the boundaries, of functioning at the edges; in other words, extremism suggests the extremities. And any organisation or group that is, in this sense, extreme will tend to manifest a tenuous link to whatever is the appropriate centre, or give evidence of a loose connection to the relevant normative tradition. In this respect, extremism expresses heterodoxy against orthodoxy. But extremism can refer to something else altogether; even, indeed, the opposite of being at the margins and that is being at, or claiming, the centre. Here the term connotes degrees of intensity or sharpness of focus; extremism suggests fanaticism. And in this case an extremist ideology or group will claim the relevant central position exclusively and, in so doing, will proclaim the apropos normative tradition intensely.

Extremism in this sense takes group identity - its religion or tradition - to an extreme; not by a move away from the centre, but conversely by intensifying its selfunderstanding and selfproclamation as representing, or being, the centre. Here extremism expresses ultra orthodoxy against orthodoxy. It is important to note, that either way extremism belongs to a tradition; extremism, by definition, has to do with the extremity or centering of an existing tradition, or religion, with which the extremist is concerned: the religious extremist thus requires specific religious identity as the primary reference for selflegitimization. By contrast, religious cults and other radical alternatives do not belong to a tradition - by definition, they are otherthan a normative tradition or religion.

Profile of Religious Extremism

In effect, the second half of the aforementioned sequential tenfeature paradigm of fundamentalism, incorporating features of the hardline phase of fundamentalism together with those of impositional fundamentalism, may be taken as a fivepoint profile of religious extremism. On the one hand, religious fundamentalism excludes, virtually automatically, anything that relative to it appears liberal; on the other this same fundamentalism can display a propensity to include, in respect to considerations of the policies and praxis of social organisation, all others that fall within its frame of reference or worldview understanding. This holding together of an ideological exclusivism with an inclusivist polity, where it occurs, comprises the contextual scope of fundamentalism which is a mark of hardline fundamentalism.

The second point of reference for religious extremism is the feature of condemnatory stance which involves the factors of negative judgemental values and a pietistic tyranny: it is in the expression of judgemental values that hardline fundamentalism displays its real stance toward any who would dissent from within, or oppose from without. In so doing, the contours and expression of piety can take a tyrannical form. Inherent in this is often a deprecating attitude towards others, whether in regard to virtually any other (the world at large), or focussed on specific others (particular groups of categories of people such as Jews, Blacks, or gays). The feature of condemnatory stance sets the seal on the hardline phase and sets the scene for the phase of impositional fundamentalism. The third point of the profile is negative value application, which is a feature of the impositional phase or type of fundamentalism. It occurs where alterity, or otherness per se is negated and, as a necessary corollary, the superiority of the self is asserted.

The other is often cast as satanic, or at least seriously and significantly labelled as a hostile opponent, and so hostilely regarded. However expressed or referenced, it will be clear that the fundamentalist is showing signs of deepening extremism in applying negative valuation to otherness as such, together with a corresponding assertion of selfsuperiority visàvis any other. As the shift from a merely hardline to an actively impositional fundamentalism takes place, we discover two critical factors at work: sanctioned imposition and legitimated violence. The former sees the very imposition of the fundamentalist s views and polity as, in fact, sanctioned by a higher or greater authority, howsoever that is conceived. This leads naturally to the legitimating of extreme violence and so a platform of justification being established, at least in the mind of the impositional fundamentalist. Sanctioned imposition and legitimated violence are the two sides of the chief coin of justification in the currency of religious extremism.

They form the feature of explicit justification which is a mark of impositional fundamentalism and the fourth point in the profile of religious extremism. The final profile point is the feature of enacted violence; here the specific values and rhetoric of the fundamentalist s ideology issue in overt behaviours. This involves the penultimate factor of manifest contempt and the end-result factor: the terrorist or otherwise violent event. On the one hand, manifestations of contempt, as an expression of negative judgements and the negation of the other, are often instantiated in various contemptible behaviours – intimidation, coercion, violent and destructive actions directed at nonhuman symbolic targets: works of art, places of worship, and so on. Such behaviours may be ad hoc, simply manifesting an underlying contempt in a comparatively spontaneous fashion. On the other hand, there is certainly the phenomenon of intentionally organised terrorism where extremism knows no bounds: the terrorising of a targeted populace is itself both means and end. For it is only so that the extremist ensures that the imposition, that has been duly sanctioned, can actually be brought about.

Political Realism and Christian Realism

In other words, the political ends justify the means. Christian Realism however, allows neither states nor leaders to hide questionable moral actions behind the excuse of political prudence. Quite the contrary, universal moral principles must be applied to states and individuals alike. Niebuhr tackles this question of moral political action in his book, Moral Man and Immoral Society. In chapter four, "The

Morality of Nations," he begins with the hypothesis that "group relations can never be as ethical as those which characterise individual relations. From there he expounds the theme that, "perhaps the most significant moral characteristic of a society is hypocrisy, concluding the chapter with this ringing indictment:

The fifth principle of political realism builds on what it understands as the amorality of states with this rule: "Political realism refuses to identify the moral aspirations of a particular nation with the moral laws that govern the universe." In other words, while not ignoring the reality of morality, Morgenthau warns against political theorist identifying with a particular version. "There is a world of difference between the belief that all nations stand under the judgment of God, inscrutable to the human mind, and the blasphemous conviction that God is always on one's side and that what one wills oneself cannot fail to be willed by God also.

In contrast, Christian Realism is identified by a philosophy and doctrine that holds the ideals of Christianity as paramount. And yet, it is also this distinction that Niebuhr, the realist, is most effective in calling his fellow Christians back from the idealism and extremism with which it is constantly tempted. Morgenthau's final principle concludes: "The difference, then, between political realism and other schools of thought is real, and it is profound." It is critical that "the political realist maintains the autonomy of the political sphere, as the economist, the lawyer, the moralist maintain theirs." In this way, the theory of political realism remains a viable tool for understanding and predicting political action and behaviour. It is a ruler, for measuring interest defined in terms of power without attempting judgments on whether the length or width meets certain moral standards. The political realist "cannot but subordinate these other standards to those of politics. And he parts company with other schools when they impose standards of thought appropriate to other spheres upon the political sphere."

Christian realism places the tape measure of political realism firmly in the hands of Christian carpenters and demand that they use it with a complete understanding of human nature; an understanding that realizes the spiritual reality underlying all of mankind's efforts, political or otherwise.

Christian Realism is a phrase often read but rarely defined. It appears in The Nature and Destiny of Man but one time in the following context: "The Renaissance movement, however, developed another stream of thought which appropriated some of the insights of Christian realism and pessimism." While not defined in this reference, the inference is that the concepts embodied in what Niebuhr called Christian Realism had been around for a long time. In fact, in Christian Realism and Political Problems, Niebuhr attributes them to Augustine:

For Niebuhr, Augustine's City of God is the foundation for Christian realist thought. Augustine presented a realistic appraisal of mankind that was in contrast with the classical view of man. The classical view idealized man's unlimited potential because of his ability to reason. According to Niebuhr, "this difference in the viewpoint of Augustine and the classical philosophers lies in Augustine's biblical, rather than rationalistic, conception of human selfhood with the ancillary conception of the seat of evil being in the self."

It comes as no surprise then that Niebuhr's Christian Realism understands first and foremost, that human nature is evil as a result of sin. "The Bible defines sin in both religious and moral terms. The religious definition of sin is man's rebellion against God, his effort to usurp the place of God."This spiritual aspect of man's existence, this spiritual reality if you will, is the distinguishing element in Christian Realism. It is a fact of human existence transcending the natural and the classical understanding of man because these philosophies neither recognize man's unique position in creation, nor the relationship that such a position implies with the Creator. "Man does not know himself truly except as he knows himself confronted by God. Only in that confrontation does he become aware of his full stature and freedom and of the evil in him."

Nor is this reality readily apparent to sinful man on his own. It is a reality, a truth, which must be revealed to him by his Creator. Only God can give mankind the insight into his nature that enables him to understand his unique place in the world and his destiny in history. This helps explain the error of classical thought which trusts man to overcome his limitations through a civilized society. In reality, the evil within each individual only becomes compounded within society. Human society can never be as moral as the individual and is, in fact, collectively worse, collectively more evil. Niebuhr's Moral Man and Immoral Society is an indepth study of this very subject. The following quote demonstrates the extent to which an individual's own sinfulness can be projected upon his relationship to the state.

This sinfulness is also evident in international relationships. "The selfishness of nations is proverbial. It was a dictum of George Washington that nations were not to be trusted beyond their own interest." For the Christian realist, selfcenteredness is a corruption of the divine stamp of individuality. Niebuhr criticizes the renaissance with providing intellectual justification for this particular malady when he writes: "If Protestantism represents the final heightening of the idea of individuality within terms of the Christian religion, the renaissance is the real cradle of that very unchristian concept and reality: the autonomous individual."

What classical philosophy might regard as a virtue, Christian Realism regards as a liability. The autonomous individual is not interested in society for the purpose of improving the world. As a sinner, this is impossible. Quite the contrary, the autonomous individual is interested in society insofar as society can improve his or her own situation. On this point, Niebuhr is often his most caustic, skewering self pretensions with comments such as: "The question therefore arises how modern man arrived at, and by what means he maintains, an estimate of his virtue in such pathetic contradiction with the obvious facts of history." The irony in this situation is that the autonomous individual must organize with other autonomous individuals for any semblance of security or civilization. In other words, order is required for a civilized society, and yet it is an order built upon the sands of doubt and mistrust. "Therefore all human life is involved in the sin of seeking security at the expense of other life." Political realism calls this dilemma a double jeopardy, using it to explain how the defensive actions of nations often escalate into conflict. But there is more to an orderly society than simply organization. Order must be enforced with power.

Christian Realism understands this need for power in a sinful world and recognizes the state as a unique creation of God to protect sinful human beings from each other. "The legitimate majesty of government is acknowledged and affirmed in the Christian doctrine of government as a divine ordinance." And yet, the power granted government must be wielded with justice. "The moral and social dimension of sin is injustice. The ego which falsely makes itself the centre of existence in its pride and willtopower inevitably subordinates other life to its will and thus does injustice to other life." The irony again is that the concept of justice in a sinful world can never be objective and fair, since those in power also define the concept of justice for their time and situation.

Consequently, "the very power which organizes human society and establishes justice also generates injustice by its preponderance of power." The inference for international relations is obvious. This balance of power, first established by individuals within a culture or society for mutual security and protection, becomes the basis for alliances between states. It is at this point that political realism and Christian Realism part company for Christian Realism insists that justice be tempered with morality. Not that political realist reject the need for morality in society, but their emphasis on "prudence" suggests that the highest standard of preserving power in a particular situation outweighs other moral considerations. Christian Realism challenges this practice and recognizes the hypocrisy inherent in it. "Such a morally neutral definition of political cohesion allows Augustine to compare the harmony of the state with the harmony which thieves maintain among themselves and to suggest that there be little difference except size, between a state and a robber band."

Christian Realism maintains that not only must the action of government in exercising power and justice be based on what is morally right, but even more importantly; this morality is best identified with Christianity. In this regard, it is important to note for this study that the concept of a sinful nature is not found in the Qur'an. It is only within Christianity that man is confronted with the reality of sin and his need for a Savior. Only within the framework of Christianity can sinful man hope to provide any semblance of justice tempered with morality, for it is only within Christianity that sinful man is confronted with the reality of God's own justice and mercy. The heart of the Christian Gospel is that God Himself, in the Person of His eternal Son, Jesus Christ, sacrificed Himself for sinful man.

In God's divine justice, Jesus overcame man's failure to live up to his created perfection, suffered the consequence of man's sin on the cross and rose from the dead to announce God's forgiveness. This is the essence of the Christian doctrine of grace. God then works through the proclamation of this Good News to change sinful, self-centered humans beings into repentant, forgiven and service oriented human beings who recognize each other's real worth and real potential. This is possible only by faith in a living Christ who empowers each individual with a new perspective on life and a new motivation for his behaviour. "For it is by grace you have been saved, through faith—and this not from yourselves, it is the gift of God—not by works, so that no one can boast. For we are God's workmanship, created in Christ Jesus to do good works, which God prepared in advance for us to do."

What was once an autonomous individual, looking out for his own interest now becomes an individual struggling by faith to live up to God's expectations of him. "This is the religious emphasis upon love as the highest virtue...The religious ethic, (the Christian ethic more particularly, though not solely) insists that the needs of the neighbor shall be met, without a careful computation of relative needs." In this Gospel, Niebuhr centers Christian Realism and declares: "The agape, the sacrificial love, which is for Christian faith revealed upon the Cross, has as its primary justification in an 'essential reality' which transcends the realities of history, namely, the character of God."

In summary then we define Christian Realism as a political theory that understands that evil exists as a result of sin and therefore, each individual is by nature sinful and evil. Left unchecked, sinful natures will eventually resort to extreme behaviour to secure their desires. Therefore, to prevent mankind's self-destruction, God divinely established government to provide order in human society and to enforce that order by the exercise of power. However, that power must be tempered with justice and that justice must be moral. The morality that best governs justice is Christianity, which seeks the ideal of Christ Himself. This is possible only by faith and therefore only exercised by Christians who understand that they are sinners who have been redeemed by the grace of God. This definition lays the foundation for understanding the difference between Christian Realism and the brand of international terrorism that justifies its violence by its extreme allegiance to Islam.

International Terrorism and Jihad

Islam is a theology of worksrighteousness. In other words, a believer enters heaven based on good works. The five pillars of Islam are centered upon the individual's responsibility to recite the Shahada, pray five times a day, give to the poor, fast during Ramadan and make a pilgrimage to Mecca at least once in one's lifetime. Doing these five things secures one's salvation. However, as with any worksrighteous theology, Muslims can never be certain of their eternal salvation. They must simply hope that they have done enough to please God when they meet Him on judgment day. It is easy to see then, how someone wanting to please God and secure their own salvation might be tempted to pursue radical, legalistic and violent reforms of culture and society deemed offensive and detrimental to Islam. The terrorists who attacked the United States on September 11, 2001, believe that we are a threat to their religion and culture. That is why they consider us hated enemies and are convinced that their only recourse is violence.

While international terrorism takes many forms, the focus of this study is the particular brand with which we find ourselves at war: the radical Islamic terrorism promoted by Osama bin Laden. Radical Islamic terrorists are extremists who demand uncompromising allegiance to Islam and advocate violence in defense of it. The goal of AlQa'ida is straightforward enough: "Cleansing of the Muslim countries from corrupt and secular leadership, and fight against the powers that threaten Muslim states and the holy places of Islam." This mission to cleanse the Muslim countries derives from the Islamic fundamentalism practiced by Osama bin Laden known as Wahhabism. The Encyclopedia of the Orient defines Wahhabism as a "movement in Islam from mid18th century, calling for a renewal of the Muslim spirit, with cleansing of the moral, and removal of all innovations to Islam."

The Taliban's destruction of the ancient Buddhist statues is just one example of this practice. But to cleanse the Muslim countries requires more than prayer and the destruction of a few historic icons. According to Bin Laden: "The Israeli forces occupied our land and the American troops are on our territory. As a result of the September 11, 2001 attacks on the World Trade Center and the Pentagon, Congress authorized President Bush to unleash whatever means he deemed appropriate to conduct America's war on terrorism. While political, legal, law enforcement and economic instruments of power continue to be utilized in this counterstrike, the most visible means of retaliation remains the U.S. military. At present there are approximately 3,000 U.S. troops in Afghanistan with thousands more in the region. President Bush has repeatedly said this is a different kind of war and that other nations harboring and supporting terrorists will face retribution. The future for the U.S. military is increased operations and the almost certain invasion of other countries such as Iraq.

The Moral Framework

The moral framework provided by Christian Realism begins with an understanding of human nature. Contrary to Islam and its militant stepchild, Wahhabism, Christian Realists understand that human nature is sinful and that human beings are inherently evil. Reason does not give us the ability to overcome this spiritual calamity. Rather, left to our own, we would easily destroy ourselves through constant conflict and chaos. However, God in His grace has provided both salvation and security: Salvation in the Person of His Son, Jesus Christ, and security in the concept of His law embodied in the State. And yet, while forgiveness for sins is granted by grace during our lifetimes, perfection is not. The world has been redeemed, not perfected. We do not live in a Christian State anymore than we can hope realistically to live in a Christian world. Jesus described this spiritual reality when He said that His disciples find themselves in the world but "not of the world." He commissioned His disciples to change the world through a proclamation of the Gospel, not by force.

Consequently, Christian Realists are neither surprised nor confused about another religion taking up the sword against what many U.S. citizens consider a benign and even benevolent society, more intent on succeeding and enjoying life than harming others. Niebuhr points out:

> Even religious communities, if they are sufficiently large, and if they deal with issues regarded as vital by their members, resort to coercion to preserve their unity. Religious organizations have usually availed themselves of a covert type of coercion (excommunication and the interdict) or they have called on the police power of the state.

Unfortunately, Christian history is also replete with

examples of similar religious fanaticism. Niebuhr illustrates this point in Moral Man and Immoral Society by quoting Waldo Frank's description of a Spanish conquistador, in America Hispana:

> Only a man who believes can do what he did. He has seen cheap wine turn to the blood of Christ; now he can understand how his own bestialities are transfigured into acts which build the Church of Rome. Within his cruelties is the intuition of his destiny as an agent of the divine. His mystic role makes his impossible adventure bearable, and makes him bearable to himself.

In the Nature and Destiny of Man we Read this Analysis:

> The fanatic fury of religious controversies, the hatred engendered in theological disputes, the bitterness of ecclesiastical rivalries and the pretentious claims of ecclesiastical dominion all reveal the continued power of sin in the life of the 'redeemed'; and the use which sin makes of the pretension of holiness.

The moral lesson for Christian leaders, especially those who find themselves wielding power over life and death, is sobering. "For the pride of the wise and the pretensions of the spiritual leaders of culture and civilization may be more productive of evil than the simpler will-to-power of the mighty and the noble." Ironically, in response to the attacks of September 11, America has embraced its own version of defensive jihad on behalf of its culture and values. The challenge is to balance the need for defense of our citizens and justice for the victims and their families without succumbing to acts of evil and terror us. And lest we think too highly of ourselves in this regard, Niebuhr's Christian Realism would remind us how fine a line separates us from Al Qa'ida and the Taliban.

The religious instinct for the absolute is no less potent in patriotic religion than in any other. The nation is always endowed with an aura of the sacred, which is one reason why religions, which claim universality, are so easily captured and tamed by national sentiment, religion and patriotism merging in the process. One has only to recall the misguided diatribe of Jerry Falwell and Pat Robertson, suggesting that the terrorist attacks were Divine judgment upon certain segments of American society (i.e., homosexuality) to realize the truth of this statement. Terrorism based on religious beliefs is an ultimate example of man's hypocrisy and sin. "Such spirit can be most simply defined as demonic. The most striking, contemporary form of it is a religious nationalism in which race and nation assume the eminence of God and demand unconditioned devotion."

The moral framework of Christian Realism insists that because we are all equally evil in God's eyes, and because God still loves us enough to redeem us, we have an obligation to love even our enemies. In the Sermon on the Mount, Jesus said: "Love your enemies and pray for those who persecute you, that you may be sons of your Father in heaven. He causes his sun to rise on the evil and the good, and sends rain on the righteous and the unrighteous." And this is precisely where Christian soldiers and officers are confronted with the struggle to understand this key element of their faith in light of their military duty. How does a chaplain advise Christian officers and commanders as they respond with force in this war against terrorism?

By acknowledging with them that life in a sinful world is not nearly as much a choice between good and evil as it is a choice between several evils. Niebuhr's advice, based on the philosophy of Immanuel Kant is that "truth is judged by its harmonious relation to a previously discovered system of truths, so the morality of an action is judged by the possibility of conforming it to a universal scheme of consistent moral actions." A perfect example would be the concept of proportionality within the Just War theory. As commanders plan attacks against terrorists with precision weapons, they are following centuries of practice founded in Christianity which teaches that restraint is a measure of morality.

The Biblical Foundation for this Exercise of Power

For rulers hold no terror for those who do right but for those who do wrong. Do you want to be free from fear of the one in authority? Then do what is right and he will commend you for he is God's servant to do you good. But if you do wrong, be afraid, for he does not bear the sword for nothing. He is God's servant, an agent of wrath to bring punishment on the wrongdoer.

It is important to note that how one bears the sword is a matter left to the ruler or State. God gives us the opportunity to wield power with justice which is in turn tempered with mercy as we reflect on His example of applying power and justice and mercy towards us. Recognizing the inherent temptation to respond to acts of evil in kind, enables the Christian realist to practice even the military art of war without resorting to extreme acts of murder and mayhem directed against an adversary's noncombatant population, their industry or culture. Indeed, it is this theological insight into man's sinful nature that ensures Christian realists will insist on strict restraints in crafting a response to international terrorism so that we do not become the very evil we claim to be fighting against.

6

Ethical Justification for Terrorism

When dealing with the ethical question of terrorism, it's important to understand the ambiguity of the word itself. What is terrorism exactly? While the meaning may be subjective, the term terrorism is traditionally described as the use of force or violence to inspire social or political change in a random, arbitrary fashion. The term terrorist has recently become a very popular word in American politics, and brings up a series of moral questions to be deliberated. Can terrorism ever be justified? Of course it can, and act utilitarianism can most certainly justify it. Again whether or not certain acts are terrorism is very much dependent on the observer's political/ moral bias. However, while expounding no moral judgment whatsoever, let's look at some instances where (by definition) terrorism was used and brought about a greater good for the society.

- The American Revolution – prior and during the War the colonists used terrorist tactics to incite fear into British tax collectors, British loyalists, and those who weren't on the side of their revolution.
- The current struggles of the Maoists in Tibet; using tactics that the West have labeled "terrorism" against an oppressive monarch.

- The resistance forces in Iraq are fighting against an unjust, illegitimate occupation and will eventually come out victorious.
- The North Vietnamese were called "terrorists" in their struggles against yet another unjust, illegitimate occupying force.
- The French Revolution has often been cited as being plagued with terrorism, yet brought about the end to absolute monarchy in France (until Napoleon).

Were the individuals who participated in these events "terrorists?" This is a highly debatable issue, for the apparent success rate of these movements is apparent in history today. The common element throughout all that data is the fact that violence was only used as a means of the last resort when all peaceful alternatives had been exhausted and no longer provided the most utility for the greatest amount of people. If the act of "terrorism" maximizes the wellbeing of the entire populace then it can surely be justified. While peaceful means should always be a consideration, and used prior to physical violence, when these means don't reach the appropriate ends, is when man is forced to turn violent. However, the act utilitarian must answer a few questions before engaging in what could potentially be considered "terrorism."

Firstly, is terrorism the most effective and efficient way to reach the desired goal? Many times terrorism is not the most effective and efficient means, such as when it hardens the opposition to your use of violence, while passive resistance may create sympathy for your cause. This is an imperative consideration. However, this doesn't mean that terrorism won't necessarily be the most effective and efficient means to an end. Often times, passive resistance can result in physical violence from the opposition, when this happens violence is going to be the ultimate solution to the problem. Secondly, is the desired goal worthy enough of justifying the terrorist act? This again is dependent on social perspective. Is the reunification of Ireland an important enough goal for the IRA to continue to fight for? Is national sovereignty a worthy enough goal for the Iraqi Resistance to continue fighting against American occupation? The question of whether or not the end result is worth the violence does not have an easy answer; a lot of consideration for all those involved has to be taken before violence is used.

The problem with justifying terrorism is that most of the time consequences aren't taken into consideration, and biases cloud the humane judgments of most human beings. If we can justify that the Iraqi resistance movement is a just struggle against occupation, then we should also be able to proclaim that the Palestinian Liberation Organization is a just struggle against Israeli occupation.

These questions and consequences need to be thoroughly considered; when these consequences are not taken into consideration, events such as the massacre of Russian students by Chechen rebels can take place. Needless violence does not fall into act utilitarian ethics though, and is only a perversion of the notion of spreading utility amongst the populace.

In conclusion, acts of terrorism are about as vague in meaning as the word itself. Subjectivity and personal biases have always flawed perspectives in morality, but we have to take an objective route in dealing with ethical questions. Is the act of terrorism justified? Only when it is in the best interest of the greatest amount of people, when the goal is worthy of the cost, and when all other means of resistance have been exhausted. In principle act utilitarian does justify terrorism, and it is through this model that we can make objective observations of the world around us today, and perhaps answer these perplexing ethical questions.

Religion and Culture as Motivations for Terrorism

The 'War on Terror', led by the USA and supported by other states, has been the main factor that shaped the international agenda over the past four years. Many financial resources, human capital and political and military efforts have been invested in the ongoing campaign aimed to obliterate terrorist organisations wherever they are. The source of this terror originates from Muslim countries in the MiddleEast and SouthEast Asia, but it threatens the entire international community and includes all human beings. This threat, which the international community identifies with Global Jihad, is by far the most dangerous threat to the world's peace and security. The questions that are often left without clear answers pertain to the unique characteristics of the regions that enable terrorism to flourish.

It is commonly believed that religion is what motivates terrorist organisations such as Al-Qaeda and its associated organisations, to perpetrate deadly attacks against civilians. However, the fact that only a small minority of Muslims around the world support or are actively involved in these kinds of attacks, raises questions of whether religion is the sole motivator behind terrorism, and what part culture plays in this phenomenon. The answer lies in the assumption that religion and culture are interlinked motivators, and that the combination of specific cultural conditions with strong religious convictions has resulted in Islamic terrorism.

The Rise of Terrorism

Terrorism is not a new phenomenon in human history. It has been an integral part of social behaviour for over 2000 years, and yet, no international consensus has yet been formed regarding what terrorism constitutes. The fact that there is no single acceptable definition imposes many obstacles on those who wish to fight terrorism effectively. Nowadays, the most commonly agreed upon definition is: "The use of [or the threat to use] violence against civilians in order to attain political goals". The emphasis put on political goals is what differentiates terrorism from other types of violence (such as criminal violence). It is widely known that the first terrorists were motivated by religious fanaticisms. David Rapoport, claimed that before the 18th century and the advent nationalism, anarchism, and Marxist ideology, "religion provided the only acceptable justifications for terror." The Jewish Zealots in the 1st century, the Muslim Hashashins and the Hindu Thugs, are the most recognised religious terrorists of the ancient times, which mainly used assassinations and scarifying people as their modus operandi.

The emergence of nationalism, imperialism and Marxist ideology led to a change in the nature of terrorism, and since the 18th century (the French revolution), until the mid 20th century (the anti-colonial movements of the 1960s), it was mainly driven by secular motives while the influence of religion declined. The main features of this kind of terrorism were guerilla tactics, political kidnappings, sabotage and mayhem. The turning point in the nature of terrorism is perceived to be in 1968. The Vietnam War and the rise of leftist movements in Europe and the USA (mainly motivated by Marxism and anarchism), together with the ascendants of Palestinian nationality after the Six Day War in 1967, generated a new wave of terrorism which expanded into global dimensions and shifted from national motives to political and ethnic ones. This form of modern international terrorism is characterised both by the secular nature of the organisations and by its lethality, indiscrimination and intention to create massive havoc and fear among the targeted population.

In the post Cold War era the world has witnessed the reemergence of religious terrorism, mainly among Islamic organisations. The collapse of the Soviet Union, which led to the discrediting of communist and Marxist ideologies, together with the rise of liberal-democratic values, contributed to the rise of religion as a substitute for secular motives. In addition, the rise of radical Islamic regime in Iran (1979), the war in Afghanistan (1979) and the rise of the Taliban regime (1996), led to a steep increase in the number of Islamic religious motivated terrorist organisations. Consequently, from the 13 known terrorist organisations identified in 1968, none was characterised as religious. Yet today, from the 42 designated terror organisations in the US State Department's list, more than half are Islamic religiousmotivated.

The threat of terrorism intensified amply in the past decade, with the emergence of Global Jihad – a more extreme mutation of international terrorism. What distinguishes international terrorism, which the world dealt with during the 1970s, 1980s and mid 1990s, from the recent Global Jihad, is a combination between two main factors: the extreme ideology inherent in the Islamic radical belief of the holiness of the personal "Jihad" (martyrdom) ; and the deadly methods employed together with the willingness to use nonconventional weapons. Global Jihadist movements led by the infamous Al-Qaeda network (which includes approximately 40 associated and affiliated organisations) headed by Osama BinLaden, pose the greatest threat to Western countries as well as to moderate Muslim regimes.

The Relationship between Religion and Culture

Before dealing with religion and culture as motivations for terrorism, there is a need to define these two convoluted terms. Many scholars have tried and are still trying to define them, and yet, like 'terrorism', there is no definition that generates consensus, rather a set of definitions that complete each other. Religion is a vague term that constitutes many different aspects, some of them not entirely objective. One of the most comprehensive definitions of religion is comprised of four domains: a discourse whose concerns transcends the human, temporal and contingent; set of practices to produce a proper world and human subjects; a community which constructs identity; and an institution that asserts eternal validity. All four domains allow every human being to apply his own subjective definition of religion and to practice it accordingly.

Culture is another intangible term that can be defined in many different ways. The traditional way to define culture is by a combination of concepts such as: group or community with collective identity that can be conveyed by language, nonverbal signals, norms of behaviour, habits, clothes, art, etc. Ernest Gellner argues that culture is a "distinct way of doing things which characterises a given community… [culture] can be defined as systems of concepts or ideas which guide thought and conduct." Culture is more flexible than religion and therefore it can emerge from events or processes and can be changed accordingly. Throughout the years religion has evolved as one of the central components of most cultures and became deeply involved in the practices of the community. Furthermore, religion is one of the most unpredictable aspects of any community's cultural identity. In many cases it is impossible to distinguish religion and culture as two separate concepts that comprise the collective identity of specific community or nation. Thus, religion and culture are directly interlinked and I will show that the symbiosis between the two have led to destructive consequences resulting in supporting and perpetrating Islamic terrorism.

The Use of Religion and Culture by Islamic Terrorist Organisations

Religion and culture are practically inseparable and Islamic terrorist organisations use this relation in order to operate in two realms. The first one is the religious realm, in which the violence first and foremost is portrayed as a sacramental act or divine duty, executed in direct response to some theological demand or imperative. The other realm is the cultural one, in which culture provides the social cohesion required for legitimising religious-motivated terrorism. Terrorism by definition is not an Islamic phenomenon. Why then have most terrorist attacks in recent years been perpetrated in the name of Islam? The main reason behind this is that Islam provides the necessary religious ground in which terrorism maybe nurtured as well as the cultural background that enables societies to accept and support terrorism.

Yet, it should be noted, that most Muslim communities in the world do not engage in terrorism nor do they support it as a mean to achieve a general aim. The absence of a certain cultural environment necessary for perpetrating religiousmotivated terrorism, explains why Islamic terrorism in most cases did not emerge from within Muslim communities in Western countries; rather it was done by outside terrorists from Muslim countries. It is impossible to determine which is the predominant instigator, religion or culture, in relation to terrorism. However, the fact that religion is an integral part of the Islamic culture provides the fertile ground for the growing phenomenon of religiousmotivated terrorism. It is essential to recognize specific aspects of the Islamic culture in order to comprehend the motives that might lead to terrorism. For instance, the glory of ancient powerful Islamic empires serves as an important factor in the Muslim's will to revive the great days of Islam.

In addition, the culture of warriors inherent in Islam since the days of the prophet Mohammed constitutes concepts of religious punishment in the name of God, blood revenge, honor and respect, and deep rooted differentiation between Muslims and infidels. These two main aspects in the Islamic culture serve as driving forces in the collective identity of many Muslim communities. Consequently, the shift to violence while using twisted religious justification seems to permeate into some Muslim communities' way of life. A twisted perception of religious decree together with particular cultural environment can be seen in the concept of martyrdom (Shahadah). This concept - the sanctification of God's name by selfsacrificing ones life - have become a popular modus operandi among several Muslim communities, owing to the fact that it is a religious duty whose glorification originates from the cultural foundation inherent in Islam. Many Muslim societies use religion to advocate martyrdom, by creating 'martyr worship cultures', which take the form of suicide attackers.

This however, creates a problem for Muslims, since although the cultural environment was ready to accept martyrs, the concept of committing suicide is unacceptable according to Islam, and whoever commits suicide is not allowed to enter heaven (another divine concept in Islam). Therefore, facing the need to use suicide terrorism, the modern "smart bomb" of Islamic terrorist organisations, a religious authorisation was required in order to justify the acts. A prominent religious scholar, Sheikh Yusuf al-Qaradawi, announced that "The operations carried out by the Muslim youth that defend the lands of Islam and the religion and dignity of Islam are the greatest forms of Jihad for the sake of Allah. They fall under the definition of legitimate terrorization…I maintain that it is wrong to consider these acts as 'suicidal,' because these are heroic acts of martyrdom, which are in fact very different from suicide." This announcement explained to Muslims that suicide attacks, although forbidden in Islam are justified if done at the will of God and it promises the suicide attackers entrance to heaven.

Another religious scholar, Sheikh Muhammad Fadlallah, was also required to explain this contradiction between heaven and suicide attacks. His solution is conveyed in the following religious ruling: "There is no difference between dying with a gun in your hand or exploding yourself. In a situation of struggle or holy war you have to find the best means to achieve your goals." All terrorist organisations cannot act effectively if the society that surrounds them does not support their activity. Mao Tse-Tung once said that: "The guerrilla must move amongst the people as a fish swims in the sea." Although he was referring to guerilla fighters, terrorists are not different in their necessity to feel comfortable in their natural habitat. Therefore, in times when the natural surroundings do not accommodate terrorism, there is a need to create the essential cultural environment in which terrorism, and especially religiousmotivated one, can operate.

Yasser Arafat, the late Palestinian leader (and symbol of the Palestinian struggle for self-determination), was not a religious leader. However, he consistently encouraged the creation of cultural conditions that would enable Palestinians to continue in their fight for their independence. One of the popular methods which Arafat adopted was using religious terminology and rhetoric in his public speeches given in Arabic (as language is a crucial element in any culture). In an interview to the Palestinian National TV in January 15, 2002,

Arafat explained that dead Palestinian children Shahids are "the greatest message to the world". After the first female suicide bomber succeeded in her attack killing one Israeli citizen and injuring 140, Arafat said: "The Fatah Movement proudly eulogize their heroine Martyr, from the Alamari refugee camp, the martyr Wafa Idris.". Perhaps his most famous public statement was made in Johannesburg in the midst of the Oslo accords when peace was within reach: "The Jihad will continue, and Jerusalem is not [only] for the Palestinian people, it is for all the Muslim nation...We are in need of you as Moslems, as warriors of Jihad [in Arabic, Mujaheddin]."

By using the words Jihad, Muslim nation and warriors in one sentence, Arafat linked religion and culture; Jihad used to illustrate the means, Muslim nation intended to provide the collective identity and warriors to represent the set of norms and behaviour inherent in Islam. The Palestinian society serves as an example of a Muslim society with a cultural environment that is an effective platform for religiousmotivated terrorism against Israel. In the peak of the Palestinian terror wave in 2002, the idolisation of Palestinian terrorists, regardless of the fact that their cause was more of a nationalist one than religious, illustrated the social cohesion of the Palestinian society and the legitimisation that it provided for terrorism. The ongoing massive use in electronic media, wallpapers, newspapers, street graffiti and more, created a culture of terrorism within a society that glorifies suicide attacks, manufactures heroes and is committed to continue the fight against the infidels (Israelis).

As a result of this cultural environment, religious motivated terrorism can flourish and the massive support it has among the people and the leaders provide the necessary legitimacy for terrorist attacks. For instance, the AlAqsa Martyrs Brigades, the armed wing of the Fatah (the main Palestinian organisation that controls the PLO), is a secular organisation which uses terrorism in order to achieve national and political goals for the Palestinian people. Yet all suicide attacks carried out by its members were done after comprehensive religious indoctrination, which provided the perpetrator with a tool to selfjustify his act - in the name of God and for the liberation of Palestine. Furthermore, even the name of the organisation, indicates that its actions are derived from religious motives or justifications, as AlAqsa mosque is one of the holiest sites of Islam and martyrdom being an Islamic concept.

Indeed, the religious culture within the Palestinian society, although most of the Palestinians consider themselves as secular, allows terrorists to use religion as a justification for their acts. There is no indication in the Qur'an for the word terrorism. However, religious sages (Faqih - an expert in Islamic law) use religion in order to meet modern political modules and to serve specific aims, by using interpretations and contemporary methods. These religious sages use fatwas (legal pronouncement that is not binding to all Muslims) and their religious authority in order to justify terrorism as a necessary means for meeting the needs of reality. According to Magnus Ranstorp: "Terrorists take refugee in religion...which determines goals; they find physical or psychological sanctuary against repression; or they may use it as a major instrument for activism and for political action." Hence, religion serves as an instrument in the hands of Muslim terrorists in order to justify their actions, and to provide moral explanations to their inhumane actions.

Culture on the other hand, provides the collective identity and the social behaviour that legitimises and supports terrorism as well as creates the necessary environment to recruit activists and to raise funds. Without the proper culture, religion by itself cannot be used as an adequate reason for terrorist attacks. Thus, the combination of religion and culture can generate the set of beliefs and values that motivate Islamic terrorism and produce social unity, regardless of the religious fervor of the community members. Although it is often believed that terrorism is a manifestation of religious fanaticism, when looking at today's Global Jihad it is clear that it cannot be separated from the cultural background as well as from daily events. As religion and culture are intertwined, one should explore them together and put them in the political and socioeconomic context in order to be able to comprehend the real nature of Global Jihad.

The Evil of Terrorism

The first thing to say about terrorism, and to say with all the firmness that one can command, is that it is an evil, a heinous crime, an attack on civilized life and on peace. This because there has been a tendency in some parts of the media and among some commentators, including not a few philosophers, to excuse the terrorists who attacked the US on September 11th on the grounds that the US brought these attacks on itself by its own foreign policy, and in particular by its policy in the Middle East. But however plausible these claims may be, we should not let them blind us to clear and manifest truths. We must state the truth and state it clearly and without hesitation.

The attacks on the US were evil deeds and those who planned and carried them out were evil men. So much is elementary. To doubt this, as some who ought to know better have done, is to betray certain confusion if not corruption of mind. Surely we all know, surely we have all known from our earliest youth that two wrongs do not make a right. Let it be, if you will, that the terrorists had grievances, even legitimate grievances, against the US. These grievances could never justify their deeds. An evil deed can never be justified. An evil deed is precisely that, an evil deed. No grievance or pretext, however strong, can ever make it not to be an evil deed. Mr. Bin Laden, however, who if not behind the attacks on September 11th certainly applauds them is able to give no other excuse for them than random accusations against US policy. But Mr. Bin Laden clearly has a corrupt mind. We should not expect better from him.

Terrorism, however, at least in its primary and typical use (and certainly in its use in the phrase "the war on terrorism"), refers to acts of private individuals or groups of private individuals and not to governments, even if these individuals receive support and succor from governments. We should also distinguish terrorism in this its primary sense from the acts, often destructive and sometimes wicked too, of rebels and revolutionaries against existing governments and peoples. By rebels and revolutionaries we mean typically people who belong to the country whose government they are attacking and whose aim is to overthrow that government and to replace it with another. As such rebels and revolutionaries are not so much a grouping of private individuals as a rival government in waiting. But terrorists as typically understood are not a rival government nor are they seeking to overthrow the existing government, even if they would not be sorry if that happened. The terrorists who attacked the US on September 11th, for instance, were not Americans seeking to overthrow the US government and replace it with another one.

There is something else also that needs to be noted about terrorism if we are to be clear about what it is. For the violence of terrorists is typically directed at civilians and civilian institutions, albeit civilians of the country against which the terrorists have a grievance, and is and is meant to be indiscriminate. It is from this feature, indeed, that terrorism gets its name. For such indiscriminate and violent acts are designed to cause terror among the people at large, and it is by means of such terror that terrorists seek to attain their goals and force the hand of governments. Such indiscriminate violence can also be a feature of the acts of certain government officials and of certain rebel groups. Members of the police force in some parts of the world engage in random acts of violence against the civilian population as part of a policy of terrorizing the people into subservience.

It matters not here what grievances the terrorists may have or what accusations they level against those countries whose people they attack. An evil deed is an evil deed and nothing can make it to be a good deed. Not even religion, not even the Muslim religion, can make it to be a good deed. Those who say it can, or who claim the support of Islam for their terrorist attacks (as we know from private letters that the hijackers did on September 11th), are simply abusing religion and Islam. Do not take my argument alone for this. Take rather the words of one of the Taliban themselves, the Taliban ambassador to Pakistan, who said of the attack on the US: "This action is terrorist action. We know this was not Islamic and was a very dangerous action, and we condemn that" (China Daily, Thursday, October 4, 2001). Mr. Bin Laden has, of course, said the exact opposite.

He has praised the attacks on the US and on civilians, and said that Islam expressly requires Muslims to engage in such attacks. But if even the Taliban deny that this is what Islam teaches, one wonders what sort of Islam Mr. Bin Laden is following or whether he is really following Islam at all rather than his own corrupt inventions. At all events decent Muslims have good reason to repudiate, and to repudiate openly and loudly, the Islam preached by Mr. Bin Laden. We can be grateful, therefore, to those Islamic countries that have done so, among whom Saudi Arabia should be mentioned. Saudi Arabia severed relations with the Taliban on the grounds that the Taliban had brought Islam into disrepute which, with their support for Mr. Bin Laden, must, even by the Taliban's own admission, be true.

Responding to the Evil of Terrorism

Terrorism then is an evil, and an evil of a particularly vicious kind which constitutes, as the Chinese permanent representative to the UN said, "a serious challenge to human civilization and dignity as well as a serious threat to international peace and security." Those countries, therefore, which love peace and care for the good of mankind, must do something to rid the world of this evil. Not to do so would be a dereliction of duty. It is everyone's duty to do good (pursuing good and avoiding evil is an elementary injunction of reason), and among the good things to be done is the removal of evils, especially grave evils—to the extent, at any rate, that this is possible. Here, however, we must be careful, for in opposing evil it is all too easy to fall into evil oneself. We are all doubtless aware, even from our youth, of how easy it is, when someone has injured or insulted us, to respond with hatred and fury and to inflict, or try to inflict, worse injury than we first suffered. We may in this way satisfy our lust for revenge but we do not in this way remove evil or make the world a better place.

On the contrary we simply add to the evil in the world, for we add our own evil to the evil of the other. One cannot defeat evil with evil. That is simply contradictory. To use evil against evil is not to defeat evil but to be defeated by it and to become evil, or even more evil, in one's own turn. This is a truth that Mr. Bin Laden has altogether failed to grasp. But we, who profess to be opposing Mr. Bin Laden and his ilk, must not sink to his level. We must not become terrorists and mass murderers ourselves. For we cannot on the one hand condemn terrorism and set out to destroy it, while on the other hand commit acts of terrorism of our own. Now it is a striking fact that in all the buildup to the war on terrorism, beginning from President Bush's first declaration immediately after September 11th, there have been repeated and persistent declarations from all sides that the war should be conducted with great prudence and caution, that it should only target the guilty, that it should not result in collateral damage or as little such damage as possible, and so forth. These declarations came first from the American Government itself.

They were then repeated by almost all countries round the world, whether friendly or hostile to the US. The hostile countries, among which we should particularly mention Talibancontrolled Afghanistan, made these declarations with certain indignation and even with fear (springing, perhaps, from secret guilt). But it is a tribute to the US that they made these declarations at all. The declarations were an admission that it made sense to appeal to justice when talking to the US; that one could reasonably expect the US to be sensitive to the claims of justice when deciding what to do; that one had some hope, indeed, of getting the US to change its mind if its policies could be shown not to accord with justice. But consider the contrast here. Has the world thought it worth appealing to justice with the Taliban or with Mr. Bin Laden? Has the world beaten a path to Mr. Bin Laden's door appealing to him to follow justice and prudence in his decisions of whom and what to attack? Has the world appealed to him, in the name of justice, to give himself up to a court of law to prove his innocence or to admit his guilt? Some appeal was indeed made to the Taliban in the name of justice to hand Mr. Bin Laden over, but we know how little regard they paid to that appeal.

Again, to change focus slightly, has anyone appealed to Mr. Saddam Hussein in the name of justice to stop the tyranny and oppression of his people, to abide by UN resolutions, to apologize and make reparation for his aggression against Iran and Kuwait? For the evil of terrorism springs from many sources, and in particular it springs from the injustices, real or apparent, committed by others against what the terrorists hold dear. Such injustices give no excuse, of course, to the evil deeds of terrorists as I have already several times remarked, but if we can, each in our own way and in our own place, will be doing our part to reduce the emergence of more terrorists in the future, as well as making the world a better place in general. But such an answer, while vital and in need of frequent repetition, is not enough. Our concern is the more specific question of whether force, in particular the force of war, is a just response to terrorism. If it is not we ought not to engage in it; but if it is we need to know what sort of force, under what conditions, subject to what limits, and so forth.

The first thing to note here is that force is a neutral term. It does not by itself connote something either good or bad. The same is true, for instance, of tolerance. That too connotes something neither good nor bad in itself. Everything depends on what is tolerated and why. Tolerating the murder of infants would clearly be bad; tolerating the expression of different opinions in the course of philosophical debate would clearly be good. That is why those who praise tolerance as a virtue are speaking too simply. Tolerance as such is not a virtue, nor is intolerance as such a vice. We need to know tolerance or intolerance of what, by whom, when, how. That is also why those who condemn force as a vice, such as pacifists, are speaking too simply as well. Is all use of force always and everywhere wrong? Is the force used by parents to discipline children wrong? Is the force used by police forces to arrsest criminals wrong? Is the force used to defend oneself against attackers wrong? It seems patent that to answer yes to all these questions is absurd. Some uses of force are clearly right and just. The only interesting question to ask is which uses are so.

Since force is in itself neutral, it can only be just or unjust according to the way it is used, that is say for what goals or ends, in what amount or kind, against and by whom, when and where, with what likely consequences, and so forth. Of these several features, the goal or end of force would seem to be the first and most important. No amount of force, used by anyone on any occasion, could be just if the end aimed at were not just. So what are the just aims for which force may be used? Well ultimately, since we are talking of the use of force by men against men, the goals must be the good of men. Only if force has as its goal the promotion of the human good could it be good. The human good is clearly a complex whole consisting of many parts, from material and physical goods, to external goods, to cultural, educational, and spiritual goods. There is no need to spell these out in detail or explain their connections and relative subordination to each other. It is enough to note them in their general outline. For our concern is less about what the human good is than about what uses of force are justified with relation to it. In particular, since the war on terrorism is directed against resisting an evil, the evil of attacks on innocent life and limb, on habitations and property, on economic and social structures, the question is what determines the legitimate use of force in resistance to evil.

The operative idea here is clearly that of selfdefense. Since the human good is the object of pursuit, whatever attacks that good or hinders that pursuit may be resisted and repulsed sufficiently to make the pursuit of the good possible again.

Suppose, however, that force is the only, or only reasonable, way to preserve and promote the good. Are we justified in having recourse to it? The answer would seem to be an unambiguous yes in the case of ordinary criminals who threaten us from within our own communities. One could hardly conceive of a community, at least a decent community, that did not protect itself and its members, using force if need be, against such criminal activities. Since such activities serve to undermine any community and threaten its viability, and the more so the more they are left to grow unchecked, a community that does not undertake to defend itself against them has, to all intents and purposes, given up the desire to survive as a community at all. By parity of reasoning, the same should hold in the case of enemies and terrorists who attack the community from without and in more violent and destructive ways. In other words, the justification for armies and wars is of the same sort as the justification for policemen and prisons.

There is, however, a paradox here, a paradox that lends considerable support to the case of pacifists. For any use of force seems always to be an attack on the good as well as a defense of it. Policemen have sometimes lost their lives in the attempt to arrest criminals by force and their families and friends have suffered all the grief of bereavement as a result. If such harm arises in these cases, how much more does it do so in time of war? Not only are more people maimed and killed in war (and in more awful ways), and more families tortured with grief, but the potential loss of civilian life, the destruction of property, the suspension of peacetime activities, the disruption of the economy and so forth make the damage to the human good so great as to render war unacceptable.

Violence and the Sacred in the 21st Century

In our world of rapidly changing borders, crosscultural business dealings and globalization, security issues between nationstates remain a priority, but terrorism is perhaps the first truly global security concern. Acts of violence by terrorists are difficult by their very nature to track, predict and counter, and as events of the past few years have shown, terrorism can strike literally anywhere. At least with political - secular - terrorism, the global community may foresee the conflict and realize that a political action of violence may be forthcoming (for example, in response to new legislation, perhaps a change in the legal status of a group defined by the nationstate in which they reside). In the case of religious terrorism, the possibility of a small group of fanatics perceiving a theological mandate to commit violence is far more difficult to predict and to prepare for and counter. In religiously motivated violence, because the mandate is from the highest power, the perpetrators are in their own minds immune from the normal laws governing us, and can commit acts of atrocity that would normally be reviled.

Yet we must find a way of approaching religious terrorism systematically, in order to construct a means of confronting it as a global society, and develop strategies to combat it. In essence, we must explore the attempts of an emerging global society to account for the phenomena of disparate faiths and valuesystems as technology brings those disparate cultures into ever closer proximity, with often explosive results. As the 21st Century marches forward into an increasingly religiously-charged society of violence, beginning with the attacks on the World Trade Towers on September 11, 2001 and continuing through the Iraq War, we need to ask ourselves some questions about religious terrorism, in order to prepare for the increase in acts of religious terrorism around the world.

Religious terrorism is usually defined as acts of violence perpetrated by members of a certain religious belief structure, against those whose different belief structures are in conflict with the terrorists. (This definition serves as a good starting point, but we shall see that is not as hard and fast a definition as it once was). Such conflicts are often deemed intractable by many, causing the interested parties (such as the United Nations, conflict resolution theorists, negotiators and other NGOs) to focus on peripheral issues, stating that religious terrorism is the hardest form of terrorism to approach - in fact, nothing could be further than the truth. Although humans vary immensely in their beliefs, the similarity is that almost everyone has beliefs, and different groups have gone through similar processes to arrive at their current belief structure; given time and opportunity, one can apply similar processes to arrive at an understanding of different religions and of religious terrorism. Such an approach must begin with the question of why violence is the usual recourse of these fanatics. If we take as a given that violence is inherent in life on this earth and has been since throughout human history, then we must realize that organized religions, mythologies and belief structures must account for violence.

Although arguments can certainly be made on both sides of the question "Is violence inherent in humanity?", it cannot be denied that violent acts occur in nature, and must be dealt with by humanity as witnesses to creation. As people are confronted with violence, they must find a way of coping with violence and its chaotic effects, and ways of restoring order to the world. French historian René Girard has discussed the idea that sacrifice restores order to society, and it is here that we must look for the means by which religious organizations justify acts of terrorism. Religion imposes order on violence, yet ironically it frequently uses violence to restore order in "extreme" situations. It is important to realize that the acts of terrorism in recent years are not random, nor are they temporary the fact is that these events are reactions against a perceived disorder, and as such are permanent fixtures in the cycle of religious belief - it is unlikely that there will be a sudden downturn in the number of religious terrorist attacks.

To understand religious terrorism, we must seek to make explicit the dynamics involved in religiously justified violence, in order to clarify and categorize theoretical issues which will then lead to a greater understanding of religious terrorism, and a greater awareness of the characteristics of religious terrorists. At the same time, we must reach a point where we move beyond irrational fears, and cease equating certain groups with terrorism as the media has often done by pounding such rhetorical formulas as "Islam=Jihad=Muslim Terrorism" into the popular consciousness. There is no doubt that acts of terrorism are perpetrated by Muslims, but it is not an ingrained aspect of the Islamic faith at least not any more than the precepts of violence which are embedded in Christianity and acts of violence easily classified as terrorism are perpetrated by people with various religious affiliations, including Hindu, Sikh, Buddhist, Christian, and Aum Shinrikyo (the cult which unleashed chemical weaponry on subway commuters in Japan).

Most acts of terrorism are considered political in nature, but many are religiously based, and even those acts which are explicitly political often have religious underpinnings. We can see a difference between "pure political" terrorism and "pure religious" terrorism by understanding the different targets for each. Politically motivated acts of terrorism are usually directed towards a clear target, either an entity or structure representing the state, with the goal being an act of destruction which will cause the state to respond in a manner conducive to the internal goals of the terrorists. In such cases the use of terrorism is often a coercive move, although not always. In an act of religious terrorism, the target is more loosely defined - it is simply some representation of those who disagree with the terrorists belief system. This began changing in the final years of the last millennium however; targets simultaneously became more diffuse on a smaller scale and more targeted on a larger scale.

The predictability of possible targets for religious terrorists began decreasing as they unleashed violence on seemingly randomly chosen victims, such as the subway commuters in Japan's Sarin attack of 1995, or the fact that AlQaeda's goals are simply to "strike at the West", meaning essentially all people and places are targets at all times. The goal of acts of religious terrorism is also less clear. Often the goal is simply to lash out at the "unbelievers" in a way which is harmful enough to be noticed throughout the community. It is rare that such acts of "pure" terrorism occur however, which is what makes religion and terrorism such a crucial topic in today's global society. Despite the acute need for broad discussion and investigation of religious terrorism, the discourse has yet to reach useful levels. We must create and place this discourse in the context of an emerging global society reacting to the telecommunications revolution both by becoming smaller and more integrated, but also by social/cultural boundaries coming into closer proximity, and chafing, in what Dr. Samuel Huntington has called "the clash of civilizations" in his book of the same name.

The Current Status of the World with Regards to Religious Terrorism

We have myriad examples of religious terrorism in the recent past both outofcontext single events and ongoing situations; the original bombing of the World Trade Center and its final reckoning on 9/11, the explosion in Oklahoma City, and ongoing conflicts in Ireland, Sudan and Bosnia are just a few of the most widely discussed. Here we see that acts of terrorism are often both political and religiously motivated. The explosion in Oklahoma City is a prime example of a terrorist event with primarily political motivation, but with roots in religious doctrine, both explicit and surmised. We have events of violence which are as yet completely unexplained - at least in public at the time of this chapter such as the Olympic pipe bomb in Atlanta in 1996, and the explosion of TWA flight 800, in which terrorism is still being discussed as a possible reason, despite final NTSB findings as to the cause of the accident.

This raises a disturbing question: Have acts of religious terrorism become so diffuse, so random in the recent past that we cannot successfully hypothesize as to their motivation and probable perpetrators after the fact much less before? If so, the security forces of the world are in a difficult situation. Even in situations where the perpetrator is caught, as in the Oklahoma bombing, we are at a loss to explain how we might have adequately been prepared for such an event, even given the widespread discussion of politically motivated splinter groups. The Oklahoma case is particularly illuminating to an examination of the role of religion and terrorism as it was immediately and incorrectly viewed as a religious terrorist attack by the most likely culprits: Muslims. It is interesting to reflect here that when terrorist events of almost unbelievable atrocity occur, victims and witnesses are most likely to suspect religious motivation; the worldwide fear of religious fanaticism is universal in its response to acts of violence, and lack of understanding of other religions.

A perfect example of this lack of understanding can be seen in U.S. President Bill Clinton's remarks immediately following the bombing of the Oklahoma Federal building in 1995: "Make no mistake; this is an attack against America and the way we live!" This was followed with additional statements regarding the status of Muslims undergoing a trial for the New York City bombing incident a year and half earlier, implying quite obviously that the assumed attackers were of MiddleEastern origin. Continued rhetoric from The White House and other organizations including Oklahoma University's professor of terrorism speculated on the perpetrators and attempted to whip up fear towards Muslims.

Clinton, the professor and other media personalities pointed a finger of blame towards unknown Islamic radical terrorists, and media reports of searches for Middle Eastern men mounted, as average citizens began to react. The effect on the populace of such rhetoric cannot be dismissed, as it furthers religiously motivated distrust and enters into the cycle of culture-clash that perpetuates radical responses to differences in religious belief. When journalist Mark Steyn was visiting Oklahoma City soon after the bomb he heard a woman working at a restaurant say that she swore if an "Islam person" were to come in she would refuse to serve him. On the internet, discussion groups and websites sprung up to track Muslim actions and suspected Islamic groups, and the electronic rooms of the world of cyberspace were ringing with hate email.

An American selfstyled patriot ultimately was found to be responsible, but the implications of the early statements and whispers in America underscore the fact that 'Islam' still strikes a chord of fear in many western hearts and minds. Clearly there is a need for greater understanding of Islamic ideals in many areas. More importantly, this event and its surrounding media coverage explicate causes of escalating religious terrorism; misunderstanding and fear fanned by an increasingly electronic mediainterconnected world which responds to media coverage so rapidly that it creates an immediate complex discourse often based on false premises.

The media refuses to learn its lesson though, and now broadcasts all sorts of opinions on why suspect Timothy McVeigh parked his fertilizer-bomb laden truck outside the Oklahoma City Federal building. Most often discussed is the date of April 19 which is extrapolated to attribute the bombing to a reaction to the situation in Waco, Texas, when the Branch Davidians eventually set their compound and themselves aflame rather than submit to federal authorities. The implication is that McVeigh was objecting to what he perceived as restrictions of freedom of religion, as well as overzealous federal power, but these are mere speculations, possibly as fatuous as those made about Islamic suspects earlier in the year. The changing of the millennium was felt as a threatening rather than encouraging event by many people as the discourse surrounding the event had somber undertones.

This helped shape a global response of fear about random acts of violence, a fear which became increasingly obvious as splinter groups began to voice concerns about the end of the millennium and those voices penetrated mainstream society. Discussion of millenarian mythology passed beyond the academic and into the mainstream; even in popular culture, on television, one of the most talked about shows of the 1996/97 season was Millennium, a gothic U.S. show about a group of men and women dedicated to fighting the random acts of violence perpetrated by society's darker, usually fanatically religious side in reaction to the approaching millennium.

Those people were terrorists in the ultimate sense of the word as it used in popular parlance: striking out with violent acts in seemingly random events, inculcating terror in those people affected. Yet this is not the actual definition of terrorism, which in fact implies a systematic use of terror, planned events of violence for a specific purpose, although the target of the violence may in fact be random. Recent religious terrorism has changed the nature of violence as it embraces less conservative weaponry. Terrorism has long brought to mind visions of bombs and hostagetaking, and although these continue to be weapons of the religious terrorist, new forms of violence are being unleashed on unsuspecting citizens. Perhaps the most shocking of these new terrorist weapons at the end of the millennium was used in Japan, by an obscure cult led by blind religious recluse Shoko Asahara. The group Aum Shinrikyo was founded in 1987 by Asahara, and rapidly began stockpiling dangerous chemicals. Eventually the cult combined these chemicals in socalled binary bombs, releasing the deadly nerve gas Sarin into the subway. Justification for the act was in the groups' Doomsday ideas as the year 2000 began to approach, the belief was that the world would end in cataclysmic events, after which adherents to the faith would find themselves in paradise.

A millennial group such as Aum Shinrikyo feels the need to become an active player in these events by hastening the demise of the unbelievers. The use of chemical and biological weapons began increasing in groups like Aum Shinrikyo, as they began to prepare for the end of the millennium. According to the judge who presided over the case of the bomb at the World Trade Center, the bomb itself was also packed with cyanide to poison the surrounding area; the plan failed because the cyanide burned during the explosion. U.S. based white supremacist groups also began stockpiling cyanide in the early 1980s, and in 1986, members of Bhagwan Shree Rajneesh's cult deliberately caused a salmonella epidemic. These types of weapons are the latest in attacking people directly, but other kinds of attacks are also on the rise: the events of 9/11 showed the world that planes with no bombs or chemicals aboard could still serve as weapons of enormous destruction; information warfare which hadn't even been considered much of a threat as recently as ten years ago is now taking on prominence in security discussions.

One of the wonders of the age is the internet, and the global society being created through the interlinking of computer systems worldwide, stimulating the flow of information. As this system makes inroads into all levels of human interaction, the potential for a whole new kind of terrorist attack emerges: information warfare. The incidents of "hacking" are on the rise worldwide, and often the perpetrator is invisible. There is no doubt that religious groups are computer-savvy, and are using the internet as a meeting and planning place, as well as a place to broadcast their beliefs and calls for action. There is ample reason to believe that they will - if they are not already doing so - use the internet and related technologies to engage in acts of destruction to further their goals. The apocalyptic aspects of some of these groups are showing up in manifestos they are publishing electronically, giving a clear indication that they will take action in the near future. One final horror also needs to be addressed in discussing the changing face of religious terrorism.

Since the downfall of the Soviet Union, a remarkable amount of dangerous radioactive material such as is used in nuclear warheads is "missing". The possibility of this material falling into the hand of a terrorist organization is not one to be ignored. It is known that Saddam Hussein had scientists working on giving Iraq nuclear capability, and although it seems that he never succeeded in actually building a WMD (weapon of mass destruction), given the state support of a variety of terrorist groups in the MiddleEast, there is the chance of a nuclear weapon being deliberately used in an act of religious terrorism. The normal restraints against using nuclear weaponry which have held its use in check by nation-states are not recognized by religious terrorists, and for that reason this is perhaps the greatest concern of any security minded global organization. Another aspect of religious terrorism which is changing most noticeably is locale, particularly in the United States. Until relatively recently religious terrorist attacks have been primarily events which occurred outside the nation's boundaries it was something that happened in troubled areas such as Northern Ireland or in Israel.

Most of the events of terrorism in Europe can be deemed political actions rather than religiously based; if religious terrorism did happen in someplace like Madrid or Paris, it was because the terrorists were making a point of striking against another government. But in recent years the spate of events inside the United States' borders has increased, and perhaps most disheartening for Americans is the fact that many of these events are perpetrated by other Americans. The 9/11 planes striking the Trade Center of course stands out as the largest of these events, but abortion center bombings, assassination of abortion doctors, and the fact that militia movements are gaining adherents contributes to a feeling of impending doom. Aum Shinrikyo and other cults also have members in the U.S., and the goals of these groups and their members' willingness to carry out bizarre attacks are suspect at best.

What is particularly interesting is the larger role that apocalyptic dialogue is having on the internal goals of these groups. Biblical ideals of Armageddon are becoming the central force in the decision making processes of many terrorist groups, and there is an increasing likelihood of previously relatively quiescent groups suddenly turning violent. Any movement which anticipates imminent, total supernatural salvation view themselves as having a divine imperative to have a participatory role in the 'last days'. Given the impetus to hasten salvation, these groups may feel that their particular role is to assist in 'judgment day', thus the predilection towards destruction. As judgment against unbelievers would clearly result in their chance at salvation being slim at best, the death resulting from a religiously motivated act of violence is not one which is inherently evil in the eyes of the deity of the terrorist group.

For years a distinction has been drawn between foreign and domestic terrorism, and that division has resulted in a weak response to religious terrorism which crosses boundaries of all sorts, political, geographical and cultural. Domestic terrorism is assigned to a nationstate's internal peacekeeping forces, often with the result that any intelligence gathering on the organization's ties to groups outside the state is somewhat lacking, and thus a response is incomplete. Foreign religious terrorism is almost deemed to be "understandable", and perhaps unavoidable in Huntington's 'clash of civilizations'. If any attempt to respond is made on a global basis, it is usually to reframe the event as political, and then pass it on to the military. This has the result of legitimizing the terrorist event, as the media picks up the story and it becomes a miniwar, played out on the television screens of the masses.

Religious terrorism can be bound up in political dissent, but the global aspects of religious terrorism outside of nationstate disputes calls for a global response outside of any nationstate's military, and outside of the United Nation' peacekeeping forces. In 1986, then ambassador Benjamin Netanyahu wrote of his theories about winning the war against terrorism in his book Terrorism: How the West Can Win; missing the crucial point that the West cannot win this war, although it can contribute a great deal to a global community response to religious terrorism. The title seems regrettable from a cultural standpoint, seeming to assert that the West stands together and disregards the East, implying that the East is either not involved (after the Aum Shinrikyo event, this would be a particularly disturbing standpoint), that the East is the origin of terrorism (after the Oklahoma bombing, also a vapid viewpoint), or perhaps worse, that the West does not need the East to successfully combat religious terrorism.

Netanyahu also strives to make clear the fact that underlying all responses to terrorism - political, economic, military there must be a moral basis upon which to build a successful strategy to combat terrorism. It would seem that for a moral response to religious terrorism to have any validity in the global community, such a basis must be worked towards by the West and the East, giving at least a moderately universal sense to the foundation of a global war against terrorism. Given Netanyahu's current position in the political arena, it will be interesting to observe his actions and see whether they dovetail with earlier assertions. Regardless, the point must be made here that Netanyahu and other contributors to his book accept as a given that everyone in the West can reach a moral understanding of universal truths. It can probably however be agreed already that acts of terrorism are found to be abhorrent by the majority, and this is a strong enough basis upon which to form a front against religious terrorism. To entangle counterterrorism in discussions of morality would merely prolong the time to reach a useful response.

So we are left with the attempt to frame an international response to religious terrorism, with the obvious understanding that the response must be universal in its agreement that religious terrorism is inherently counter-productive to the global community, and that a response must be unified at the political, military and economic layers of the world society. A task immense in scope and unprecedented but not impossible. Should an international organization be formed with full funding from a variety of nations? Without a doubt, the answer must be an emphatic 'Yes'. Should such an organization be organized under the United Nations as many have suggested? The answer here must be just as emphatic, but must be 'No'. Regrettably, the UN has lost a great deal of credibility, and its topheavy bureaucracy and entangling web of missions would be at best detrimental to a focused global response to religious terrorism.

As Netanyahu pointed out, it is doubtful that many would disagree with Churchill's dictum that protection of its citizens is a government's first obligation, but we must now extrapolate Churchill's idea and state that a civilized world's first obligation is to protect its lawabiding citizens against the acts of those who would endanger those citizens and as a result would hinder the creation of a just, participatory and sustainable societywhere sustainability is at least partially measured by stable, relatively permanent peace. It is possible that even the existence of an organization proven to be taking into account the phenomena of disparate faiths in as part and parcel of an ongoing, determined struggle against terrorism would be useful in curbing the need of religious terrorists to make themselves heard through violence, as long as it was clear what the response to that violence would be.

More importantly, it must be understood that the response would not vary from event to event depending on locale, victims, and supposed motivation. Herein lays perhaps the most critical aspect of any organization devoted to fighting terrorism: the response must be pre-determined, rugged, and it must be known to the terrorists of the world. The form of the response itself can of course be argued, but it would behoove the founders of such an organization to examine historical evidence, leading them to the realization that there are several keys to a relatively successful response to terrorism. Netanyahu and others have pointed out that simple noncapitulation is the most important factor in dissuading terrorists, as terrorism sets out to make a point, after which demands will be made. This is not always the case in religiously motivated terrorism. An act of religious terrorism may simply be a 'judgment', as was discussed earlier. So refusal to deal with the terrorists is a moot point in many cases of 'pure' religious terrorism, where no 'deal' is envisioned. In fact, as has been discussed earlier, the diffusion of religious terrorism would indicate that the perpetrator may not even be known.

We are left with the one relatively proven successful response to terrorism being somewhat useless with regards to religious terrorism. However, it does point to the immense need for intelligencegathering on the part of all nations, and the immediate sharing of that intelligence. This in turn requires a forum, and necessitates the need for a singleminded organization to be formed. Once intelligence is placed in the hands of an international organization with some power to act internationally, the knowledge can be applied in a variety of counter-measures, including infiltration prior to an act of terrorism, or at the very least informed military response. Details of this remain to be studied and formulated, but to state the obvious, knowledge often is power.

The Intellectual Roots of Terrorism

Terrorism, in the sense of aggression and terrifying an opponent, is an old human practice since traditional communities knew the blind solidarity for the clan, tribe or sect. It took a new shape and context in the second half of the 20th century. The motivations for terrorist acts are complex and intertwined: psychological, social, religious, cultural and political. In this chapter, we are concerned with the intellectual roots which constitute the strongest drive for a terrorist act, nevertheless it may also be mixed with other factors such as: cultural, social or religious. It deals in more details about the intellectual roots of Islamic groups, which commit violent and terrorist actions, inside and outside the Muslim world. Such actions are exploited by some to brand Muslims as terrorists and Islam itself as a religion that justifies terrorism against innocent people. Some studies speak about other reasons which enhance terrorism such as: culture of violence, social conditions, role of media and intelligence agencies.

The international community, headed by the United States, failed to reach an agreement on a comprehensive definition for terrorism; the reason is the disagreement on two important points: 1- is the right of people to resist occupation by force which may cause damage to civilians a terrorist act? Does the use of excessive force by the State against its civilian citizens or against others a terrorist action? The United States stands in an opposition to most countries of the world, in calling armed resistance against occupation terrorism while defending State terrorism against resistance movements as self defense. The purpose is to protect itself, its allies in NATO and Israel against the attacks of resistance movements in Iraq, Palestine, Lebanon and Afghanistan. The Secretary General of the United Nations, Kofi Anan, tried to strike a compromise between the United States and the majority of U.N. members, by defining 'terrorism' as follows: "any action constitutes terrorism if it is intended to cause death or serious bodily harm to civilians or noncombatants, with the purpose of intimidating a population or compelling a government or an international organization to do or abstain from doing any act".

The Organization of Islamic Conference (O.I.C.) failed, in several conferences, to reach a comprehensive definition of terrorism that links terrorism with violence that is intended to terrify people, whatever its motives. However, it said that armed struggle against occupation is not terrorism but it should not target civilians or innocent people. The big terrorist activities committed in the last few decades are not random incidents in reaction to direct provocation, but well planned acts by small organized extremist groups which hold religious, ideological, or nationalist doctrines. They aimed at inflicting the biggest number of victims to attract a wide media attention, the purpose is to put high pressure on governments or organizations or groups in order to respond to certain political or material demands. Although those extremist groups may succeed in executing some of their planned terrorist actions, but in most cases they failed to achieve their political objectives.

Most countries of the world reject to be blackmailed by such acts that may encourage more of them in future. Contemporary experience has shown that peaceful political actions are more successful in achieving political objectives in the long run, no matter how oppressive or totalitarian the ruling regime is. The world is less strict with states which use excessive military force to terrify and deter their adversaries, whether combatants or civilians, on the basis that states have the legitimacy to use violence against outlaws. However, a double standard criterion is practiced by some big powers in judging the military force used by Israel against Palestinians and Lebanese resisting occupation, compared by the violence used by the Sudan government against rebel movements in Darfur. The political consideration is more crucial in defining terrorism rather than the legal or moral one.

Nature of Terrorist Groups

To speak about the intellectual roots of terrorism, we need to identify some of these groups which are considered 'terrorist' in order to analyze their motives. Otherwise, our analysis shall be theoretical and not relevant to the actual situation on the ground. We do not know all the terrorist groups in the world, besides the definition of terrorism is controversial even at the level of the United Nations organizations. This is to select randomly the list of organizations, which is published in 2006 by the United States and branded as active terrorist groups. Nevertheless, the bias of the United States against those who took arms against its imperial policies or against its despotic allies in the Middle East and South Asia is well known. The reason being that it is the most concerned State with terrorism, it collects information and conducts studies about violent groups more than any other country, it refines and updates its data regularly; the United Nations and the European Union tend to accept the list provided by the United States in most cases. That does not mean we agree with the American classification of terrorist groups, but their list is useful as a random sample that has a practical nature upon which we establish our analysis on the intellectual roots of terrorism.

The American list includes 87 terrorist groups, 44 of them are considered active in 2006; they commit acts of terrorism from time to time. We attempt to define the nature of those active groups and find out the objectives behind their actions. The list may be divided into five categories according to the ideologies and objectives of the groups.

1. Ten of those groups are Islamic liberating organizations; they struggle to liberate their homeland from a foreign power which, in their understanding, occupies their land by force without justification. Those groups exist in Palestine, Kashmir, Iraq, Afghanistan and Philippine. They hope also to establish an Islamic system of government after the liberation of their land, and expect to take the responsibility of that government.

2. Eleven Islamic radical organizations are committed to change secular dictatorial regimes to Islamic ones that implement Shari'ah laws. Those organizations work from within their countries or from outside in order to over through governments in the following countries; Egypt, Algeria, Indonesia, Morocco, Kurdistan, Iraq, Libya, Uzbekistan and Pakistan. In all those countries, democracy is non existent or it is only a formal frame without a real possibility to change the ruling elite, its policies or methods.
3. Eleven socialist liberating organizations, working in: Palestine, Spain, Northern Ireland, Sri Lanka and southern Turkey. Like the Islamic organizations, the leftist groups aspire to establish a socialist regime after liberation.
4. Ten leftist radical organizations, aim to set up communist or socialist rule instead of the rightist dictatorial and corrupt government in the country, they operate in: Iran, Colombia, Philippine, Greece, Turkey and Peru. In some countries, there is more than one leftist radical organization which reflects the multiple visions and differences among leaders.
5. Two extreme religious groups, work under democratic systems in Israel and Japan, to reform the conditions of their countries through terrorist activities. They are very small and ineffective.

In analyzing the situation of these groups which commit terrorist activities, we observe the following:

a. Half of them work to liberate their countries from states, which they believed usurped their land by force. Most of the states are dictatorial or semidictatorial, for the few which enjoy democratic systems (Spain, Northern Ireland & Philippine), the demographic distribution makes it impossible for the marginalized minorities to liberate their regions through the democratic process, or to have an effective role in the rule of the country.

b. In the case of aiming at a radical reform, the leftist organizations work under conservative rightwing governments which adopt policies imposed by the United States. However, more than half of these countries enjoy a reasonable degree of democratic freedoms such as: Philippine, Greece, Peru and Colombia. The terrorist organizations in these countries do not command popular support, which will enable them to take part in the executive or legislative branches of government. There are other moderate leftist parties, which participate in the democratic system and have considerable public support; they block the way before the small radical groups. However, the moderate leftists did not succeed in changing the system in favour of the poor classes in society.

c. In the case of radical Islamic organizations, all of them operate in majority Muslim countries but the systems of government are secular, even when the constitution includes some Islamic references such as: 'Islam is the State religion', or legislations should be in accordance with 'the principles of Islamic Shari'ah'. The regimes are dictatorial or, at best, quasi-democratic, but prohibit Islamic parties from operating in a legal way while they allow leftist or even communist parties to work legally and openly. The Islamic trend, with its different groups, masters a significant public sympathy despite the harassment of governments.

d. With the exception of three Islamic organizations, which work on regional or international level, all other organizations, Islamic or socialist, operate in their own countries either for liberation or for radical reform. That means, all those violent groups have national objectives which are related to their own countries and not to international schemes.

e. The number of organizations working in Muslim countries is 29 and those working in other parts of the world are 15. That means twothirds of the organizations are within the Muslim world which constitutes one quarter of countries in the world. That may be explained by the fact that the Muslim world is the least democratic region in the world, in addition to the fact that the terrorist list used in this chapter is set up by the United States which is known for its intervention and clashes with many Muslim countries.

f. From the above analysis, we may conclude that the end of occupation of other people's lands, giving regional autonomy to distinct minorities, and adopting plural democratic system of government will solve most of the grievances that motivate ultra nationalist organizations to practice terrorism.

General Intellectual Roots

Concerning national liberation organizations, the use of the term "terrorism" is not applicable because international treaties and contemporary political history, since the establishment of national states, have accepted the right of the indigenous population to use armed resistance in order to liberate its land from an occupying foreign power. The American classification is biased in branding the organizations which work against America or one of its allies, especially Israel, as terrorists. This includes all the Palestinian groups and Hizb Allah of Lebanon which took arms against occupation, and the Kurdistan Workers' Party (PKK) in Turkey. However, the American definition of terrorism does not apply on organizations that use violence against adversary governments in the former Soviet Union, Cuba, Cambodia or some Latin American countries.

The American definition clearly speaks about 'Foreign Terrorist Organizations' (F.T.O.s), which "threaten the security of the U.S. nationals or the national security (national defense, foreign relations, or the economic interests) of the United States." Nonetheless, we need to speak about the intellectual roots, which motivate some national groups to use violence against an occupying foreign power or against a power that dominates over their region that has a separate national or religious character, without giving the people of the region their full national or religious rights. This is the case in some countries like: the basks in northern Spain, the

Muslims in southern Philippine, the Kurds in southern Turkey, the Tamil in Sri Lanka and the Chechnyans in Russia.

The main intellectual factor among those groups is the strong national solidarity in the cases of occupied countries, or the strength of the religious or ethnic commitment among minorities who live in a distinct region dominated by a majority of different ethnicity or religion. The fighting groups link between their national, ethnic or religious solidarity and the dignity of their country or region or people, as if the continuation of foreign occupation or the majority domination means a national, ethnic or religious humiliation that is more painful than death itself. The Catholics of Northern Ireland (one third of the population) reject the hegemony of the United Kingdom and the Protestant population (two thirds) who came from Scotland and England more than 150 years back and settled in their country, despite the fact that being part of the United Kingdom give them a stable democratic system and a higher standard of living than what they could get in the Republic of Ireland which they wanted to join. However, for the Irish Republican Army (IRA), which took arms against the United Kingdom and the Protestant settlers, the national dignity and the religious identity is more important than political or material considerations. Usually, the occupied nation or the suppressed minority feel that they are superior to the power which colonized or dominated them.

The strong feeling of injustice felt by the group, which has been ruled by another state, nation or a religious community and that feeling becomes more acute and widespread if the country or the region is underdeveloped or marginalized and its indigenous population is not sharing in the government. The frustration and despair that the prevailing unjust conditions will not be changed by peaceful means, because the occupying state or the dominating group insist that the situation should remain as it is even by force. If the occupied country or the suppressed group do not enjoy democratic rights, as was the case in Chechnya or in Kurdistan of Iraq (during the era of Saddam) or in Palestine, the resort to violence becomes an obvious option. Psychologists argue that frustration and despair is the major factor motivating people towards violence. A strong belief of the group, that their war against the enemy is right and justified according to their national and religious beliefs, international law and human experience.

They believe that their case is fair and clear and cannot be denied except by somebody who is ignorant or allying himself with the enemy. That their enemy has no right whatsoever to occupy their land or dominate them, he is an evil criminal who will not hesitate to kill women, children and elders of minorities or other nationalities. As they represent absolute right the enemy represents absolute evil, thus he deserves every cruel punishment. The propaganda of violent groups concentrates on exposing the injustices befallen on their people and the criminal acts of the enemy, thus their violent reaction is a legitimate self defense. The belief that human freedom deserves any cost, no matter how much it is, is a common argument used by violent groups to justify their terrorist acts and the sacrifices paid by their members and innocent people. For their members it is a voluntary sacrifice; for their people they should pay their due share in the liberation struggle which they did not do enough to defend it as a just cause; but for the enemy constituency they deserve what happened to them because they benefited from the maltreatment of the suppressed nation or group, and they mostly supported the wrong policies of their unjust government. At worse, there are 'collateral' victims in any war and the liberation struggle is no exception.

The rooted faith of the group that eventually they will win their struggle against the enemy despite all the odds against it and the big difference in human and material resources between them and the enemy. Since they believe in their just cause and have the carriage and resilience to continue fighting till the end, they are bound to succeed. The belief that the blood of the 'martyrs' who were killed for the cause requires that the battle should continue till it achieves its objective, any wavering from the course means betrayal for those martyrs. The argument continued to be used by hardliners, even when it becomes clear to the leadership of the group that the armed struggle will not achieve its objective, or its cost is too heavy for their nation or community whom they want to defend. Furthermore, to think of a negotiated settlement with the enemy, is likely to lead to a split within the group. Many would like to stay on the bloody hopeless course rather than risk a split of the group which stayed together in good and bad times.

Considering the violent groups which advocate radical change, 11 of them are Islamic, 2 religious (one Jewish & one Buddhist) and 10 are communists. They share some of the intellectual roots known among the liberating organizations; below we mention the roots which are particular to the radical change groups. The most important factor is the ideology of the group, whether it is religious or secular, there is no one example of a liberal or capitalist organization that is included in the American list as terrorist. The group earnestly believes that its ideology is the absolute truth; it is the only doctrine which will establish a paradise on earth. The rationalization of the armed struggle against unjust and despotic regimes comes from inside the ideology. For the religious groups, it is the wish of God to establish a political system on religious teachings. It is the duty of the believer to work for such a state; otherwise he is not a true believer. For communists and socialists, the violent revolution against feudalism or capitalism is part of the doctrine itself.

The democratic means of change are considered slow and ineffective; they give false legitimacy to an exploiting system which is created for the benefit of the few at the expense of the majority. The existing regime is considered despotic, oppressive and unjust. It will never accept peaceful change; it will use all means of force to defend the ruling class which ally itself with foreign powers and interests at the expense of the interest of the country and its sovereignty. The radical groups agree with the liberation organizations on the following ideas: despair of peaceful change that they are absolutely right and the ruling regime is absolutely wrong, they are eventually bound to succeed and the majority of population who are scared or deceived will side with them when the change comes. The religious groups believe that God will grant them victory, and that the struggle or jihad should continue as long as necessary in loyalty to the martyrs who passed away and to bring the desirable change.

The Intellectual Roots of Islamic Groups

We will deal in some details with the Islamic groups mentioned in the American list because they concern us more, they work mostly in the Muslim world, and they brought upon Islam and the Muslims the serious charge of terrorism. The western and Jewish media have worked relentlessly to stigmatize Muslim and Islamic groups as terrorists, by designed repetition, blunt exaggeration and international coordination. As the violent Islamic groups are aware of the serious religious responsibility in killing a human being which is equivalent to the killing of all people, and the aggression against innocent people; they attempted their best to justify theologically their violent acts against civilians.

We take three examples for those Islamic groups: the Egyptian Jihad organization which was active between 1979 till 1981 when it assassinated President Anwar alSadat; the Egyptian Islamic Group which was established in 1969 and was the most active in terrorist acts till the middle of 1990s; and the Muslim Jama'ah which was founded by Mustafa Shukri in 1969 from inside his prison, it is the most extreme organization. These three organizations represent the most important violent trends; they produced a coherent religious thought; as a matter of fact other organizations including Al-Qa'idah have borrowed their theology from those groups. Ayman al-Zawahri, the second man in Al-Qa'idah, was a senior member of Al-Jihad before joining Al-Qa'idah. The important theological works produced by the leaders of those organizations are:

- Risalat al-Iyman (the Message of Faith), by Dr. Salih Sariyyah who was executed in 1974 after a failed coup attempt in Cairo.

- Al-Faridah alGha'ibah (the Absent Doctrine), by Muhammad Abdusalam Faraj who took part in the assassination of al-Sadat and was executed in 1981.
- Kurasat (the Manual), written by Mustafa Shukri , the head of the Muslim Jama'ah who participated in the killing of the minister of Awqaf, Muhammad Husain al-Dhahabi, in 1977 and was executed with others in 1978.
- Manhaj Jama'at al-Jihad (the Jihad Group Manual), by Abud al-Zumur who became the leader of the Jihad organization after the death of Abdulsalam Faraj.
- Mithaq al'-Amal alIslami (the Charter of Islamic Action), written by Ibrahim Najih in 1984. He was considered the faqih (jurist) of the Islamic Group which killed several policc officers and European tourists; latter on he headed the team which revised most of the organization's thought. His late writings led to the end of violence by the group in 1997.
- Hatmiyat al-Muwajah (the Inevitable Confrontation), published by the Islamic Group. The major ideas of the Islamic groups to justify violence, with minor differences among them, are as follows:

Considering the Muslim state in which they live, as 'nonIslamic' or 'Dar Harb' (Enemy Land) because the rulers do not implement the Shari'ah laws; thus the government and its members are infidels on the basis of an old fatwa issued by Ibn Taymiyyah. Those rulers are worse than polytheists because at one time they were Muslims and then they apostatized, they deserve a severer punishment than nonbelievers. The Muslim Jama'ah which was harshly persecuted in prison went even further to say that the whole society became infidel by its acquiescence towards such a situation. Hassan al-Hudaybi, the leader of the Muslim Brotherhood, wrote from within his prison a book called 'Du'atun La Qudat' (Preachers not Judges) rejecting the ideas of those groups; at one time they were members of his organization. To rebel against the rulers who apostatized by changing the Shari'ah laws and suspending the rulings of

Islam, is a religious duty. Those rulers lost their right to rule and be obeyed, according to a saying by the Prophet who link the obedience for rulers by not committing a clear denial of an authentic religious principle. Those despotic rulers who remain in power by force can only be removed by force.

The establishment of an Islamic state in a Muslim majority country is a religious duty incumbent on every Muslim, because some religious rulings can only be implemented by the government. They quoted the Quranic verses: "And whosoever does not judge by what Allah has revealed, such are the disbelievers." "And so judge (you O Muhammad) among them by what Allah has revealed and follow not their vain desires." If the Islamic state can not be established except by fighting, so it is the duty of every Muslim to take part in that fighting.

The groups strongly believe in their eventual victory, because of the good omens promised by the Prophet Muhammad who said that the Muslim Ummah will reign between the far east and the far west, and their religion will cover the same. To enjoin the good and prevent the evil is a religious duty, that is mentioned in many Quranic verses and traditions of the Prophet. One means of doing this effectively is by force, which means rebelling against the government that does not allow the practice of this duty. The Islamic groups answer the objections to their extreme attitude which remind them of the many verses and traditions of the Prophet that urge Muslims to: allow freedom of religion, adopt forgiveness, pardoning and tolerance etc. They answer that all these teachings were abrogated by the verse of the sword, "Then when the sacred months have passed, then kill the polytheists wherever you find them."

Islam and the Issue of Terrorism

This perception is not due to any intrinsic resentment of Islam by the American people. It is understood that the mainstream of Muslims, the vast majority of them, like in every other faith, is peaceful and pay their taxes, trying to make America a better society, trying to improve relations with neighbours and colleagues. But images and terminology influence public opinion, and a bitter taste is left when Islam is reported in the daily headlines. The term "Islamic fundamentalism", whatever it means, has been repeated enough times in relation to violent incidents that naturally, any thinking human being has to be uncomfortable with the fact that America is home to a vibrant Muslim community. The problem stems from negative images about Islam. In the court of public opinion, Islam is guilty until proven innocent.

Even though the Middle East was home to fewer terrorist incidents than Latin America and Europe, for example, it is still regarded as the region where terrorism is rooted. According to a recent US State Department report, Patterns of Global Terrorism, issued earlier this year, 272 terrorist events occurred in Europe, 92 in Latin America and 45 in the Middle East. Sixty-two anti-US attacks occurred in Latin America last year, 21 in Europe and 6 in the Middle East. These numbers represent the terrorist trend and not an anomaly, whereby the majority of perpetrators are not linked to the Middle East or Islam. The Red Army Faction in Germany, the Basque Separatists in Spain, the Tamil Tigers in Sri Lanka, the Shining Path in Peru and the National Liberation Army in Columbia are not viewed with the same horror as terrorist groups of Muslim background.

There is no moral justification for terrorism regardless of the ethnic or religious background of the perpetrator or the victim, but the factual basis of terrorism has been either hidden or twisted in the public's perception of this policy problem, especially in congressional hearings on terrorism. The countries with the worst terrorist records in the world are not in the Middle East either. They are not even Muslim countries outside the Middle East. They are Columbia and Germany, havens for drug lords and neo-Nazis. The negative association of Islam with terrorism exists, but no one has ever asked

"Why?" Could it be that American society cannot overcome the Khomeini phobia, even though he is dead? The US Congress found it necessary to push $20 million towards covert operations in toppling the Iranian government even at the dissent of people in the CIA. The Arab countries, both friend and foe, are run by tyrants who kill more of their own people than those outside their countries. The presumption that these countries represent a threat to American interests or that any one of them can dominate the region or even rival the only remaining superpower is indeed generous. So the issue is not these countries' hegemony in their region or the world, but about who can dominate their people and exploit their resources.

The perception in the Middle East is that US policy does not serve the peoples interests; it protects Israel and friendly Arab dictators even when they violate human rights, while it slaps sanctions on and takes military actions against countries whose dictators misbehave, resulting in suffering, starvation and even slaughter, all in the name of teaching the tyrants a lesson. The priorities in the Middle East for the US are not human rights and democracy, but rather oil and Israeli superiority. Consequently, antiAmerican sentiment increases. This mood of the general public is then characterized as "Islamic fundamentalism", even though the resentment is not rooted in religion. When it turns violent, it is termed "radical Islamic fundamentalism" or "Islamic terrorism." The various "terrorism experts" promote linkage to the Middle East before any other possibility every time terrorism is speculated. They exploit the human suffering of the victims, their families, and the fears of the American public.

Indeed, extremists of Muslim backgrounds are violating the norms of Islamic justice and should be held accountable for their criminal behaviour, but we in America should not be held hostage to the politics of the Middle East or biased reporting. An Israeli journalist, Yo'av Karny, reporting on the events in Chechnya made a striking observation about this development: "The West will be told—and will be inclined to believe—that the oppression of the Chechens is part and parcel of a cosmic struggle against 'Islamic extremism' that rages from Gaza to Algeria, from Tehran to Khartoum. Russians will seek Western sympathy. They should not be given it." The issue is not Chechnya, and it is not even about Islam and the West. Debates about religious wars and cultural clashes only distract us from the real issue: the powerful want to continue dominating the powerless, manipulating facts to influence public opinion, hence maintaining the status quo.

A bomb goes off in a marketplace in Jerusalem. A suicide bomber launches himself into a bus full of women and children in Tel Aviv. Foreign tourists get massacred at a holiday resort in Luxor, Egypt. Villages upon villages get annihilated in Algeria. The list of events worldwide which have come to symbolise the 'Islamic terror' are endless. From the times in the 70's and 80's when Pan Am and TWA aeroplanes would be hijacked, to the mid 80's in war torn Lebanon where Americans and Europeans would be held as hostages for years; all such incidents have come to be identified with the religion of Islam.

Such incidents from past and present have undoubtedly affected Muslims worldwide and more so in the West. Any Muslim, who wants to practice his/her religion and expresses the pious desire to live under the banner of Islam, is labelled a fundamentalist or extremist. Any Muslim man who walks down a busy street in London or Paris (and Paris more so) with a beard and a scarf on his head, is looked upon as being a terrorist who's probably got an AK47 stashed somewhere on his person. Muslim women who are veiled can't go anywhere in the Western world without being taunted as being oppressed or being mad (for covering up). However, are such beliefs and opinions about Islam really justified?

Exploding the Myth

One of the many short comings which have arisen in the West is judging Islam by the conduct of a minority of its people. By doing this, segments of Western society have deliberately played off the desperate actions of many Muslims, and have given it the name of Islam. Such behaviour is clearly not objective and seeks to distort the reality of Islam. For if such a thing was done Judge a religion by the conduct of its people) then we too could say that all Christianity is about is child molesting and homosexuality whilst Hinduism was all about looting and breaking up mosques. Generalising in such a manner is not seen as being objective, yet we find that the Western world is foremost in propagating this outlook on Islam. So what is the reality of Islam? How does one dispel the myths which have been created and spread so viciously?

The only way to examine Islam is to simply examine its belief system. Look at its sources, the Qur'an and Sunna, and see what they have to say. This is the way to find the truth about what Islam says about terror, terrorism and terrorists. One, who is sincerely searching for the truth, will do it no other way. The very name Islam comes from the Arabic root word 'salama' which means peace. Islam is a religion which is based upon achieving peace through the submission to the will of Allah. Thus, by this very simple linguistic definition, one can ascertain as to what the nature of this religion is. If such a religion is based on the notion of peace, then how is it that so many acts done by its adherents are contrary to peace? The answer is simple. Such actions, if not sanctioned by the religion, have no place with it. They are not Islamic and should not be thought of as Islamic.

Jihad

The word jihad sends shivers down the spines of many Westerners. They readily equate this term with violence and oppression. However, it must be said that the meaning of jihad, as a 'holy war', is something which is totally foreign and not from Islam. If anything, such a description belongs more so to Christianity and its adherents. It was terms like this which were used to justify the slaughter and pillage of towns and cities during the crusades by the Christians. By simply looking into the sources of Islam, one is able to know that the true meaning of jihad is to strive/make effort in the way of Allah.

Thus striving in the way of Allah can be both peaceful and physical. The Prophet Muhammed (saws) said: "The best jihad is (by) the one who strives against his own self for Allah, The Mighty and Majestic". In the Qur'an, Allah also says: "So obey not the disbelievers, but make a great jihad (effort) against them (by preaching) with it (the Qur'an)".

By controlling and fighting against ones desires, the Muslims can then also physically exert themselves in the path of Allah. It is this physical or combative jihad which receives so much criticism. Because of the sheer ignorance of this type of jihad Islam is regarded as terror, and Muslims are regarded as terrorists. However, the very purpose of this physical jihad is to raise the word of Allah uppermost. By doing this, it liberates and emancipates all those who are crying out for freedom all over the world. If the likes of the pacifists of this world had their way, then the world would indeed be full of anarchy and mischief. The combative jihad seeks to correct this as Allah says in the Qur'an:"And if Allah did not check one set of people by means of another, the Earth would be full of mischief. But Allah is full of bounty to the worlds".

Such would be the corruption on this Earth if there had never been a combative jihad that Allah says: "For had it not been that Allah checks one set of people by means of another, monasteries, churches, synagogues and mosques, wherein the name of Allah is mentioned much, would surely have been pulled down. Indeed Allah will help those who help His (cause). Truly Allah is All strong, All mighty". This combative jihad being both defensive and offensive is something which is commanded by Allah upon the Muslims. Through this command the oppressed and weak are rescued from the tyranny of the world:

"And what is the matter with you that you do not fight in the cause of Allah and for those weak, ill treated and oppressed among men, women and children whose only cry is; 'Our Lord, rescue us from this town whose people are oppressors and raise for us from you one who will protect and raise for us from you one who will help".

Anyone who knows the early history of Islam will know that all those nations and empires which came under the fold of Islam were indeed previously oppressed. When the companions of the Prophet Muhammad (saws) went out for the offensive jihad against the Egyptians, the Persians and the Romans, we find that the people did not resist against them at all. Rather, they accepted Islam on such a scale, that it is inconceivable that the jihad of Islam could be anything other then a liberation for these people; a liberation from centuries of tyranny. In fact, with the Byzantine Egyptians and the people of Spain, the Muslims were even beckoned to come and liberate these lands from the oppression of their kings. This is the glorious track record of the Muslim jihad Compare this with the brutal track record of warfare in the Western world over the centuries. From the crusades against the Muslims to the days of colonial warfare, the Western world has killed, destroyed and plundered everything which has come in its way.

Even today this merciless killing goes on by the Western nations. While claiming to be about world peace and security, Western nations are ready to bomb innocent civilians at the drop of a hat. The classic example of this is the recent bombings of Sudan and Afghanistan. Whilst claiming that Sudan and Afghanistan were havens for Islamic terrorists, the bombings of these two nations could not have come at a better time for the American president Bill Clinton. The destruction of innocent lives which were a result of these bombings clearly seem to have been an attempt by Clinton to avert attention away from his sexual misdemeanours; something which he so often gets caught up in. Without doubt this was the reason for such terror from the American military upon innocent people. This is the same American military which claims to enter the world's trouble spots under the guise of being peace keepers. But "... when it is said to them; 'Make not mischief on the Earth', they say; 'We are only peace makers'. Indeed they are the ones who make mischief, but they perceive it not".

The hypocrisy of the West is indeed astounding. By looking at the rules and regulations of this combative jihad it will be clear to any sincere person that this is indeed the religion of truth. When fighting an unjust enemy, no matter how unjust they are, it is forbidden by Islam that their retreating forces are mutilated, tortured or slaughtered. The treacherous violation of treaties and carrying out assassinations after a cease fire, are also prohibited. Allah says in the Qur'an:

"And fight in the way of Allah those who fight you. But do not transgress the limits. Truly Allah loves not the transgressors".

Not transgressing the limits means not to kill women and children, for the Messenger of Allah (saws) "forbade the killing of women and children". Not transgressing the limits means that the elderly, the sick, monks, worshippers and hired labourers are not attacked. Not transgressing the limits means not killing animals wantonly, burning crops and vegetation, polluting waters and destroying homes, monasteries, churches and synagogues:" Allah does not forbid you to deal justly and kindly with those who fought not against you on account of religion, nor drove you out of your homes. Indeed, Allah loves those who deal with equity" (Surah AlMumtahinah 60:8)

After reading such passages from the Qur'an and knowing about what Islam commands and prohibits in jihad, the rules of warfare are given a new meaning; a meaning of justice. How sad it is then, that whilst Islam is condemned for striking terror into the hearts of the people, the likes of the Serbs, the Indian army in Kashmir and the Israeli soldiers in Palestine are left untarnished for the atrocities they have committed in the name of warfare so what about suicide bombing, is this too a part of jihad in Allah's path? From what has already been stated above, it can be deduced that this is not from the religion. However, unfortunately many Muslims have taken suicide bombing as being a virtuous act by which one receives reward. This could not be further from the truth. The Prophet (saws) said: "Those who go to extremes are destroyed".

Suicide bombing is undoubtedly an extremity which has reached the ranks of the Muslims. In the rules of warfare, we find no sanction for such an act from the behaviour and words of the Prophet Muhammad (saws) and his companions. Unfortunately, today (some misguided) Muslims believe that such acts are paving the way for an Islamic revival and a return to the rule of Islam's glorious law. However, we fail to bear in mind that the Prophet (saws) said:" Do not be delighted by the action of anyone, until you see how he ends up". So, for example what is the end of a suicide bomber in Palestine? A leg here, an arm there. Massive retaliation by the Israeli's in the West Bank and Gaza. More Muslims killed and persecuted. How can we be delighted with such an end? What really hammers the final nail in the coffin of this act, is that it is suicide; something which is clearly forbidden in Islam. The Messenger of Allah (saws) said: "He who kills himself with anything, Allah will torment him with that in the fire of Hell".

Some are under the misconception that by killing oneself for an Islamic cause, one commits an act which deserves Paradise. Once when a man killed himself, the Prophet (saws) said: "He is a dweller of the Fire". When the people were surprised at this, the Prophet (saws) said:" A person performs the deeds which to the people appears to be the deeds befitting the dweller of Paradise, but he is in fact one of the dwellers of the Fire." The taking of ones life which Allah has given as a trust to the human, is a great sin. Likewise the taking of other lives (which is so often the case with suicide bombing) is also forbidden, as human life is indeed precious:"...If anyone killed a person not in retaliation for murder or to spread mischief in the land, it would be as if he killed the whole of mankind. And (likewise) if anyone saved a life, it would be as if he saved the whole of mankind". Thus, all other types of extremities such as hostage taking, hijacking and planting bombs in public places, are clearly forbidden in Islam.

The Media

By going through the teachings of Islam, it is clear that such a religion has only come to benefit mankind - not to destroy it. So why is there so much hatred for this noble religion in the West? The answer is simple, the media. It is the Jewish influenced media of the West which has portrayed Islam to be something that it is not. During the 70's and 80's when the PLO (Palestine Liberation Organisation) was carrying out daring hijacks on the world's airways, the media in the West portrayed it as being Islamic. When the Shi'ite suicide bombers of the 80's were causing so much havoc in the Lebanon and in the Gulf region, the media in the West portrayed it as a part of Islam. However, it is known by the heads of the media that the likes of the PLO were not an Islamic organisation, and that according to Islam, Shi'ites are outside the fold of Islam.

Yet such facts are never portrayed by a media which seeks to cover the truth of this religion. A number of years ago, when the Oklahoma City bomb went off, a headline in one of the newspapers, 'Today', summed up this attitude. With a picture of a fire fighter holding a dead child in his arms, the headline read: "In The Name of Islam." Time has of course proven that this bigoted assumption was incorrect, as Timothy McVeigh, a right wing radical now faces the death penalty for the crime. Likewise the bombs which went off in the Paris metro in 1995 were also blamed on Muslim fanatics. It has now emerged that the Algerian secret service who having routinely bribed many European journalists and MPs, were actually behind it. The desire to throw a veil over Islam is immense by these people:" They intend to put out the light of Allah with their mouths, but Allah will complete His light even though the disbelievers hate (it)". Whilst trying to destroy Islam through this instrument of the media, the Jews clearly try to portray an image of themselves as being the oppressed people. Every year, we are reminded as to how many Jews perished under the Nazis in World War II.

We are made to feel sorry for these same people who have gone on to commit so many crimes upon the Palestinian people. Some may say that this is a racist and biased viewpoint. But we say; If this media was not run and orchestrated by the Jews and was truly neutral, then why are Menachem Begin and Yitzhak Shamir, two former Israeli prime ministers, not held aloft as being terrorists? Anyone who knows about the history of the Palestinian occupation will tell you that these two men were members of the Stern Gang and Irgun, two notorious Jewish terror groups who killed many innocent people. If this media was truly impartial, then why does it not tell about the extent of the Israeli bombardment and illegal occupation of Southern Lebanon and its people? And if this media really had nothing against the religion of Allah, then why does it not inform the people that every day hundreds are entering the religion of Islam? Such things will never be highlighted in the Western media, simply because to do so would be against their very interests.

With such immense pressure against it, it is indeed a blessing from Allah that Islam goes from strength to strength. It continues to grow faster then any other religion in the Western world, conquering the hearts and minds of thousands. All this should not even surprise us though, for Allah has promised us that this religion will prevail: "It is He who has sent His Messenger with the guidance and the religion of truth, so that He may make it victorious over all other religions, even though the disbelievers detest it". It is a must that humanity comes towards the religion of Islam. Without it, we will continue to slip down the road of inequity and darkness. With it we can establish a society of justice and peace. "There is no compulsion in religion. The right path has indeed become distinct from the wrong. So whoever rejects false worship and believes in Allah, then he has grasped the most trustworthy handhold that will never break. And Allah is All Hearing, All Knowing" Surah AlBaqarah.

The Fight against Terrorism and Human Rights

Counterterrorism measures that fall outside the framework of the rule of law and human rights standards effectively roll back wellestablished norms and lay the foundations for further insecurity. The 2004 OSCE Ministerial Council adopted the Sofia Ministerial Statement on Preventing and Combating Terrorism. This Statement reemphasizes the determination of the OSCE participating States "to combat terrorism in all its forms and manifestations, as a crime that has no justification, whatever its motivation or origin, and to conduct this fight with respect for the rule of law and in accordance with [their] obligations under international law, in particular international human rights, refugee and humanitarian law." The OSCE also notes the declaration on the issue of combating terrorism contained in the annex to UN Security Council Resolution 1456 (2003), in particular the statement that states must ensure that any measures taken to combat terrorism comply with all their obligations under international law and should adopt such measures in accordance with international law, in particular international human rights, refugee, and humanitarian law.

Human rights are sometimes violated during the conduct of the fight against terrorism. These violations may take many forms including the limitation of fundamental freedoms such as freedom of religion and belief, freedom of expression and freedom of assembly. The right to life has also been threatened in certain circumstances and certain other non-derogable rights, as set forth in Article 4 of the International Covenant of Civil and Political Rights, such as the right to freedom from torture or inhuman and degrading treatment or punishment and the right to a fair trial have been limited by certain legislation and practices in the fight against terrorism.

A strong and active civil society that is actively engaged in promoting democracy and tolerance is instrumental in combating terrorism. This must go handinhand with civil society's support to legitimate measures of the State's authorities aimed at protecting everybody under their jurisdiction from terrorist acts. The OSCE approach is one of co-operative security based on democracy, respect for human rights, fundamental freedoms, the rule of law and social justice. This concept's key elements are the comprehensiveness and indivisibility of security and the allegiance to shared values, commitments, and norms of behaviour. Respect for and compliance with international human rights law remains central to the efforts to prevent and combat terrorism. This Meeting is designed to devise ways that participating States can enhance their efforts to fulfill these mutually reinforcing goals and OSCE commitments.

Religious Freedom

Freedom of religion or belief is a nonderogable right. In the aftermath of 11 September 2001 and 11 March 2003, a number of religious communities in the OSCE area have experienced growing distrust and hostility. As the fight against terrorism has been stepped up and the perceived threat of religious extremism has become a major focus of public debate, religious and immigrant communities have increasingly felt stigmatized or targeted for discrimination or abuse because of their beliefs. This session will aim to look at how certain communities have felt that freedom of religion or belief has been undermined in the aftermath of 11 September 2001 and 11 March 2004, and how they have reacted to this new security climate. Also, the session will examine how governments can balance security concerns while allowing individuals and communities of believers to meet freely for worship, educate their followers and provide information about their beliefs to the public at large.

Torture and the Fight against Terrorism

The right to life and the right to freedom from torture or cruel, inhuman and degrading treatment or punishment are absolute non-derogable rights in all circumstances. Unfortunately these rights have been threatened and limited by certain legislation and practices in the fight against terrorism. Any discussion of human rights in the context of preventing and combating terrorism must recognise the basic premise that state authorities must take steps necessary to protect society from terrorism but that the fight against terrorism cannot provide a justification for the use of or for collusion in torture or cruel, inhuman or degrading treatment or punishment. States must be vigilant to ensure that security measures taken and investigatory techniques used in the context of the fight against terrorism protect against torture and ill-treatment. Allegations of torture in prisons and interrogations in the context of the fight against terrorism and trends in jurisprudence on the admissibility of evidence which may have been extracted through torture are of great concern in this regard.

The Role of Civil Society

The development of a strong and active civil society is essential for a wellfunctioning and stable and democratic State. This can be achieved through strengthening democratic institutions and nongovernmental organisations that aim to promote human rights, tolerance and respect for diversity. Freedom of association and assembly, freedom of expression and freedom of religion or belief are human rights that states must respect. Since 11 September 2001, a number of participating States have introduced specific antiterrorism, crime and domestic security legislation. There is a growing concern over prohibition and dissolution of political groups on account of their alleged extremist or terrorist activities. Some antiterrorist measures may be open to abuse restricting certain fundamental freedoms by targeting, e.g. minority or religious groups, NGOs and independent journalists. A vibrant civil society is essential to combating terrorism, to promote democracy and tolerance and to hold governments accountable.

Holy Terror

Religion and terrorism share a long history. Indeed, many of the words we use in the English language to describe terrorists and their acts are derived from the names of religious groups active several centuries ago. The etymology of "zealot," for example, can be traced back to a millenarian Jewish sect who fought against the Roman occupation of what is now Israel between 66-73 A.D. The Zealots waged a ruthless campaign of both individual assassination and wholesale slaughter, employing a primitive form of chemical warfare: poisoning wells and granaries used by the Romans and even sabotaging Jerusalem's water supply. The word "assassin" is similarly derived from a religious terrorist group, in this case a radical offshoot of the Muslim Shi'a who, between 1090-1272

A.D., fought the Christian Crusaders attempting to conquer presentday Syria and Iran.

Literally "hashisheater," the assassin would ritualistically imbibe hashish before committing murder: an act regarded as a sacramental or divine duty designed to hasten the new millennium. An additional perhaps even more compelling-motivation was the promise that, should the assassin perish in the course of his act, he would immediately ascend to a glorious heaven: thus fostering an ethos of selfsacrifice and suicidal martyrdom that is apparent in some Muslim terrorist movements today. Terrorism assumes a transcendental dimension, and its perpetrators are thereby unconstrained by the political, moral, or practical constraints that seem to affect other terrorists. Whereas secular terrorists generally consider indiscriminate violence immoral and counterproductive, religious terrorists regard such violence not only as morally justified, but as a necessary expedient for the attainment of their goals. Thus, religion serves as a legitimizing force conveyed by sacred text or imparted via clerical authorities claiming to speak for the divine.

Religious and secular terrorists also differ in their constituencies. Whereas secular terrorists attempt to appeal to a constituency variously composed of actual and potential sympathizers, members of the communities they purport to "defend," or the aggrieved people they claim to speak for; religious terrorists are at once activists and constituents engaged in what they regard as a "total war." They execute their terrorist acts for no audience but themselves. Thus the restraints on violence that are imposed on secular terrorists by the desire to appeal to a tacitly supportive or uncommitted constituency are not relevant to the religious terrorist. Moreover, this absence of a constituency in the secular terrorist sense leads to a sanctioning of almost limitless violence against a virtually openended category of targetsthat is, anyone who is not a member of the terrorists' religion or religious sect. This explains the rhetoric common to "holy terror" manifestos describing persons outside the terrorists' religious community in denigrating and dehumanizing terms such as, "infidels," "non believers," "children of Satan," and "mud people." The deliberate use of such adjectives to condone and justify terrorism is significant, in that it further erodes the constraints on violence and bloodshed by portraying the terrorists' victims as either "subhuman" or "unworthy" of living.

In addition, where the aims of the "secular political" terrorists can be described as utilitarianseeking to bring about changes to achieve the greatest benefits for the greatest number the aims of "religious political" terrorists are more accurately defined as the attainment of the greatest possible benefits for themselves and their coreligionists only. This further engenders a tremendous disparity between ends and means. Where the secular terrorist sees violence primarily as a means to an end, the religious terrorist tends to view violence as an end in itself. Finally, religious and secular terrorists have starkly different perceptions of themselves and their violent acts. Where secular terrorists regard violence as a way of instigating the correction of a flaw in a system that is basically good or as a means to foment the creation of a new system, religious terrorists see themselves not as components of a system worth preserving, but as "outsiders," and therefore seek vast changes in the existing order. This sense of alienation also enables the religious terrorist to contemplate far more destructive and deadly types of terrorist operations than secular terrorists and indeed to embrace a far more openended category of "enemies" for attack. Taheri, for example, ascribes three key differences in this respect between Islamic terrorism and secular forms of terrorism:

First; it rejects all the contemporary ideologies in their various forms; it sees itself as the total outsider with no option but to take control or to fall, gun in hand...

The second characteristic that distinguishes the Islamic version from other forms of terrorism is that it is clearly conceived and conducted as a form of Holy War which can only end when total victory has been achieved...

The third specific characteristic of Islamic terrorism is that it forms the basis of a whole theory both of individual conduct and of state policy. To kill the enemies of Allah and to offer the infidels the choice between converting to Islam or being put to death is the duty of every individual believer.

7

Religion, Terrorism and Public Goods

Can rational models, once theological explanations are discredited, explain why certain radical religious rebels are so successful in perpetrating suicide attacks? The fundamental barrier to success turns out not to be recruiting suicide attackers; there is a rational basis for volunteering. Rather, the barrier is the danger of other operatives defecting. A club model, portraying voluntary religious organizations as efficient providers of local public goods explains how they weed out potential defectors by requiring sacrifices as signals of commitment. They are thereby able to succeed in risky terrorist attacks. The model has testable implications for tactic choice and damage achieved by clubs and other rebel organizations.

Data spanning a halfcentury on both terrorists and civil war insurgents, much from Middle East sources and Israel/ Palestine, reveal that: a) missions organized by radical religious clubs that provide benign local public goods in the absence of competing provision by government are both more lethal and are more likely to be suicide attacks than missions organized by other terrorist groups with similar aims and theologies; and b) suicide attacks are chosen when targets are "hard," i.e., difficult to destroy. Our results suggest benign tactics to counter radical religious terrorism and insurgency. Why are religious radicals such lethal terrorists? Why would anyone choose suicide terrorism, which is very rare in civil wars? And why do suicide attackers generally target members of other religions? These questions seem to pose a challenge to modeling that assumes rational choice, suggesting instead an irrational group of psychopaths motivated by hatred and religious zealotry. Yet members of these radical religious groups are hardly typical "bad guys."

They exhibit productive, constructive and noble behaviours: acts of piety, charity and selfsacrifice. Their organizations are often efficient providers of valuable local public goods. Hamas, Hezbollah and Muqtada al-Sadr's Mahdi Army all provide social services. The Taliban restored law and order to Afghanistan, halting poppy cultivation (for opium) and reducing crime. By securing trade routes they restored commerce (both legal and illegal) in Afghanistan. Hamas is a theological descendant of the Egyptian Muslim Brotherhood, which at its peak actively provided social services through charitable institutions. The Palestinian Muslim Brotherhood efficiently provides health care, schooling, welfare, disaster relief, and community services to needy communities in Gaza and the West Bank. Psychological research indicates that suicide attackers are neither mentally disturbed nor motivated primarily by theology. Ariel Merari carried out interviews with failed Palestinian suicide attackers and their families. He found that all the attackers were psychologically healthy, and that none mentioned religiosity or promises of rewards in the afterlife as their main motivating force.

The Tamil Tigers, who carried out the most suicide attacks in the 1980s, are nominally atheists. Yet when they choose violence, religious radicals are devastatingly effective. The Taliban, who were not experienced fighters, managed to conquer and hold most of Afghanistan, an accomplishment unmatched by the Soviet military and not attempted by Western forces today. Hamas quickly evolved into the deadliest terrorist organization in Palestine, in the number of attacks conducted, the proportion of attacks which destroyed their targets and the number of casualties per attack. By these measures it is much more effective than its secular rival, the

Fatah's Tanzim, or than the more experienced Islamic Jihad. Hezbollah quickly became the dominant militant organization in south Lebanon, expelling its secular Shia rival, Amal, and eventually forcing the withdrawal of Israeli forces. Why suicide attacks? The suicide attack is a gruesome tactic of rebellion which necessitates losing a loyal cadre. Why would leaders of rebellions employ it? Under what conditions will suicide attacks succeed? What kinds of rebels use it most effectively?

This chapter attempts to resolve those puzzles, the effectiveness at violence and the choice of suicide attacks, using an approach which assumes rational choice by individuals. Our argument draws on three literatures: the economic theory of clubs, the sociology of religion and the political science of insurgencies. We claim that the radical religious terrorists and rebels are best understood not as theologically motivated (most religious radicals are nonviolent) or as psychopaths, but as public good providers. We argue that their operational secret is an organizational form which deters defection, allowing them to penetrate highvalue targets. We take a unified analytic approach to extreme religious groups, applying the same club model to radical Islamists that has been used to explain the behaviour of Christian and Jewish sects. That club model is extended here to explain not only the benign activities of religious sects, but also their effectiveness at violence. Rationalizing behaviour is not merely an analytical tool, but has practical implications.

If we cannot explain destructive behaviours in a model in which individuals respond to incentives, what policy solutions could we recommend that are not themselves inherently destructive? Before proceeding, some definitions will be useful. A religious radical is an individual who belongs to a group which distances itself from the mainstream culture by creating some sort of tension. The words radical and sect will be interchangeable in that sense. In this usage a radical religious group need not be politically active or violent. Indeed, most radical religious Muslims, Christians and Jews are nonviolent and apolitical. We will also distinguish between two types of violent tactics chosen by rebels: insurgency and suicide attacks, as explained below. Why belong to a sect? Imagine a community for which neither government nor markets function well. Local public goods usually provided by government such as public safety, law and order and welfare services are poorly provided or absent, while neither public nor private sectors efficiently deliver education, health services or insurance. It would be efficient for individuals in such a place to band together into communities which provide public safety, education, welfare services, and other local public goods through mutual aid.

Iannaccone (1992) pointed out that religion is a natural organizing node for community provision of local public goods. Moreover the most puzzling features of religious sects, their propensity to limit choices (prohibitions) and to destroy resources and options (sacrifices), can be explained as internal incentive policies which allow clubs to efficiently provide services to members. Since members engage in joint production of local public goods during their hours of no market time, market work is a distraction with a negative externality for other members so efficient clubs should tax market wages. Lacking tax authority they turn to prohibitions on consumption as a crude but feasible method of lowering wages. Sacrifices can be explained as a costly signal of "commitment" to the community, or (less prosaically) a signal of relatively poor economic options outside the club. A sacrifice serves as an initiation rite, securing membership and with it access to club goods. Iannaccone provides supporting evidence for the club model from data on Christian denominations, showing that more extreme prohibitions and sacrifices predict greater provision of public goods to members. Berman (2000) extends the club approach to UltraOrthodox Jews, showing that subsidies to sects dramatically increase prohibitions and sacrifices.

The resulting reduction in the effective wages of UltraOrthodox women in Israel caused fertility to increase by over a child per woman. Duration of Yeshiva (full time religious seminary) attendance increased by over ten years, all within two decades. Berman and Stepanyan (2003) document high fertility and generally low returns to schooling among Muslim sects in five countries. This chapter applies that club approach to the puzzles of rebel effectiveness and suicide attacks. First, religious clubs are well suited to coordinated violence. Insurgency and terrorism are crucially sensitive to defection, so a club which extracts sacrifices as signals of commitment has an advantage. Second, we invoke the literature on insurgencies to explain clubs choosing suicide attacks. Where states are strong enough to protect targets well, rebel organizations cannot successfully use standard insurgency tactics. Yet under those conditions, suicide attacks remain effective. While recruiting suicide attackers is easier than many surmise, recruiting operatives resistant to defection in these highstakes attacks is a firstorder tactical problem. Radical religious clubs are better able to insulate themselves against defection. In section 1 we provide background, describing violent behaviour and public good provision by Hamas, Hezbollah, and Taliban–unusual institutional material for economists.

We also use a newlyconstructed dataset to describe two patterns in suicide terrorism. First, though the environmental conditions favouring insurgency are poor countries with rough terrain, the use of suicide attacks is not predicted by either. Second, while rebels tend to attack coreligionists, suicide attacks tend to target members of other religions. Our approach is also informed by a third finding from FL on factors that do not predict insurgency: Grievances, religious differences and ethnic differences. That last finding motivates an organizational rather than theological approach to studying radical religious rebels. We present a more formal version of the club model, extending Iannaccone's public goodproviding sect to include violent activity and the possibility of defection. We also formalize the concept of "hard targets" to explain when rebels choose suicide attacks. As targets are hardened (i.e., chances of successful destruction and escape are reduced) suicide attacks are increasingly chosen because they allow even well defended targets to be destroyed without apprehension. This is a critical concern for rebels in asymmetric conflicts since a strong state can use information from captured attackers to expose the network and arrest or kill its members.

For hard enough targets this advantage outweighs the cost of losing a cadre (the attacker) with certainty. Thus as states become more powerful and better able to defend targets – the first pattern – suicide attacks are used more often. Coreligionists tend to look similar. Thus attackers of the same religion as targets are hard to distinguish by profiling, making coreligionist victims soft targets because they are harder to defend; consequently — now for the second pattern — attackers can kill coreligionists without resorting to suicide attacks. We also ask why religious radicals so often choose suicide attacks. Rather than the conventional explanation, which is based on theological motivation, our approach emphasizes the tactical difficulty of operating against hard targets. We model the choice of tactics by rebels when targets can be either hard or soft and rebels are concerned about capture and defection. We first outline the beliefs that suicide attackers would need to hold for their actions to be deemed rational. We then consider the attacker and his organization in a rational choice framework. The model, extending Iannaccone (1992) and Berman, explains why hybrid "clubs" (which provide benign local public goods such as education and welfare) of a certain type (most easily formed through religious membership) are able to complete highstakes suicide attacks despite strong incentives for operatives to defect.

We find that hybrid clubs are in fact more lethal than other terrorists, regardless of the type of attack. We also find that, as the Hard Targets argument predicts, suicide attacks are chosen against better defended targets. Combining the logic of clubs with that of suicide attacks, we find that radical religious clubs do in fact carry out suicide attacks more often and more effectively than do secular terrorists. Thus, our evidence suggests that theological motivations are overrated. Among three radical religious organizations with very similar theologies about Jihadist conflict, those with active local public good provision (Hamas and Hezbollah) are more lethal suicide terrorists than that without (the Palestinian Islamic Jihad). We also discuss how this approach might extend to Iraq, Sri Lanka and Chechnya.

The better states and markets are at providing social services, the harder it is for insurgencies to organize around a socialservice provision base and conduct high stakes attacks without fear of defection. These implications differ from those of conventional development economics (and political science) in critical ways. Another general conclusion for counterterrorism is that the threat of defection is a powerful force limiting the tactical choices of terrorists. For instance, the assassination of Al-Qaeda leader Abu Musab Al-Zarqawi in June 2006 was based on information from a captured Al-Qaeda source transmitted to U.S. interrogators. In the Southern Philippines Abu Sayyaf terrorists have been killed or captured using intelligence obtained in return for generous rewards. In conclusion we suggest future empirical extensions.

The Taliban, Hamas, Hezbollah and Muqtada alSadr's Mahdi Army are examples of highly ritualistic, extremely conservative Muslim groups. They belong to a family of radical sects whose religious behaviour represents a clear break from traditional practice. They augment the prohibitions of mainstream Islamic practice, such as dress codes and shaving. They tend to segregate themselves from other Muslims and to be intolerant of deviation, in contrast to the historical tolerance of Islam. Though often termed "fundamentalist" - as if returning to some historic norm of practice, these groups actually practice norms unprecedented in their extremism. The roots of current Radical Islam date back only to the 1920s with the establishment by al Banna of the Muslim Brotherhood (hereafter MB) in Egypt and Mawdudi's subsequent founding of the JamaatalIslami in Pakistan.

The core beliefs of Radical Islamists clash with those of Western liberalism in their view of an individual's place within society. In the Western liberal approach individuals have rights and obligations in a direct relationship with the state. Public Economics, for example, typically designs policy for states in relationship to individuals, not groups. In contrast, Radical Islam derives from a more historically relevant approach: an individual's primary relationship is with a clan, sect or tribe, and through that with the sovereign. Clans, sects and tribes tend to be suspicious and jealous of competing affiliations. The strong affiliations that individuals seek with clans, sects and tribes are easier to understand if we bear in mind that these groups thrive in places where government is a poor provider of local public goods such as health care, education and public safety and the market is an inefficient provider of income and insurance. In that environment, group affiliation is a source of mutual insurance, providing protection, health care, income, food, clothing and the like. Though money needs not change hands, that insurance relationship is nonetheless economic. Such relationships with a group much smaller than the state have been ubiquitous historically.

They survive in the West in the form of radical religious sects like Ultra-Orthodox Jews and Christian Anabaptists (such as Hutterites and Mennonites) who provide extremely high levels of community mutual aid to members. An efficient market economy and a functioning state are both threats to these affiliations as they reduce the need for the services which these groups provide and reduce the non market hours available to members to provide services to others. Like Radical Islam, radical Christian and Jewish sects often seek to distance members from market economies. We turn now to the puzzle of effectiveness at violence among Radical Islamic rebel organizations. Taliban Afghanistan is a famously ungovernable country which has suffered 23 years of civil war at an appalling cost of one and a half million lives. The *Mujaheddin*, a loose tribe-based alliance of Islamic militants conducted a successful insurgency which eventually expelled a Soviet occupation. They had U.S. and Saudi aid, administered by Pakistani intelligence (ISI). Those subsidies were remarkably effective in expelling the Soviets, but radicalized Afghani society: "Prior to the war the Islamicists barely had a base in Afghan society, but with money and arms from the CIA pipeline and support from Pakistan, they built one and wielded tremendous clout".

By the mid 1990s, the Pashtun south had collapsed economically. It was run by former *Mujaheddin* warlords in fiefdoms ranging in size from a few provinces to single villages. During this particularly chaotic period, the Taliban emerged in Kandahar, the largest city in the south. Rashid (2000) emphasizes economic factors contributing to their formation. He describes a chaotic scene of warlords battling each other, looting businesses and infrastructure (including even telephone poles), and kidnappings and raping children. Banditry on the roads was an expensive obstacle for traders and smugglers. With alternate routes in northern Afghanistan blocked by heavy fighting, a route through Kandahar and Herat was the best chance for trade from Pakistan to Iran and Turkmenistan. By the fall of 1994 the Pakistani government backed an effort by the ISI (Pakistani Intelligence) and Pakistani truckers to open this route.

When a trial convoy was held up by warlords near Kandahar, a small, largely unknown group of radical Islamists, the Taliban, conveniently emerged to free it, and to conquer Kandahar with minimal casualties. The second largest city in Afghanistan was taken by simply bribing the local warlords to surrender. The Taliban were wellarmed with rifles, mortars, ammunition and vehicles acquired by raiding an ammunition dump on the Pakistani border. The Taliban were soon operating a safe single-toll road through the Kandahar region, a feat the warlord could not accomplish. By December they had recruited 12,000 students from the religious schools of the radical Islamic Juma'at al Islamiya (JUI) of Pakistan, mostly the sons of Afghan refugee families. Within three months the Taliban had efficiently conquered 12 of 31 provinces of

Afghanistan, either by fighting, intimidating, or bribing local warlords to surrender. They collected arms, imposed law and order, and opened roads.

The increase in commerce was significant, immediately lowering the price of food. The Taliban proceeded to conquer and control some 90% of Afghanistan, a feat unmatched by the Soviet Union. With Taliban protection, smuggling prospered. The Taliban protected most of the $1B AfghanPakistani drug trade, their control so complete that they could ban opium cultivation in 2000. The truly remarkable aspect of this period bears emphasis: A few hundred seminary students with relatively little military experience created a militia effective enough to conquer Afghanistan, a country in which Western forces have had trouble securing even the capital. Of all the allies that the ISI could have (and did) choose, why is it that the group with the most extreme religious practices was the most efficient at securing the safety of convoys and ordinary people, and at conquering and controlling Afghanistan? Hamas Just as the Taliban militia are an offshoot of the nonviolent JUI, Hamas is a descendant of the MB, the first modern radical religious movement in Islam.

The MB was founded by Hasan al Banna in Egypt in 1928 with the aims of reinvigorating Islam through individual piety and self improvement, fighting the insidious force of assimilation into materialist Western culture, and establishing an Islamic state. Members met weekly in small groups, reinforcing a set of basic prohibitions on gambling, alcohol, adultery and usury. The MB established a broad network of mosques, boys and girls' schools, youth groups, clinics, hospitals, charities, trade unions, night schools for workers, and even factories. These drew considerable public support both as social service providers and as a focus of religious and political expression. In 1948 a splinter terrorist organization of the MB, the "Secret Apparatus," carried out a campaign of bombing and political assassination, including among their victims the Egyptian Prime Minister. The government suppressed the MB.

AlBanna was shot in the street, apparently by a government

agent. Since then the MB has been illegal but tolerated in Egyptian society and politics, sometimes courted by government but often suppressed. In the 1950s an imprisoned member, Sayyid Qutb, developed the theology of militant radical Islam. He preached that religious communities could only survive if segregated from insidious secular culture. Moreover, Qutb preached that violent revolt was a religious duty, both against the secular West and against the secular government of Egypt. His call to violence was rejected by most Muslims, including the Egyptian MB. Muslim theology is generally tolerant of other cultures, permitting warfare only in self-defense and rejecting violence in religious matters. Branches of the MB appeared in Gaza and the West Bank in the 1950s. In 1971 Sheikh Ahmed Yassin founded an MB affiliate Congress (Mujamah) in Gaza. Though Muslims in the West Bank and Gaza were relatively secular at the time, Sheikh Yassin soon gained popular support by establishing a social service network of medical clinics, schools, charities, and support for orphans, drug treatment centers, youth clubs, sports clubs and mosques.

The filled gaps in the social services provided by the Israeli occupational government, charities and international organizations especially among refugees. Congress was financed by tithing (zakat) and by support from Arabs abroad. Yassin's Congress shared AlBanna's agenda: personal ethical conduct, personal piety and the eventual establishment of a local Islamic government. In contrast to their secular rival, the Fatah, (the dominant party within the Palestinian Liberation Organization or PLO), the MB saw the liberation of Palestine as a long term goal to be deferred till ethical conduct and local Islamic government were established. The MB was nonviolent, except for some skirmishes with Fatah supporters. They contributed to an increase in religious practice in the 1980s in the West Bank and Gaza: dress codes were more stringently observed and outward signs of piety increased, including the frequency of prayer.

This occurred especially in Gaza which is poorer and

where the MB has more support and institutions. Hamas was founded in1988 as a result of the first Palestinian Intifada, a spontaneous revolt against Israeli occupation. Sheikh Yassin's local organizers urged him to endorse the revolt and establish a militia, lest the MB lose popular support to Fatah, which was harnessing the outburst of nationalism. Yassin eventually agreed, establishing a secret militant organization, Hamas, separating it to protect the social service institutions from reprisal. Hamas called for violent opposition to Israeli occupation. It underwent an ideological shift, adopting a nationalist position more extreme than that of Fatah, making the immediate conquest of all Palestine (not just the West Bank and Gaza) a religious obligation. This expensive change in ideology predictably provoked a campaign of arrests and suppression by the Israeli army, putting members at high risk of arrest.

That ideological shift would eventually also put members at risk of arrest and provoke reprisal by the Fatahled government after the 1993 Oslo accords. Hamas soon became a singularly effective rebel organization: hard to penetrate, disciplined, adequately funded, well trained and committed. Members regularly risked arrest and endangered their lives by confronting soldiers, assassinating collaborators, organizing and carrying out terrorist attacks. Hamas suicide bombings of buses in Israel in 1996 delivered a close Israeli election to the political right, hobbling the Oslo process which Hamas opposed. Hezbollah Hezbollah is another radical religious group which shocked Western forces with its capability. It seemed to emerge from nowhere in 1982 in South Lebanon. Hezbollah surprised Israeli forces, U.S. and French peacekeepers with a consistently deadly series of attacks, including the October 1983 suicide attack on a U.S. Marine barracks in Beirut which killed 241 servicemen.

Hezbollah was formed by a group of former seminary students. Many of them had studied in the Shiite holy cities of Najaf and Qom and had subsequently been expelled by either the Iranian government of the Shah or by Saddam Hussein's Iraqi government. In the eastern Lebanese city of Baalbek and later in the poor Shiite neighbourhoods of Beirut, they organized mosques, schools and charities, with generous support from the new Iranian Islamist government of Ayatollah Homeini. Between 1982 and 1987 Iran spent more than a hundred million dollars annually on hospitals, mosques, schools and charitable organizations affiliated with Hezbollah. Baalbek, which had been a fairly liberal city and a popular tourist attraction in the Bekaa valley of eastern Lebanon, was radicalized over a few short years. Burka, the cloaks worn by traditional Muslim women, became ubiquitous, first in Baalbek, then in the Shiite neighbourhoods of Beirut and after that in south Lebanon, as Hezbollah displaced the more secular Shiite Amal movement.

Religious radicalization was accompanied by massive increases in social service provision. While Hezbollah expanded its social service provision rapidly, it also expanded its territorial control by force, pushing the rival Shia Amal organization out of Shia neighbourhoods in a serious of battles, sometimes involving artillery. In their confrontations with Israeli forces in South Lebanon, Hezbollah developed and improved many of the tactics which plague coalition troops in Iraq today: roadside bombs, suicide attacks and rocket attacks. They demonstrated their tactical effectiveness in October 2001 and again in July of 2006 with the kidnap of Israeli soldiers patrolling within Israel. When Israel retaliated for that second kidnapping with air strikes within Lebanon, Hezbollah responded with a month of rocket attacks on Israeli civilians.

Literally trenched in positions within southern Lebanon, Hezbollah retained their tactical capacity to fire rockets into Israel despite massive Israeli air strikes, artillery fire and were eventually expelled only by a ground invasion. Hezbollah would eventually run candidates in Lebanese elections, becoming the dominant Shia party by 1998 and the core of the proSyrian coalition threatening to topple a proWestern Lebanese government. To summarize, the Taliban, Hamas and Hezbollah are radical Islamic groups that turned violent. While their geographical and theological origins are distinct, they share several functional characteristics which suggest investigating their behaviour in parallel. All three formed from affiliates of venerable nonviolent radical Islamic organizations, Hamas from the MB and the Taliban from the Jamiat-e-Ulema-Islam (JUI) in Pakistan, and Hezbollah from the clerical culture of the Shia holy cities in Iraq and Iran.

All three grew by providing local public goods in an environment where local public good provision by government was exceptionally weak. Each developed into an effective insurgent organization which produced the specific local public good—security, using violence. All three received generous subsidies from abroad, whether for geopolitical reasons, out of ideology, or in return for services. Younger members undergo some costly personal sacrifice in the case of the Taliban and Hamas (we know less about initiation of Hezbollah fighters). There are differences: Hamas and Hezbollah regard all local coreligionists as potential members, while Taliban treated most Afghans as a conquered people. Yet the common elements, common puzzles, and parallels to a wide set of terrorist groups, seem to justify a common framework.

Insurgency and Suicide Attacks

The Taliban, Hamas and Hezbollah have at different times used both suicide attacks and more conventional forms of insurgent violence. In all three cases their objective is apparently local political power, which Hamas and Hezbollah have pursued through both elections and violence, and which the all three have pursued by capturing territory, just like conventional insurgents. That behaviour invites a question: When do rebels choose suicide attacks? To answer that question it is useful to first review some key facts about insurgencies, and then contrast predictors of insurgency to those of suicide attacks. Insurgency is a technology of rebellion through guerrilla warfare that has been successful in challenging regime domination in many countries. It has been hitched to various ideologies: communism, nationalism, religious fanaticism, and even to no ideology at all.

Between 1945 and 1999, 127 civil wars in 69 different countries accounted for more than sixteen million deaths. Many of these relied upon the technology of rural insurgency. FL shows that civil wars cannot be explained by: (a) level of grievances in the society or (b) degree of ethnic or religious difference or any form of civilizational clash. Rather, the best predictors of civil war are conditions favouring the success of the rural insurgency technology: bad roads, rough terrain, poor state armies, lack of more remunerative employment for young men, and weak or new governments.

Suicide Attacks as a Tactic

Guerrilla warfare by insurgents encompasses a variety of tactics - most typically a network of self-sustaining rural militias that first intimidate populations and then govern them, providing alternate sovereignty. Suicide attacks –in which the attacker will almost certainly die if the attack succeeds - are here interpreted as a tactic of rebellion distinct from typical insurgency tactics - in which the attacker has at least some chance of survival. Although they are an ancient tactic in interstate warfare, suicide attacks are relatively rare. They were not used in modern internal rebellions until 1982 when Hezbollah launched suicide attacks to challenge the Israeli occupation of South Lebanon. The Liberation Tigers of Tamil Eelam (LTTE) in Sri Lanka followed suit with the second major series of suicide attacks taking place beginning in 1987 (combined with conventional insurgency tactics). Suicide attacks have been employed (at least twice) in civil wars in only five of the sixty-nine countries facing insurgencies in the last half of the 20th century.

Why are suicide attacks so rarely used by rebels? Consider the profile of a suicide bomber as culled from the literature. He (or she) appears to be quite distinct from the typical recruit in a rural insurgency. The suicide bomber is more upscale economically and more highly educated on average. The country of his victim is typically richer, and typically has a competent army. The country's terrain is more easily accessed by the state. The list of countries sending suicide attackers in the 20th century is consistent with the idea that suicide attackers come from places where the government and military are well organized to suppress insurgency: Israel, Sri Lanka, Lebanon, Turkey and Saudi Arabia. The increase in suicide attacks since 1999 is associated not with increased rebellion but with rebels choosing suicide attacks over other tactics. To illustrate the trend increase in suicide attacks, in the first four years of this century 196 suicide attacks were reported, one third more than in the entire second half of the 20th century.

While the increase in fatalities is mostly due to the 9/11 attacks, the increased incidence of suicide attacks is almost entirely due to rebellions against well organized, well funded militaries: the second Palestinian Intifada against Israel, the Iraqi insurgency against Coalition forces, and the Chechen rebellion against Russia. Comparing existing research on insurgencies with that on suicide attacks suggests a conjecture: When conditions disfavour insurgency leaders chose suicide terrorism when possible. The intuition is straightforward. Suicide bombing is a costly tactic, as it strips the insurgent organization of motivated, committed cadres. Moreover, an organization with political aspirations must explain the loss of a son or daughter to the family and community. If sustaining the insurgency were easy, such wasteful losses would be avoided.

To explore the conjecture we combined the FL data on civil wars with the data on suicide attacks, aggregating the latter into countryyear observations of civil war onsets with those of suicide attacks, across countries. Our measure of insurgency is the one commonly used in the civil war literature, the onset of civil wars. The first two columns reproduce findings familiar from literature. A cross sectional linear probability regression of a civil war onset indicator on GDP/capita and the estimated proportion of mountainous terrain yields a negative coefficient on GDP/capita and a positive coefficient on mountains.20 Doubling GDP/capita predicts a probability of suffering a civil war 810 percentage points lower. Doubling the proportion of mountainous regions predicts a 0.44 percentage point lower probability of a new civil war, about one quarter of the mean.

These regressions suffer from potential endogeneity bias as discussed in the literature. They are reported here only for comparison. The next two columns, in contrast, show that GDP/capita predicts a small and statistically insignificant change in the number of annual suicide attacks between countries. Mountainous terrain does not predict suicide attacks either. Taken together, these results indicate that the predictors of civil wars do not predict suicide attacks: poor, mountainous countries are no more likely to suffer suicide attacks than richer, flatter countries. Perhaps the difficulty of conducting conventional insurgency forces the choice of suicide attacks, despite their cost. Israel, for example, suffered from 146 such attacks during the sample period. Israel is a developed, relatively flat, small country with a well equipped army that has invested heavily in information.

The conditions for insurgency in Israel, given the FL results, are not propitious. Standard insurgency tactics are unlikely to succeed; making suicide attacks a relatively effective tactic. To further pursue that example, when Hamas – the major perpetrator of suicide attacks in Palestine, turned its sights on the weak military of the Palestinian Authority in Gaza in June 2007, it chose conventional rather that suicide attacks, achieving a quick victory. Yet not all outgunned rebels in flat countries choose suicide attacks. These cases include South Africa (the ANC), Spain's Basque Country (ETA), Japan (Aum Shinrikyo), Italy (Red Brigades), and Germany (Baader Meinhof). One factor that does predict the use of suicide attacks is, as we mentioned at the outset, a difference in religion between perpetrators and victims. As with the case of the kamikaze pilots (Shinto pilots and largely Christian victims), the suicide attackers in our dataset most often targeted victims of other religions.

In Israel (Muslims vs. Jews), Sri Lanka (Hindus vs. Buddhists), Russia (Muslims vs. Eastern Orthodox Christians), and China (Muslims vs. Buddhists), religious difference marked perpetrator from victim. In the nine cases perpetrated by Saudis, although the forces of Al-Qaeda seek to overthrow their coreligionists, their suicide attacks typically targeted Christians. In Egypt, the suicide attack was by Muslim fundamentalists against secular Muslims housed in the Egyptian embassy in Pakistan. Only fourteen attacks perpetrated by the PKK (the Kurds) in Turkey are clearly disconfirming. To be sure, insurgents target coreligionists much more often than they do members of other religions; they just seldom use suicide attacks to do so. In three of these cases, suicide attacks were used: Sri Lanka, Russia (Chechnya), and China (Xinjiang). Cases such as Nagorno Karabakh in Azerbaijan, Srpska Republic in Bosnia, and rebellions in Nigeria, Philippines, Sudan, Cyprus and Bangladesh all pitted guerrilla armies against states led by people of a different religion. In these cases, however, conditions favouring insurgency were better, perhaps lessening the need for expensive suicide attacks.

Only the IRA in Northern Ireland is an example not promising for insurgency, along with religious difference, yet no suicide attacks. Hezbollah, Taliban and Hamas often attack coreligionists themselves, though never with suicide attacks. Insurgents tend to operate in poor, mountainous regions and against coreligionists. Suicide attackers tend to come from countries that are not particularly poor or mountainous and they tend to attack members of other religions. While much has been made of the radical Islamic aspect of suicide terrorism, the greatest wave of suicide attacks in the 20th century was by (nominally atheistic) neoMarxist Tamil separatists against the Hindu Sri Lankans.

Rational Martyrs and Terrorist Clubs

Why are religious radicals such successful rebels? Why do they so often choose suicide attacks? And why are members of other religions so often the targets of those suicide attacks? The conventional answers rely on theology: promises of eternal grace motivate radical religious rebels to battle fiercely.

Rewards in the afterlife will compensate them for losing their lives in suicide attacks, but not if they kill coreligionists. Recalling the discussion in the introduction, careful work in psychology and political science has largely rejected those notions: suicide attackers do not appear to be motivated primarily by religious beliefs, and religious radicals often kill coreligionists–though by other means. So rather than focusing on theological motivations we model a rebel organization with rational members, whose payoffs could be in the hereafter. We analyze the unique agency problems that an organization has in providing public goods (both violent and nonviolent) and consider how it chooses among violent tactics.

Rational Martyrs

Judging by press coverage, much of the terror generated by terrorists' attacks comes from the idea of an army of theologicallymotivated suicidal drones. Yet suicide attackers could be rational, given either: a) a belief that their suicidal act will be rewarded in the hereafter; or b) altruism toward family or compatriots combined with a belief that the suicidal act will benefit family, community or some larger cause; or c) a desire to maximize social solidarity achieved by sacrificing one's autonomy for group goals. A given population is likely to contain at least some individuals who hold the necessary beliefs and preferences. Belief in the hereafter and in rewards in the hereafter is dispread. Islam, like all major religions sanctifies human life and rejects suicide. Yet Qutb justified suicide attacks as a sacred defensive act of Jihad. So while mainstream religious beliefs preclude suicide, aspects of religion could be useful in recruiting a suicide attacker who was so inclined. Preferences for altruism or group solidarity, combined with a belief that the welfare of others will be improved by the act, may apply to both religious and secular terrorists. Recall Merari's interviews with failed Palestinian suicide attackers and their families, which suggested that religiosity and promises of rewards in the afterlife were not their main motivating force.

If anything, altruism seems to be a more likely

motivation. For suicide attackers altruism would need to be accompanied by an exaggerated belief about the benefit to their cause resulting from a successful attack. For instance, the 9/11 terrorists may have believed that their act would help topple the Saudi government. A Hamas suicide bomber might believe that a single destructive act would significantly contribute to creating an Islamic state in Palestine. These beliefs stretch credulity but reflect a common bias of decisionmakers in overestimating their potential to affect change. The belief that through suicide one can experience the ultimate oneness of individual and group goals, as suggested by Wintrobe is also plausible.

While we lack estimates of the incidence of different beliefs, only a very small proportion of the population need be committed believers if an organization can identify and recruit them. Iannaccone points out that despite conventional wisdom about "brainwashing," research reveals that indoctrination played only a minor role in recruitment to US sects in the 1970s. Recruits were predisposed to belief. Thus it may not be difficult to find volunteers who prefer martyrdom to life, even without indoctrination or radical religious beliefs. That is disturbing, considering how easy it is to train and arm terrorists for extremely lethal attacks. Yet only a few organizations in the world have managed to activate suicide attackers and consistently carry out attacks. Of those most (though not all) are religious radicals. So what is so hard about organizing suicide terrorism and why are religious radicals so effective at it?

Prohibitions and Sacrifices

To explain the puzzling effectiveness of religious sects when they rebel, and their choice of suicide tactics, we turn to the sociology of religion and draw on a theory developed to explain Christian and Jewish sects. Sects (and even mainstream denominations) pose a puzzle for rational choice theory: they prohibit common pleasurable behaviours and require sacrifices. Prohibitions involve food, Sabbath activities, dress codes, driving licenses, sexual practices and medical care, for instance. Sacrifices are an irreversible destruction of resources, such as burnt offerings. In the recent history of European Jewry, circumcision irreversibly labelled a child as Jewish, an act that might put his life at risk by destroying the option of disguising him as a gentile. A vow of fidelity or abstinence is also a form of sacrifice, as it represents a permanent restriction of activities. Years of volunteer work required of Mormons can be thought of as a sacrifice of time, especially considering the foregone opportunity to accumulate human capital.

Years of study in a religious institution sacrifice alternative potential uses of that time—accumulating human capital in secular studies or accumulating earnings and work experience. Limiting choices and destroying resources is puzzling to an economist, yet people voluntarily join groups which enforce prohibitions and require sacrifices. These groups stubbornly defy price theory, persisting in timeintensive activities like communal worship, Sabbath observance and intricate food preparations, despite the historical increase in the shadow price of time. Strict sects show no sign of disappearing and those with the most demanding practices seem to be growing fastest. The modern Anabaptist traditions are holding their own while Ultra-Orthodox Jewry and Radical Islam are thriving, despite a multitude of time intensive requirements. Iannaccone offered a creative solution to the puzzles of prohibitions and sacrifices, proposing that they are efficient institutions in the context of an economic club which provides services to members.

Religion's Role in the Terrorist Attack of September 11, 2001

The central role of religion in the terrorist attacks on New York and Washington, D.C., is addressed. The terrorists were motivated by a militant fundamentalist worldview, which rejects modernism. According to Osama bin Laden, corrupt Western values and mores are not to be tolerated, making attacks justified. Religion's role in coping with the attacks also is described using Pargament's theoretical framework. Steps that individuals can take to deal constructively with the situation are listed. Four planes were hijacked on Tuesday, September 11, 2001.

Two of the planes were crashed deliberately into New York City's World Trade Center towers, causing their collapse. A third plane was flown into the Pentagon, outside Washington DC. The fourth plane, after a struggle between hijackers and passengers, crashed in a field before hitting its target. An untold number of people are dead as a result of these actions, which also are expected to affect people throughout the world as its repercussions are felt in the economic and political spheres. Clearly, this coordinated, concerted attack was intended to bring down symbols of US economic and military might. Early reports also indicate that important centers of US political power the White House and the president's airplane also were targets.

Militant Fundamentalist Worldview

Evidence currently points to militant Islamic fundamentalists affiliated with Osama bin Laden. One may expect that their actions were motivated by several factors, but we are left with an incomplete understanding of this group without an effort to grasp the central role of religion in their lives and how it influences their perception of the world. Osama bin Laden, a tall man in his midforties, grew up in Saudi Arabia, where his father became rich in the building industry. From his father's inheritance bin Laden gained $250 million, which he has used to finance and support his view of Islam. The Sunni branch of Islam is most common in Arabia and in the world, and bin Laden adheres to a radical fundamentalist interpretation of it. Like all of Islam, the Sunnis believe in one God, and that Muhammad was God's last prophet. Islam encourages people to be devoted to God, but also to be generous, hospitable, and to demonstrate care for others. So, the important questions for us to understand regarding the terrorist attack are "What makes something fundamentalist?" and "How did this worldview influence the terrorist actions?"

The overarching theme to the fundamentalist, whether Muslim or Christian, is that God is to be worshipped, respected, feared & obeyed above all else. All other considerations take a back seat to God. This intense and abiding devotion means that there are some things that are completely, utterly non-negotiable. In this way, it is like viewing the world as being black and white, with little if any grey between that which is good and that which is evil. Accompanying this is a tendency toward literalism. If scripture says that Noah built an ark, put two of each type of animal throughout thc world on it, and that they sailed on that boat while the entire earth was flooded, then it happened.

No questions need be asked; it happened, regardless of whether it is logically consistent with what we know about animals, floods, ancient ships or the geological record. An important element of the fundamentalist mindset is the rejection of modernism. Contemporary western values are inconsistent with God's values and with His will for humanity. People's duty is to worship God, not to ignore or ridicule Him. God's rules are clear and they are to be enforced and respected, not flaunted. As a result, fundamentalists have very conservative views on social issues. The fundamentalist finds media portrayals of sex, inappropriate gender roles, and many other elements of Western culture to be abominations completely out of harmony with God's will. God does not like it, doesn't tolerate it, and neither do God's devoted followers.

Bin Laden

Bin Laden was exiled from Saudi Arabia for his views in 1991, during the Gulf War. Bin Laden objected to the Saudi government policy that allowed infidels, US and other nonMuslim military troops, on their sacred soil (Saudi Arabia is considered sacred because the most holy of Islam's sites are located there.). By exiling bin Laden, the Saudi government avoided complications within its borders and with its allies. Bin Laden went to Sudan, where he used his inheritance to help the country's poor (by developing jobs, etc.), and also is said to have continued his efforts against the west. In 1996, Sudan bowed to international pressure and exiled him. From Sudan, bin Laden went to Afghanistan where he has stayed until the present time. For bin Laden, this was a return to Afghanistan.

He went there earlier, in the mid1980s, during the country's tenyear war with the Soviet Union. In 1989 the Soviet Union left, defeated, and an intense civil war raked the country. During that ongoing war, a group known as the Taliban gained control of the majority of Afghanistan; a separatist faction remains in northern Afghanistan. The Taliban, who share a deeply rigid, radical fundamentalist view of Islam, are sympathetic to bin Laden, and have allowed him to maintain training camps to support members of his group al Qaeda. It also is important to note that most countries never recognized the Taliban's government. Indeed, the civil war continues. Bin Laden formed the group al Qaeda (Arabic for "The Base") as a vehicle to help him achieve his goals for Islam.

The consistent theme of the group has been to fight against the West, most chiefly against the US, but also against countries that aid US interests. Among other things the group has been implicated in several terrorist attacks, perhaps most notably the 1998 US Embassy bombings in Kenya and Tanzania which killed 224 people. Frequently these attacks have come after a declaration (fatwa) denouncing the US and its socio-political agenda. For example, a May 1998 declaration entitled "The Nuclear Bomb of Islam" included the statement that "it is the duty of Muslims to prepare as much force as possible to terrorize the enemies of God". A few months later, the embassies were bombed; the US responded with cruise missile attacks in Afghanistan (bin Laden's suspected training camp) and Sudan (where he stored or made the weapons believed to have been used in the attack).

It is worth mentioning that in August, 1996, bin Laden issued a declaration of jihad. Its lengthy title makes clear bin Laden's position: "Message from Usama bin Laden to his Muslim Brothers in the Whole World and Especially in the Arabian Peninsula: Declaration of Jihad against the Americans Occupying the Land of the Two Holy Mosques; Expel the Heretics from the Arabian Peninsula". This declaration of jihad reflects the meaning that most westerners have come to associate with the word. Jihad, however, has been called the most misunderstood word in religion today. Although we may read of it in this context, its common, usual meaning is that of a struggle to purify oneself. In many ways, it is more appropriate to consider jihad as having the connotation similar to that of a fast, or going on a retreat, to a Christian. People who view bin Laden as a typical Muslim, make a serious mistake, as do those who view any single individual as a prototypic example of any group.

For example, a selection of public figures who profess Christianity might include: Jerry Falwell, Pope John Paul II, David Koresh, Bill Clinton, and George W. Bush. Each claim Christianity, but few would consider each of these men to represent Christianity equally well. More broadly, Aryan Nation groups that use Christianity to further their social cause of racial separation and hatred are not considered by most people to be prototypic Christians. Likewise, bin Laden is not a typical Muslim, and militant fundamentalist Muslims are not representative of Islam. Regardless of whether it was bin Laden or someone else who coordinated the attacks, there are more general questions for us to consider. Why are we surprised when people act in accordance with their religious beliefs? This certainly isn't the first time it has happened; examples abound. In 1997, a group of 39 people known as Heavens Gate committed suicide. "Heaven is a beautiful place," they said, and they wanted to go there. It shocked the country. During World War II, some Japanese pilots went on Kamikaze missions.

Many people learned with disbelief that these pilots, with just enough fuel to reach their targets, flew directly into the enemy and sacrificed themselves in order to serve the emperor, their God. This was not the first time that extreme views have resulted in extreme behaviour. Nor will it be the last, because attitudes do affect behaviour. In light of this, it is instructive to ask about attitudes and behaviour regarding the attack. How do individuals use religion to cope with disasters such as this?

Religious Coping

Ken Pargament (1997) describes many different ways that religion helps people deal with traumatic, lifechanging events. Examining his theory will help us make some sense of people's reactions to the attack. The basic assumption underlying Pargament's theory is that people search for significance in their lives. We are goaldirected, and try to find and hold on to the things that give our life a sense of significance and meaning. For many people, religion provides a way to do this. It gives us something to strive for, and tells us how we can obtain it. Crises, however, threaten one's sense of significance. They put at risk the things that are valued, and many people use religion in order to regain and maintain that which is significant. It does this in two basic ways. The first method, which Pargament calls conservation, maintains the same items as being significant. People prefer conservational strategies because they involve less change, less stress. The alternative, transformation, is used when people determine that their current sense of significance is untenable, that they must change their source of significance.

Conservational coping comes in four general types. Religious prevention helps us maintain the sense of significance by declaring certain things as being off limits. Drug use and extramarital sex, for example, may be determined to be out of the bounds of acceptable behaviour. Avoiding these activities helps people maintain an ongoing sense of purpose, that they are headed in the right direction, so to speak. Although it often refers to reduced rates of behaviour that put one at risk, comments from Jerry Falwell and Pat Robertson, who suggested that overly permissive societal norms are the root cause of the terrorist attack, also illustrate this perspective. Religious support maintains the sense of significance by helping people feel as though they are not alone in their struggle or stress. God may be viewed as a helping partner, and a group of likeminded people may lend a sense that they are receiving help during a time of need. Many people's comments, such as "God is with us," reflect this form of religious coping.

Ritual purification offers a way for people to address personal failures and inadequacies. By participating in purification rites such as confession or repentance individuals can reconcile their ideal, their sense of significance, with the reality that they don't always measure up to those ideals. The countless prayer services and candle-light vigils that have been performed, and the millions of people who have participated in them, demonstrate the importance of ritual purification as a coping method to people distressed by the terrorist acts. Religious reframing enables the individual to reinterpret (or "reframe") things so that the sense of meaning and significance is maintained. This occurs, for example, if the negative events take on a new meaning, and perhaps even become an opportunity to grow. Many of the messages heard from political leaders, such as the idea that terrorists and bombs can not destroy freedom, fit into this category. They reaffirm core values and identities, and in so doing maintain individuals' views of themselves and what they consider to be important.

Transformational coping strategies are more difficult to deal with because they require more change. If for some reason individuals cannot maintain their sense of significance, if the things that they value actually lose value, then people will opt for transformational coping. An example of this is a conversion or apostasy experience. Suppose that, after learning of the attacks and the tremendous loss of life, a person lost faith in God and humanity, forsaking them for a new belief system. This would be a transformational coping strategy. Changing one's belief system is a major undertaking, and typically comes only reluctantly, after conservational coping strategies have been tried and failed. Recent media reports have not yet reflected this type of coping but because people first attempt conservational strategies, we may expect such accounts in the future.

Religion provides a powerful way to cope with stress. Pargament's research shows that religion adds additional resources to the other coping resources that a person has available. Even if one has a closeknit family, the feeling that one is part of a religious group helps the individual to weather difficult times. Also, because religion is abstract and symbolic, one can reinterpret events so that they make sense within the core belief system. It lends itself to reframing.

The Future

Where do we go from here? Clearly, typical citizens are not empowered with the ability to strike back at the terrorists, whoever they are. Nevertheless, there are some things that people may do to benefit themselves and their communities. Individuals can reach out to those in need. Many reasonable persons feel that we have a moral obligation to offer help to those who suffered personally in the attacks. There also are many legitimate relief agencies that can use your time or monetary contribution. Talk about the attacks, about their implications for daily life. There will be debates about the nature of freedom and democracy, and what freedoms people might be willing to forego for the hope of greater safety. Think about these important issues and discuss them with other people. In all likelihood these debates are going to become increasingly important in the future.

Individuals can be involved in the political process where they live by writing to their elected officials, urging them to use care in responding to these heinous acts. For example, some commentators in the US and in the world remind us that much of the world sees the US as being hypocritical for preaching the virtue of democracy, at the same time that it refuses to encourage elections in countries led by what amounts to dictatorships. Do people in the US believe deeply in democracy, or do short-term expediencies win out? These are questions that American citizens should be debating. Discuss these issues, and write to your elected officials, urging them to do the same. Ask what the US can do to help its actions match its lofty ideals. Finally, people can learn about Islam and share that knowledge with other persons.

During World War II, the US held captive many of its citizens simply because of their race. The US, as a society, has learned something during the 60 years since that war. Let us show each other and the world that we reject prejudice and hate. William James (1902/1985) suggests that we can judge religion by its effects. If religion helps people deal with tragedy, then that is good, but we also must recognize that religious ideology played a role in initiating the tragedy. Like many things, religion is complex and multifaceted, with many different effects. Religion's complexity challenges psychologists to understand its nuances and to communicate that knowledge to our fellow human beings. The attack of September 11, 2001, reminds us of the importance of this task.

Historical Perspectives on Religious Violence

Terrorism carried out in the name of the faith has long been a feature of human affairs. The histories of people, civilizations, nations, and empires are replete with examples of extremist true believers who engage in violence to promote their belief system. Some religious terrorists are inspired by defensive motives, others seek to ensure the predominance of their faith, and others are motivated by an aggressive amalgam of these tendencies. Religious terrorism can be communal, genocidal, nihilistic, or revolutionary. It can be committed by lone wolves, clandestine cells, large dissident movements, or governments. And, depending on one's perspective, there is often debate about whether the perpetrators should be classified as terrorists or religious freedom fighters. The following cases are historical examples of religious violence.

This is a selective survey (by no means exhaustive) that will demonstrate how some examples of faithbased violence are clearly examples of terrorism, how others are not so clear, and how each example must be considered within its historical and cultural context.

Judeo-Christian Antiquity

Within the Judeo-Christian belief system, references in the Bible are not only to assassinations and conquest but also to the complete annihilation of enemy nations in the name of the faith. One such campaign is described in the Book of Joshua. The story of Joshua's conquest of Canaan is the story of the culmination of the ancient Hebrews' return to Canaan. To Joshua and his followers, this was the Promised Land of the covenant between God and the chosen people. According to the Bible, the Canaanite cities were destroyed and the Canaanites attacked until "there was no one left who breathed." Assuming that Joshua and his army put to the sword all the inhabitants of the 31 cities mentioned in the Bible, and assuming that each city averaged 10,000 people, his conquest cost 310,000 lives. To the ancient Hebrews, the Promised Land had been occupied by enemy trespassers. To fulfill God's covenant, it was rational and necessary from their perspective to drive them from the land, exterminating them when necessary.

Other passages in the Bible are arguably examples of religious communal violence or terrorism, such as the following story from the book of Numbers: While Israel was staying at Shittim, the people began to have sexual relations with the women of Moab... Just then one of the Israelites came and brought a Midianite woman into his family... When Phineas… saw it, he got up and left the Congregation. Taking a spear in his hand, he went after the Israelite man into the temple, and pierced the two of them, the Israelite and the woman, through the belly.

Christian Crusades

During the middle Ages, the Western Christian (i.e., Roman Catholic) church launched at least nine invasions of the Islamic east, the first one in 1095. These invasions were called the Crusades because they were conducted in the name of the Cross. The purpose of the Crusades was to capture the holy lands from the disunited Muslims, to whom they referred collectively as Saracens. Christian knights and soldiers answered the call for many reasons. The promise of land, booty, and glory were certainly central. Another important reason was the spiritual promise, made by Pope Urban II, that fighting and dying in the name of the Cross would ensure martyrdom and thereby guarantee a place in heaven. Liberation of the holy lands would bring eternal salvation. Thus," knights who with pious intent took the Cross would earn a remission from temporal penalties for all his sins; if he died in battle he would earn remission of his sins." This religious ideology was reflected in the war cry of the early Crusades: Deus lo volt! (God wills it!).

During the First Crusade, Western knights—primarily Frankish soldiers—captured a broad swath of biblical lands, including Jerusalem and Bethlehem. When cities and towns were captured, most of the Muslim and Jewish inhabitants were killed outright, a practice common in medieval warfare. When Jerusalem was captured in July 1099, Frankish knights massacred thousands of Muslim, Jewish, and Orthodox Christian residents. An embellished Crusader letter sent to Pope Urban II in Rome boasted that the blood of the Saracens reached the bridles of the Crusaders' horses. Not all Christian Crusades were fought in Muslim lands. The Western Church also purged its territories of Jews and divergent religious beliefs that were denounced as heresies. The zealousness and violence of these purges became legendary. During the brutal Albigensian Crusade in southern France during the 13th century, the story was told that concerns were raised about loyal and innocent Catholics who were being killed along with targeted members of the enemy Cathar sect. The pope's representative, Arnaud Amaury, allegedly replied, "Kill them all, God will know his own!"

The Church-sanctioned invasions and atrocities were deemed to be in accordance with God's wishes and therefore perfectly acceptable. An extreme and unquestioning faith in the cause led to a series of campaigns of terror against the nonChristian (and sometimes the Orthodox Christian) residents of conquered cities and territories. In a typical and tragic irony of the time, the Greek Orthodox city of Constantinople, center of the Byzantine Empire and one of the great cities of the world, was captured and sacked by Western Crusaders in 1204 during the Fourth Crusade. The Crusaders looted the city and created a shortlived Latin Empire, which lasted until 1261.

The Assassins

The Order of Assassins, sometimes referred to as the Brotherhood of Assassins, was founded by Hasan ibn al-Sabbah (d. 1124) in 11thcentury Persia. Al-Sabbah was a caliph (religious head) of the Ismaili sect of Islam.He espoused a radical version of Ismaili Islam and founded the Order of Assassins to defend this interpretation of the faith. Beginning in 1090, he and his followers seized a string of fortresses in the mountains of northern Persia, the first of which was the strong fortress of Alamut near Qazvin. Because of these origins, alSabbah was called The Old Man of the Mountain. The word assassin was allegedly derived from the drug hashish, which some commentators believe al-Sabbah's followers ate before committing acts of violence in the name of the faith. They referred to themselves as hashashins or hashishis, reputedly meaning hashish eaters. During the early years of the movement, Assassin followers spread out of the mountains to the cities of Persia, modern Iraq, Syria, and the Christian Crusader–occupied areas of Palestine.

The Assassins killed many people, including fellow Muslims who were Sunnis, and Christians. Suicide missions were common, and some Crusader leaders went so far as to pay tribute to the Assassins so that the Assassins would leave them alone. The Assassins were very adept at disguise, stealth, and surprise killings, and thus the word assassination was coined. A key component of the Assassins' beliefs was the righteousness of their cause and methodology. To kill or be killed was a good thing, because it was done in the name of the faith and ensured a place in paradise after death. This belief is practiced by many of today's religious terrorists. Although their political impact was negligible and the organization was eliminated in 1256, the Assassins left a profound psychological mark on their era, and in many ways on ours.

A Secret Cult of Murder

In India during the 13th through the 19th centuries, the Thuggee cult existed among worshippers of the Hindu goddess Kali, the destroyer. Members were called by various names, including Phansigars (noose operators), Dacoits (members of a gang of robbers), and Thuggees (from which the English word thug is derived).They would strangle sacrificial victims—usually travellers—with a noose called a phansi in the name of Kali, and then rob and ritually mutilate and bury them. Offerings would then be made to Kali. The British eventually destroyed the movement during the 19th century, but the death toll of Thuggee victims was staggering:" This secretive cult is believed to have murdered 20,000 victims a year. . . perhaps dispatching as many as several million victims altogether before it was broken up by British officials." There are few debatable counterpoints about this cult—the Thuggees waged a campaign of religious terror for centuries.

Modern Arab Islamist Extremism

The Arab world passed through several important political phases during the 20th century. Over lordship by the Ottoman Empire ended in 1918 after World War I. It was followed by European domination, which ended in the aftermath of World War II. New Arab and North African states were initially ruled primarily by monarchs or civilians who were always authoritarian and frequently despotic. A series of military coups and other political upheavals led to the modern era of governance. These phases had a significant influence on activism among Arab nationalists and intellectuals, culminating in the late 1940s, when the chief symbol of Western encroachment became the state of Israel.

Postwar activism in the Arab Muslim world likewise progressed through several intellectual phases, most of them secular expressions of nationalism and socialism. The secular phases included the following:

- Anticolonial nationalism, during which Arab nationalists resisted the presence of European administrators and armed forces.
- PanArab nationalism (Nasserism), led by Egyptian president Gamel AbdelNasser, which advocated the creation of a single dynamic United Arab Republic.
- Secular leftist radicalism, which activists often adopted to promote Marxist or other socialist principles of governance, sometimes in opposition to their own governments.

Many activists and intellectuals became disenchanted with these movements when they failed to deliver the political reforms, economic prosperity, and desired degree of respect from the international community. In particular, several humiliating military defeats at the hands of the Israelis—and the seemingly intractable plight of the Palestinians—diminished the esteem and deference the secular movements had once enjoyed. Arab nationalists—both secular and sectarian—had struggled since the end of World War II to resist what they perceived as Western domination and exploitation, and some tradition-oriented nationalists began to interpret Western culture and values as alien to Muslim morality and values. As a result, new movements promoting Islamist extremism began to overshadow the ideologies of the previous generation.

This has placed many Islamists at odds with existing Arab governments, many of which are administered under the principles of the older ideologies. In the post–Cold War political environment, adopting Islam as a vehicle for liberation is a logical progression. When radical secular ideologies and movements made little progress in resisting the West and Israel, and when secular Arab governments repressed any expressions of domestic dissent, many activists and intellectuals turned to radical interpretations of Islam. There is a sense of collegiality and comradeship among many Islamists, but there are also differences within the ideologies of many leaders, as well as between the Sunni and Shi'a traditions. The Islamist movement, however, has transcended most ethnic and cultural differences and is a global phenomenon.

Christian Perspective on Islam and Terrorism

Since September 11, people around the world have been asking this question. The atrocities of that day shocked and astounded. As horrific as they were, Christians must still be guided by the wisdom of our Lord Jesus who said, "Why do you look at the speck that is in your brother's eye, but do not notice the log that is in your own eye? … You hypocrite, first take the log out of your own eye and then you will see clearly to take the speck out of your brother's eye." Sadly, church history is replete with examples of evil perpetrated in the name of Christianity. There have been far too many times when Christians have blatantly violated the example and teachings of Christ. Perhaps the ugliest, most relevant and wellknown example is the Crusades of the middle Ages, when true Christians and "professing" Christians engaged in "holy" war. They brutally tortured and slaughtered thousands of Muslims to regain a piece of territory both groups deemed holy.

Without diminishing the horror and inhumanity of the suicide bombings, Christians must admit that in the misguided name of "religion," we have also committed atrocities. We can't point the finger! As Christians, we not only need to get the logs out of our eyes, but we also need to speak truth and not bear false witness. This means that we must be accurate and fair when we describe another religion. So, why did the Muslim terrorists feel they were right in committing these atrocities in the name of Islam? It is common to read articles and hear speeches in the present crisis that describe Islam as a peaceloving religion. But is this really accurate? It is one thing to say that there are many peace-loving Muslims and quite another thing to say that Islam is a peaceloving religion.

First, Muhammad rode into Mecca on a stallion with a sword in hand to conquer by force. By contrast, Jesus saddled up a donkey to ride into Jerusalem to humbly suffer and die for the sins of the world. Herein lays the difference. Jesus founded a religion based on moral persuasion. From the beginning, Islam has condoned the use of the sword. Historically, not all Muslims have used it. Thankfully, many modern Muslims refrain from it. But Islam is a religion which sanctions force, if necessary, to advance its purposes. One other aspect of Islamic faith also has the potential to fuel the fire of evil. The Islamic faith (at least at a popular level) puts a strong emphasis on salvation by works. Muslims have no assurance of heaven. However, if a Muslim dies while engaging in holy war (jihad), he is assured of entering heaven. According to the Encyclopedia of Islam, jihad "'is an act of pure devotion'; it is 'one of the gates to Paradise;' rich heavenly rewards are guaranteed for those who devote themselves to it; those who fall in the jihad are the martyrs of the faith."

The deluded terrorists who crashed into the World Trade Center and the Pentagon thought they were in a holy war against America. In fact, they saw themselves in a battle against infidels everywhere, including moderate Muslim governments. They were willing to lose their lives in this attack in order to secure paradise. Thus, these tragic acts represent an earthshattering clash of worldviews. The terrorists' perspective of the world, filtered by a radical interpretation of Islam, sees only two sides: "true Islam" and "infidels." This narrow viewpoint resulted in these unforgettable atrocities.

Terrorism Interfaith Harmony

One thing for which the world would like to forget 2008 is the rise of fanaticism and religious terrorism. Though the world has lived with terror for years, it became more pronounced in 2008 with acts of terror linked to religion or belief system. The perpetrators of the Mumbai carnage targeted Jews for their faith. It's a tragedy that religion, which has been the source of superior virtues such as honesty, love, compassion, justice and peace, is being used as a motivation to spread terror and kill innocents. Though motives and reasons vary from attack to attack, religious terrorism runs on the fuel derived from a misplaced belief that 'my way is the only way' and it's God's ordained duty to take up arms against those who have gone astray.

What can prevent fanaticism and religious terrorism in the New Year? Fortunately, there is light at the end of the tunnel as religious leaders are coming out against terrorism and pushing for interfaith harmony. In November, over 6,000 Muslim clerics gathered in Hyderabad to denounce religious terrorism and tell the world that there is no place for extremism in Islam. Earlier, the orthodox Islamic seminary Darul Uloom at Deoband issued a fatwa against terrorism. More importantly, leaders from other religions were roped in for the Hyderabad meeting of the Jamiat Ulema-e-Hind. A positive signal to unitedly fight terrorism is being sent to the larger community.

Taking the call for interfaith harmony a step further Sri Sri Ravi Shankar of Art of Living, who was chief guest at the gathering of the most influential body of Muslim clerics in India, offered to work with them to isolate fanatical elements abetting terrorism. A month later, over 500 imams and rabbis gathered in far away Paris for the 3rd World Congress of Imams and Rabbis for Peace where they searched for ways to resolve differences between Islam and Judaism, the main cause of violence and conflict in the Middle East. These events may not immediately make religious fanatics desist from doing what they are doing in the name of religion. Yet they represent a serious attempt to find an alternative solution to religious terrorism. While religion seeks to bring uniformity in a multifaceted world, the goal of spirituality is to celebrate the diversity. To save the world from this pitfall of religion, the time has come to spiritualise religion. One of the most notable aspects of contemporary spirituality has been its accent on educating people to a proper understanding of religion.

This is vital as the wrong understanding of the verses of scripture has caused upheaval and is used to justify narrow-mindedness. Religious terror arises when someone reduces his or her identity to a single affiliation based on a religion and a sense of victimisation. The events of the last few years have shown that stringent laws and rules of society can go only so far in containing fanaticism in a society that loses spiritual values. The approach of offering spirituality as the only sensible response to terrorism addresses the problem at its roots. Terrorism stems from wrong ideas and the struggle against it should be fought on the level of ideas. It's essential that people's consciences against terror are enlisted as a vital arsenal in the fight against it.

For this, a mass spiritual awakening is imperative. Spirituality nourishes the human values of compassion, love, caring, sharing and acceptance and honours the values found in all religions. This explains why spirituallyevolved people have never been at odds. The time has come for people of all faiths to unite against terror and educate people against misinterpretation and misuse of religion. This can happen only when people are made to realise that God loves variety and diversity and that many different schools of thought exist in this world. This can happen only when people remember that truth is multi-dimensional.

8

Interpretation of Post-modern Religious Terrorism

Terrorism, the use of force by private actors or organizations to intimidate others to achieve political and ideological goals, is a significant menace to contemporary democracies. In the preceding decades, terrorism was perpetrated for the sake of a piece of land (geographical terrorism) or the realization of political goals (political terrorism). Nowadays, we are confronted with religious terrorism: people commit violent acts and justify their deeds with reference to religious ideas or passages of Holy Scripture. There is a difference between religious terrorism as it manifests itself in the United States of America and religious terrorism as it has become known in Europe. First, European religious terrorism is perpetrated by nationals, not by foreign forces or organizations—"homegrown terrorists," as they are called. Mostly, the aggressors are youngsters estranged from the societies and ideals of their countries. They seek solace in an international religious community with radical ideas, such as that an appropriate punishment for blasphemy is death, as happened in the case of Theo van Gogh, not a small fine or a short prison sentence.

A second characteristic of European religious terrorism is that the aggression of the terrorists is directed at individuals. This is not the only religious terrorism that has manifested itself on European soil: the Madrid bombings of March 11, 2004, and the London Metro bombings of July 5, 2005, were indiscriminate in their attacks on large numbers of persons. Nevertheless, it is an important phenomenon in Europe that terrorism sometimes targets specific individuals. The most wellknown example is, again, Van Gogh. Third, terrorist attacks in Europe cannot be explained as a reaction to military intervention in foreign countries that may be motivated by humanitarian concerns.

The terrorists themselves point to what they see as the state of decadence in their local and national communities. They do not criticize their own government for becoming involved in Iraq or Afghanistan but for having made legislation that deviates from holy law. An important factor in their discontent is the freedom in Western societies to criticize and even mock religious ideas so religious terrorism is explicitly directed at the principle of free speech, as the "cartoon crisis" that began in Denmark makes abundantly clear. Dutch authorities are in a state of bewilderment. For many years, the official credo of the Dutch government was multiculturalism, an approach that fitted well with Dutch history and culture.

Multiculturalism is nowadays affiliated with a post-modern outlook. The pivotal ideas of this vision of life are relativism (cultural relativism, in particular), a negative attitude toward Western political tradition, the cultivation of collective guilt for the transgressions of the colonial past, and other real or presumed black pages in Western history. For multiculturalists, European civilization has been fundamentally on the wrong track since the Enlightenment. The Holocaust, Nazism, communism, slavery—these are seen not as deviations from the generally benign development of Western culture but as inevitable products of the European mind, which is inherently oppressive. Multiculturalists also reject the universality of Enlightenment ideas of democracy, human rights, and the rule of law, viewing them instead as isolated preoccupations of no universal appeal. It is preposterous and a manifestation of cultural arrogance, on this view, to invade foreign countries to export democracy and other Western ideals; it is likewise ridiculous to expect that religious and ethnic minorities in Western societies should be expected to adopt these ideas and integrate into liberal democracy.

Minorities should live according to their own customs; and, insofar as national culture is at variance with nonWestern ideas, the national culture should adapt itself to new conditions. This attitude has grave consequences for the way liberal society is organized. Think of the principle of free speech. The answer of post-modern cultural relativism is: refrain from criticism. Be reticent to comment on unfamiliar religions. Let reform come from within and avoid provocation and polarization. The consequences of this approach are far-reaching. It would lead to a bowdlerizing "purification" of the whole Western tradition of literature, art, cinematography, and even science. Postmodernism does not hold the Western tradition of rationality in high esteem, but would it also deny the right of the Western world to defend itself? The whole outlook that advocates the ideals of the Enlightenment, including democracy, human rights, and the rule of law, is to be replaced by the glorification of "otherness," by non-Western cultures, and especially by the conviction that all cultures are equally valuable.

Every predilection in favour of Western ideas has to be smashed to excoriate, in Roger Scruton's phrase, the "West" in favour of the "Rest." A good illustration of this outlook on life can be found in the work of Stuart Sim, a professor of critical theory at the University of Sunderland (Great Britain). The core of the problem is fundamentalism, a concept he was inspired to analyze after the attack on the World Trade Center. So the only way to escape from the indictment of "fundamentalist" and "fundamentalism" is to adopt the post-modern relativistic outlook that Sim himself favours. What Sim wants to encourage is a kind of skepticism toward all ideas of authority. Sim favours radical skepticism ("the more scepticism the better"). Defending Enlightenment values of democracy, free speech, and the rule of law as "universal principles" is one more kind of fundamentalism that has to be rejected.

Because every commitment to universal values is a kind of fundamentalism, the world is seen as one great clash of "fundamentalisms," with none superior or inferior to any other. For the post-modern relativist, all life stances and worldviews are of equal value. Sim's solution is to reject commitment to universal values. But is that sensible advice? This attitude, it seems to me, would make Western societies very vulnerable to the ideological challenge that religious terrorism poses. Liberal democracy, with its institutions of free speech is, not necessarily better than alternatives. The only thing that the postmodernist wants to argue against is evangelical zeal. What this attitude leads to can also be gauged in Murder in Amsterdam, a recent book on the Van Gogh killing written by the Dutch-American journalist and scholar Ian Buruma. Like Sim, Buruma holds a post-modern relativistic outlook. He tries, again like Sim, to apply post-modern relativism to the problem of religious terrorism. He also contends that an orientation toward the ideas and ideals of the Enlightenment is not significantly better or preferable to an orientation toward radical Islamic ideology.

Radical Islam is a fundamentalist position, but the same could be said about "radical Enlightenment." Both are to be rejected. This relativistic stance comes to the fore when Buruma constructs a comparison between the worldview of Mohammed Bouyeri, Van Gogh's murderer, and the people he considers the most outspoken critics of radical Islam in the Netherlands: Ayaan Hirsi Ali and law professor Afshin Ellian. While Bouyeri defends radical Islam, Hirsi Ali and Ellian defend "radical Enlightenment." According to Buruma, they are basically the same. The first point of agreement is that they are all "warriors." Bouyeri is a warrior with the sword and the knife that he used to try to decapitate Van Gogh. Hirsi Ali and Ellian are warriors with the pen. But these differences are less important than the similarities for the post-modern relativist: all are warriors.

A second point of agreement is that all are "radical." Islamists are radical in the sense that they do not shy away from radical interpretations of their holy scripture. If scripture calls for the death of unbelievers and apostates, the true believer should not shy away from fulfilling the will of God and killing the unbelievers and apostates, in particular if they have committed the crime of blasphemy. Adherents of what Jonathan Israel called "radical Enlightenment" are "radical" as well. The one is "radically secular, the other radically religious," but both are "radical." A third point of agreement is that both radical parties believe in universal values. Both parties believe they are struggling for a righteous cause and for that very reason are not relativists so both are fundamentalists from the perspective of post-modern radical skepticism.

After he sketches the tenets of the ideas of the protagonists of radical Enlightenment, Buruma writes: "The same could be said, in a way, of their greatest enemy: the modern holy warrior, like the killer of Theo van Gogh." With his qualification "in a way," Buruma seems to have hesitated. And, of course, every judicious writer would feel uncomfortable with this silly exercise in semantics. Are these two positions really "the same"? Is someone who is a warrior with the pen really the same as someone who conducts his war by killing people and decapitating them? Both Chamberlain and Hitler had moustaches, but it would be absurd to attribute any significance to this similarity. Of course, both radical Islam and radical Enlightenment are "radical," but that does not make them any more the same than a radical plan to alleviate hunger and suffering in the world is really the same as a radical plan to eradicate the Jews or any other ethnic or religious minority from this world.

Finally, it may be true that radical Islamists believe, as do adherents of the Enlightenment, in "universal values." But so did Immanuel Kant; so did such twentiethcentury philosophers as Nicolai Hartmann and R.M. Hare. Most moral philosophers believe in universal values. That does not make Kant, Hartmann, and Hare "fundamentalists." The Universal Declaration of Human Rights presented by the United Nations in 1948 is also a "universal creed." The United Nations proclaims this list of human rights as a "common standard of achievement." That does not make the United Nations an assembly of fundamentalists or dangerous terrorists. Or are they, in the eyes of postmodernist critics of modernity? The reasonings of Buruma and other post-modern relativists have preposterous consequences, but these consequences logically flow from the post-modern outlook.

Buruma also plays with the word purity. He writes that "the promised purity of Islamism" is not really different from "radical Enlightenment." That would imply that Sayyid Qutb, the ideologue of radical Islam, would not be any different from the godfather of "radical Enlightenment," Baruch de Spinoza. What worries me about this relativistic—or rather, nihilistic—position is that it makes Western societies easy prey for the ideology of radical Islamism. If Western societies think they have no core values important enough to fight for (by peaceful means), then there is no reason for immigrant minorities to accept them. If the dominant ideology in Western societies is that democracy, the rule of law, and human rights have no specific quality that makes them superior to theocracy, dictatorship, and Authoritarianism, there is no need to oppose the radical assault directed at Western democracies by the teachers of hate. Post-modern-value relativists not only deny the superior quality of Western values but even contest that people may defend those values against the assault that is being made on them.

Demonizing every criticism on religious mentalities as "polarizing" and "provocation" denies even the right to defend democratic institutions. That would be a suicidal position. What remains a mystery is why many intelligent people stick to the post-modern frame of mind, even though so many intelligent writers—Terry Eagleton and John Searle, to name just two—have thoroughly deconstructed its tenets. They hope that, if we abstain from radical criticism of the terrorist mindset, we can pacify the most radical elements. For Buruma profiles not only protagonists of radical Enlightenment but also

Amsterdam alderman Ahmed Aboutaleb and the city's mayor, Job Cohen. Buruma writes that he met Aboutaleb—a Moroccan-born Muslim who advocates pluralism—"surrounded by bodyguards. Like Ayaan Hirsi Ali, he needed fulltime protection." That should have stimulated Buruma to further reflection on the nature of religious terrorism. As for Cohen, he has a reputation of being much too soft. He never employs strong language against ethnic and religious minorities.

Contrasting Secular and Religious Terrorism

Since Iran's 1979 Islamic revolution, there has been a steady rise in Islamist terrorism. Too many analysts underestimate the ideological basis of terrorism and argue instead that rationalstrategic rather than ideological principles motivate Islamist terror groups. Comparison between terrorist groups with secular and religious agendas, however, suggests that ideology matters for both and that downplaying religious inspiration for terrorism in an effort to emphasize tactical motivations is both inaccurate and dangerous. Some researchers suggest that to understand terrorism it is more important to study what terrorists do rather than what they say. University of Chicago political scientist Robert Pape argues, for example, that Islam has little to do with suicide bombing.

Rather, he suggests, that suicide bombers, wherever they are in the world, are motivated much more by tactical goals. He juxtaposes the suicide terrorism of the (non-Islamic) Liberation Tigers of Tamil Eelam (LTTE) with Islamist suicide bombing to demonstrate that a desire to end occupation is the common factor rather than religion. Therefore, he suggests focus upon religion is a distraction and that policymakers seeking to stop the scourge of suicide attacks should work instead to address root causes, which he sees as the presence of troops or interests in disputed or occupied lands. Despite the revisionism advanced by Pape and others, the fact remains that most suicide bombings since 1980 in the world in general and in the Middle East in particular are sponsored by Islamist and not secular terrorist groups. Pape avoids this conclusion by gerrymandering his data so that he does not need to include the significant numbers of suicide bombings conducted by Sunnis against Shi'a in Iraq.

Middle East expert Martin Kramer suggests that Pape's theses may be comforting to Western readers who want to believe that if only the United States were to pull its military forces from the Persian Gulf and if only all occupation in the Middle East would end that there would be no more suicide bombings. Western thinking admires empirics, metrics, and pie charts. The secular emphasis of Pape's theories also comforts. But comfort does not correlate with reality. Islamism is an ideology, and that it does not fit neatly into existing political theory should be beside the point.

Ideological Underpinnings of Terrorism

Inattention to the ideological upbringing of terrorists is counterproductive. Although the empirical tools of political science are ill-equipped to assess culture, ideology, and motivation, difficulty in quantifying these factors does not mean they do not exist. Rather than filter evidence to fit the model, responsible political scientists should adjust their models to accommodate the evidence. Important differences exist between those terrorist groups striving to implement secular revolutionary principles based on the thinking of Vladimir Lenin, Mao Zedong, or Ernesto "Che" Guevara and the groups motivated by the religious revolutionary theories of Muslim Brotherhood theoretician Sayyid Qutb, Iranian ayatollah Ruhollah Khomeini, or Palestinian theologian Abdullah Yusuf 'Azzam, whose concept of defense of Muslim lands as every Muslim's personal obligation had major influence on Al-Qaeda founder Osama bin Laden.

Islamists have supplanted these with a new canon including Egyptian Muslim Brotherhood founder Hasan alBanna's essays, the writings of the Muslim Brotherhood's main theoretician Sayyid Qutb, essays on Islamic governance by Ayatollah Ruhollah Khomeini,Abdullah Yusuf 'Azzam's Join the Caravan, and bin Laden deputy Ayman alZawahiri's Knights under the Prophet's Banner. After analyzing the religious foundations of suicide bombing, David Bukay, a lecturer in political science at the University of Haifa, explains, "Suicide bombing in the Muslim world cannot be separated from religion. The ideological basis of such an interpretation has deep roots in Islamic theology, but it came to prominence with the twentieth-century rise of Muslim Brotherhood theorists such as Banna and Qutb and was further developed by their successors."

Secular Agenda Terrorism

There is nothing new about terrorism inspired by secular agendas. Although Plato, Aristotle, and leading Christian theologians such as Thomas of Aquinas, John of Salisbury, and George Buchanan discuss political violence, most terrorism experts mark Maximilian Robespierre's "Reign of Terror" during the French Revolution as the beginning of modern, political, systematic terrorism. Beginning in the early nineteenth century, German and Italian radicals embraced terrorism and, in the 1880s, Narodnaya Volya (People's will), which conducted a violent campaign of assassination to fight autocracy in Russia, became a role model for similar groups established by Armenians, Macedonians, Bosnians, and Serbs prior to World War I.

Between 1914 and 1939, there was a visible decline in terrorism perpetrated by independent political groups although Fascist governments and the Soviet Union sometimes sponsored terror against their own populations for internal political objectives. During World War I, British operative T.E. Lawrence's assistance to the Arab revolt in the Hijaz laid the foundation for modern guerrilla warfare, a subject later developed by Chinese revolutionary Mao Zedong. Between 1945 and 1979, there were three principle types of terrorist entities: organizations struggling for independence from colonial occupiers such as the Front de Libération nationale (FLN) in Algeria or the Mau Mau in Kenya; separatist groups such as the Irish Republican Army (IRA) in Northern Ireland and the Basque Euzkadi TaAskatasuna (ETA) in Spain; and socioeconomic revolutionaries such as the Montoneros in Argentina, the Sandinistas in Nicaragua, the Baader Meinhof Gang in West Germany, and the Red Brigades in Italy.

A commonality among all groups, though, would be an attempt to justify their actions in economic or social theory. In most if not all cases, the definition of the opponent by secular agenda guerrillas and terrorist groups was confined to a socioeconomic concept such as "Yankee" capitalism or resisting the imperialism of countries such as Great Britain or France. Even the Palestine Liberation Organization (PLO) infused its national liberation agenda with Marxist rhetoric. Among anti-colonial movements, a terrorist group's victory did not seek to shatter the nationstate system or eradicate the defeated side. Although many left-wing radicals sincerely believed in universal change with respect to the individual and his role in society, their actual policies were oriented more toward local rather than global interests. Guevara's attempt to export the Cuban revolution to Congo and Bolivia floundered, and all attempts by Latin American guerillas to unite failed.

Nor did Mao Zedong and Ho Chi Minh seek global export of their ideology or practice although neither of them was averse to utilizing instruments of state power to aid proxy groups in neighboring states. Further, in almost every case, if a terrorist group seized a government or defeated a colonial power, it, nevertheless, found it in its interest to restore diplomatic and economic relations quickly. In Algeria, for example, the FLN reestablished close ties with France upon winning Algerian independence. In 1963, the year after Algeria won its independence, Paris provided it with 1.3 billion francs (US$260 million) in loans. In no instance did the enemy associate with a particular civilization or culture, as now occurs with pan-Islamist terrorism. While it was popular to talk about the internationalization of terrorism in the 1970s, incentives for terrorist groups to cooperate had more to do with tactical concerns than with ideological motivation.

For example, when George Habash, leader of the Palestinian Front for the Liberation of Palestine (PFLP), assembled representatives in May 1972 from the Irish Republican Army, the Baader Meinhof Gang, and the Japanese Red Army for a meeting in northern Lebanon's Badawi refugee camp, he sought to trade PLO and Libyan offers of training bases for European and Asian terrorist groups in exchange for facilitation by European groups of PLO operations in Europe. The PFLP's participation in a January 31, 1974 Japanese Red Army attack on a Shell oil refinery at Pulau Bukom, off the coast of Singapore, was motivated less by PFLP ideology than by an agreement to pay the Japanese Red Army for its May 30, 1972 attack on the Lod (later renamed Ben Gurion) Airport outside of Tel Aviv.

Secular Terror Tactics

Terrorist goals shape tactics. Groups immersed in the rhetoric of liberation, for example, target governing officials and foreign residents. The Viet Minh initially targeted only the French and those they deemed to collaborate with the French before expanding their campaign to drive out all foreigners. The Mau Mau and FLN pursued similar patterns of attacks. Among terrorist groups seeking autonomy or separation, favourite tactics included the kidnapping and murder of government and military officials. The IRA targeted British policemen, soldiers, and the British intelligence apparatus while the Basque ETA concentrated its attacks on local politicians and judges. Warnings prior to attacks that might harm the general population show that these groups sought more to make a political statement and less to cause a blood bath.

Social and economic revolutionaries targeted businessmen and bankers. In 1975, for example, the Ejército Revolutionario del Pueblo (People's Revolutionary Army) kidnapped wealthy

Argentine heirs for a $60 million ransom. The Italian Red Brigades seized and, on March 16, 1978, executed Aldo Moro, a former Italian prime minister. Baader Meinhof did similarly with HannsMartin Schleyer, a West German businessman. Controlling time is a unifying characteristic of secular agenda terror. Hostage taking and voicing demands against a deadline leads many governments to negotiate and some, such as the West German government, to capitulate, as Bonn did when it freed three Black September terrorists who remained alive after the September 1972 Munich massacre of Israeli Olympians. Hostagetaking also amplifies media coverage into what Gabi Weiman, a Haifa University professor of communication, calls "the theater of terror."

British Prime Minister Margaret Thatcher recognized the same phenomenon when she declared after a terror attack in 1985, "We must find ways to starve the terrorists and hijacker of the oxygen and publicity on which they depend." The most common secular agenda terrorist demand, at least historically, is for the release of prisoners. Between 1972 and 1980, most European negotiations with PLO terrorists involved the PLO's demands to free imprisoned terrorists. Moro's Red Brigade kidnappers and the Black September terrorists, who on March 1, 1973, seized the U.S. embassy in Khartoum, also demanded prisoner releases. Suicide bombing was never and still is not as frequent a tactic for secular agenda terrorists as it is for Islamist groups. While a few secular agenda terrorists starved themselves to death in prison in Germany or Ireland, their suicides were not part of operations but came only after capture. However, there have been three secular terrorist campaigns that have embraced suicide terrorism: proSyrian secular groups in Lebanon in the early 1980s, the Tamil Tigers in Sri Lanka, and the Kurdistan Workers Party (Partiya Karkerên Kuridstan, PKK) in Turkey.

Between 1983 and 1986, the Syrian Social Nationalist Party was responsible for ten suicide bombings; Syrian Baath Party members conducted seven, and the Socialist Nasserite party executed two suicide bombings. Although the LTTE was founded in 1972, it did not launch its first suicide attack until 1987; four years after Hezbollah pioneered such tactics in Lebanon. The change in Tamil strategy came when the Sri Lankan army forced their collective backs against the wall, arresting most of the LTTE leadership in 1981 and making significant military inroads. While the Tigers initially provided their fighters with a poison capsule in order to enable them to avoid interrogation, between 1981 and 1987, they began to attack targets with explosiveladen trucks, the driver exiting the vehicle moments before the explosion. Such attacks were imprecise and so, between 1987 and 2000, some 200 Tamil terrorists, 30 percent of whom were women, conducted 168 suicide bomb missions.

The PKK only began using suicidebombing tactics in 1995, targeting government and military installations rather than populated areas. Suicide bombing was never a major component of its terrorist operations; it launched only fifteen suicide attacks between 1995 and 1999, some of which were particularly deadly; gunfire, land mines, and delayed fuse bomb attacks account for the majority of its operations, which have killed thousands since 1984. Again, suicide attacks have been the exception rather than the rule. Too little is known about the motivation of the attackers, here. Some may have been terminally ill or promised significant financial reward to support their families; others may have believed they could escape alive. PKK suicides are few and far between.

Islamist Agenda Terrorism

Parisbased sociologist Farhad Khosrokhavar's Suicide Bombers: Allah's New Martyrs has been at the forefront of efforts to emphasize the tension between religious motivation and more rational and temporal strategic considerations. Khosrokhavar, perhaps because of his greater familiarity with Islamic tenets, is correct to see it as a function of jihad. There has been an evolving and, perhaps, dominant strand of modern Islamist thought which finds Western culture to be inimical to Islam and, therefore, a legitimate target for jihad.

One of the biggest ideological differences between religious and secular terrorists is their definition of the enemy: While secular terrorists see their opponents as representatives of a certain socioeconomic order or regime, Islamist terrorists espouse a broader definition. Qutb, for example, revived the Qur'anic term jahiliya, the pre-Islamic age of ignorance in which paganism flourished, to describe the state of any society not by his definition Islamic.

Abdullah Yusuf 'Azzam's understanding of dhimmi (subjugated religious minority) status also inserted into modern political discourse the early Islamic bifurcation of the world into the dar alIslam (abode of Islam) and dar alharb (abode of war). In the former, where Muslims ruled, Jews and Christians could convert or accept second class status while Muslims conducted violent jihad to bring minorities under their control. While traditional theologians might argue that Muslims had a duty to protect dhimmis so long as they continued to pay inflated taxes and adhere to special codes, 'Azzam, bin Laden, and their fellow travelers have argued that Jews and Christians have gone astray from their "original religions," and are agents of the modern West, undeserving of any protection. Arab Sunnis returning from fighting the Soviet occupation in Afghanistan as well as various Palestinian groups such as Hamas and Palestinian Islamic Jihad inaugurated a new phase in religion-inspired terrorism.

'Azzam spun a mystique of invincibility around the Muslim warrior following the Soviet Union's defeat in Afghanistan. One of his most famous slogans during the Afghan war was, "Jihad and the rifle alone. No negotiations, no conferences, no dialogue" On March 6, 1995, Hamas spiritual leader Sheikh Ahmad Yasin declared that any suicide bomber who had received the blessing of a certified Muslim cleric should be considered a shahid (martyr) who had fallen in the service of jihad rather than one who had committed suicide by personal intent, something forbidden in Islam. Sheikh Yusuf al-Qaradawi, an influential Sunni cleric based in Qatar, affirmed Yasin's approach the following year. Then, on February 23, 1998, bin Laden announced the establishment of the International Islamic Front for Jihad against the Crusaders and the Jews and declared it legitimate to kill any American, whether military or not.

While Qutb provided the theoretical basis for modern Sunni Islamism, Khomeini provided the exegesis to legitimize Shi'i theocracy in his 1970 essay, "Hukumati Islami" (Islamic government). Permeating Khomeini's writing is a perception of the West as an opponent to Islam, the concept of martyrdom, and the self-identification of Shi'a as oppressed people. He saw the superpowers as responsible for all the world's wrongs and suggested that it was the obligation of all Muslims to mobilize the oppressed to remove the superpowers from the global arena. Khomeini's linkage between asceticism and suicide is crucial to understand the rise of suicide bombing into the principal tactic by Islamic terrorist organizations. He believed humanity can only crush its selfish desires by spiritual devotion to the umma or community, which is being threatened by the West. The only way to cope with the human obsession with materialism is total denial. Khomeini, in fact, goes to the extreme of justifying the deliberate giving of one's life for the Islamic cause insofar as death is the ultimate denial of one's material self. While martyrdom has long been a theme of Shi'ism, Khomeini's teachings and charisma led many Shi'a to rationalize the justification of suicide on religious grounds.

Islamist Terror Tactics

The major Islamist terror tactic has, since the early 1980s, been the suicide bomber. In contrast to secular terrorists, Islamist suicide terrorists need not escape; their planning focuses instead on how to deliver the perpetrator to the target area. Suicide bombers are walking smart bombs, able to position themselves among crowds or in restaurants to achieve maximum carnage. During the 2001-02 terror waves in Israel, Hamas and Islamic Jihad bombers, for example, made last minute target selections in order to bolster the number of civilians they could kill. Islamist terrorists also need not use time to augment their demands. While the Marxist groups of the 1970s might have threatened hostages against concrete demands, Islamists seek to kill first and lecture later. Islamists do take hostages but, in such cases, their goal is as likely to be to draw out terror in a 24-hour news cycle as to win concessions.

The 9-11 hijackers, for example, resisted U.S. air traffic control attempts to communicate because their goal was not a wish to transmit demands but rather the desire to kill as many people as possible. AlQaeda's decision to launch the attacks cannot be disengaged from ideology and the dream of renewing a lost caliphate. One of bin Laden's most important objectives were to accelerate recruitment of new volunteers for global jihad and Islam. Bin Laden said that the "war in Afghanistan has exposed America's weakness. Despite the clear technological advantages of its war machine, it cannot defeat the Muslim mujahideen.... The number of people who embraced the Islamic faith after the campaign was greater than the number who had grasped Islam in the past eleven years." Hijacker Muhammad Atta's last will and testament, found in the trunk of his car, suggests very different considerations than a secular agenda terrorist event.

Self-Sacrifice and Suicide

There remains much controversy, at least in the United States and Europe, about the origin and motivation of religiously justified terrorism. Pape and University of Georgia political scientist Mia Bloom, author of dying to kill: The Allure of Suicide Terror, are among the most influential revisionists. But, despite the popularity of their theses in a field which seeks to mitigate if not exculpate the influence of religion, their arguments fall short. Pape makes two major assumptions about suicide bombing: first, that it is motivated primarily by resistance to foreign occupation and, second, that religious ideology has only a minor role in suicide attacks perpetrated by Muslims. Bloom also argues that suicide bombers kill themselves only as a means to an end, using suicide only "to outbid rival militias through the use of shocking tactics" and, in the Palestinian case, to "compete for leadership." According to Pape and Bloom, strategy and political objectives rather than religion are the primary incentive for suicide attacks. But religion, rationalism, and strategic planning are not incompatible. The Tamil Tigers may have embraced suicide bombing in their separatist fight against the Sri Lankan army; however, suicide bombers in Casablanca and London were not motivated by occupation but rather by jihadist ideology. While Western scholars may have internalized the separation of church and state legislated in the United States and practiced in Europe, for Khomeini, Hezbollah's Hasan Nasrallah, bin Laden, and Qaradawi, no such separation exists. They are rational but see the world differently. Unlike Pape and Bloom, Khosrokhavar looks for the deeper, individual rather than organizational motivations behind suicide bombing. With comparative analysis of martyrdom in Christianity and Sikhism, Khosrokhavar argues that it is particularly Islamic to sanction sacred death for the sake of the community (umma).

Perhaps this is why Khosrokhavar warns that political science and economics are not sufficient to understanding the human factor in religioninspired terror. Both individuals and terrorist organizations see suicide bombing as a rational and integral aspect of ideology, strategy, and tactics. Israel counterterrorism expert Boaz Ganor elaborates on this self-image of the suicide bomber and his supporters. Ganor explains, "The term suicide attack is misleading. In the eyes of the attacker and his community this phenomenon has nothing to do with committing suicide ... Committing suicide is forbidden in Islam but instead, he is seen as a shahid—a martyr who fell in the process of fulfilling the religious commandment of jihad." Khomeini's influence on Islamist terror suggests that suicide bombing has a wider ideological and strategic foundation than just opposition to occupation. Rather, the basis for suicide bombing is threefold: First, suicide for jihad cleanses the perpetrator of the world's evils. Second, suicide for the community purifies the umma. Third, suicide bombing serves the goal of opposing Islam's enemies.

Pape's interpretation of cause and effect is questionable. He claims that terrorism forced Israel to withdraw twice from

Palestinian areas during the 1990s: in April 1994, when Israel withdrew from parts of Gaza, and between October 1994 and August 1995, when Israel pulled back from portions of the West Bank. He also credits terrorism with Jerusalem's decision to release Hamas spiritual leader Ahmed Yasin from prison in October 1997. His assumption is faulty, though. Pape neglects to mention that Israeli leaders agreed upon this withdrawal policy in the Oslo accords' "Declaration of Principles." The Israeli public persuaded its leadership to seek peace with the Palestinians, not because of terror—Israeli forces had contained if not defeated the first intifada—but rather because they thought the Oslo adventure might achieve a reasonable political solution.

By focusing only on occupation and national liberation, though, Pape overlooks a complicated web of incentives and motivations that undercuts his argument. Marc Sageman, a former CIA case officer, psychiatrist, and University of Pennsylvania political scientist, pursues a different thesis in his book *Understanding Terror Networks*. Sageman seeks to refute the regular notions regarding causes for terror, such as poverty and brainwashing, and emphasizes instead social bonds and networks. He argues that the best way both to understand and to counter global jihadism is by mapping and analyzing the Islamists' social structure. Although Sageman argues that social bonds among terrorist networks play a stronger role then ideologies, he avoids Pape's mistake of seeking to claim exclusivity for his theory, and so encourages counterterrorist intelligence communities to train case officers versed in Muslim cultures and language and acknowledges the individual dedication of the 911 terrorists, which, as their "martyrdom" videos and Muhammad Atta's last will and testament show, was rooted in religion.

Supporters of Pape's revisionism blur the difference between self-sacrifice and suicide to downplay the dissimilarity between secular terrorism and Islaminspired suicide bombing, that is, to downplay the distinction between readinesses to sacrifice oneself for a cause as opposed to a conscious decision to carry out a suicide attack. Every soldier who enlists to a combat unit knows that he or she could be killed in action; many young men and women are willing to take that risk, not because of a desire to die but rather because of the conviction that under certain circumstances it may be necessary to lose one's life in the line of duty. Secular terrorists also acknowledge risk without expressing the desire to kill themselves. Guevara writes, for example, "The guerrilla combatant ought to risk his life whenever necessary and be ready to die without the least sign of doubt, but at the same time, he ought to be cautious and never expose himself unnecessarily. All possible precautions ought to be taken to avoid defeat or annihilation."

Jamal al-Gashay, one of the three Black September terrorists captured by West German police after the Munich massacre and later released in exchange for the return of hostages on a hijacked Lufthansa jet, gave a television interview subsequent to his release. "We knew that achieving our objective might cost lives," he said, "but since the day we joined up, we had been aware that there was a possibility of martyrdom at any time in the name of Palestine." Motivation and readiness for sacrifice is not the same as willingness to embrace certain death. There is a huge difference between the Latin American battle cry, Viva la Muerte! (Hail Death!) and the declaration suicide bombers make on video prior to their mission, Ana ashshahid alhayy, "I the living martyr." For the suicide bomber, such words are not a mere slogan but rather the expression of deep religious values.

Ganor defines a suicide attack as "an operational method in which the very act of the attack is dependent upon the death of the perpetrator ... This is a unique situation in which the terrorist is fully aware that if he does not kill himself, the planned attack will not be carried out." While in the 1970s, terrorists devoted much effort to establishing escape routes or to releasing their fellow terrorists from prison, for the suicide bomber such efforts are unnecessary. Although Pape and Bloom argue that religioninspired terrorists do not kill as an end in itself, Al-Qaeda strikes suggest otherwise. Regardless, the difference in modus operandi between religious and secular terrorists differs enough that they should be considered distinct groups which do not necessarily share the same temporal motives.

Analyzing the differences between secular agenda terrorists and their religious counterparts is crucial to understanding the special nature of contemporary terror. Unlike the activities of secular guerrillas and terrorists between 1945 and 1979, the war against the enemies of Islam is not limited by time, territory, or a specific socioeconomic agenda, and it is being waged against an entire culture and civilization. Therefore, "resisting occupation," as Pape suggests, is only one limited stage in a much larger scheme for a new world order. This is evident in Khomeini's vision of a wide Shi'i crescent extending from Iran through Iraq and linking up with Lebanon, or in Al-Qaeda's dream, of a new Islamic caliphate stretching from Spain in the west to Iraq in the east and eventually including Southeast Asia and Europe as well. Far from being empty slogans, these objectives reflect deep ideological commitment to a new world order. In order to better understand the political mindset of Islamist terrorist organizations, the formative texts of the Sunni and Shi'i leaders should receive as much if not more attention than the strategies and tactics they apply. Giap, the mastermind of North Vietnamese guerrilla operations, once said, "Political activities are more important than military operations, and fighting is less important than propaganda." In confronting Islamist terror, ideology is perhaps even more crucial.

Indian "Secularism" or "Sickularism

India's "secularism" has been a much touted feature of its political, administrative, cultural and intellectual life. For much of the Indian media, and for many political parties, it is has become the ultimate litmus test for membership or acceptance. Its adherents wear it as a badge of superiority and international appeal. Indian movie stars, artists, musicians, academicians and other professionals are routinely judged by their espousal and advocacy of "secularism" which brings with it all the connotations of intellectual and ideological sophistication that any successful Indian might be desirous of. Bringing with it an air of comfort, authority and access to better jobs, to enhanced funding of projects, and above all, international credibility, the secular tag has many takers, both young and old. As a ticket to personal advancement, it offers improved status, a stamp of respectability, and often, greater financial wealth (howsoever dubiously gotten).

For young well-bred Indians, it is an important enabler for appointments that are based on subjective qualities (as opposed to those based on more objective criterion, or concrete scientific/technological skills) and can also smooth the entry into the most 'hep' of social circles. To be "secular" is to be "sophisticated", and to not be "secular" is seen as backwards, almost Neanderthal - and in some circles, even akin to being a "fascist". To be confused or muddled on the subject can lead to illconcealed exasperation "you aren't one of those...are you?" The underlying implication being that to be "secular" is such an obvious choice that only those gravely intellectually challenged could desist from professing a clear point of view. That it is fashionable to be "secular" goes without saying but there are several subtle codes that the genuine Indian "secularist" must faithfully follow. It is not sufficient to be a self-described "secularist" - ones "secularism" must also prescribe to the dominant political and media currents as determined by (often unseen and unheard) "secular" ayatollahs.

Contrary to India's supposedly rich "democratic traditions" the correct "Secular" position is almost never a matter of debate, or discussion, or independent thinking. Stray from the norm, and excommunication is almost inevitable. Therefore, India's "secularists" are almost never nonconformers. Once the position of the "secular" Ayatollahs has been articulated, there can rarely be two views on the correct "secular" position. Very quickly, Indian "secularism" achieves a remarkable sameness and homogeneity of opinion. Politician after politician speak in one voice, as do media anchors and pundits; professors from elite universities like JNU, Jamia, AMU or DU - all echo the dominant stand.

So what is Indian "secularism"? It is certainly NOT separation of church and state as required by the American constitution. Nor is it the absolute requirement for a uniform secular public education system where all religious symbols are banned (without exception) as in France. Neither is it like the secularism of China where all religious practice must be vetted before the state authorities. Nor is it like the secularism of the erstwhile Soviet Union where atheism was actively encouraged and promoted. Instead (and curiously), in India, "secular" practioners from the "left" and "right" agree that there need be no separation of church and state if the church in question is Christianity or Islam. Separation of the state from Hinduism is however seen as eminently desirable, even mandatory in some quarters. (Nevertheless, if otherwise "secular" politicians are obliged to attract Hindu votes through participation in "bhumipujans" and other popular rituals, it is usually met with a benign wink and nod).

Similarly, a good Indian "secularist" will never attempt to demand an end to madrasah or convent education, or to restrict public funds to openly communal minority institutions (such as Jamia). However, it is usually acceptable to brand educational institutions led by Hindu groups as potential breeding grounds for "communal fascists". To demand monitoring, or restriction, or even outright bans on Hindu institutions is considered quite appropriate, in fact, the very hallmark of a genuine secularist. Likewise, while India's Maoists are usually the first to applaud how China has banned "reactionary" religious groups (particularly biblethumping Christian evangelists) from destroying the "socialist" unity of China, they have no qualms in actively allying with the most aggressive of Christian missionaries in India (note Kandhamal, Orissa). And of course, India's once Sovietinspired CPI could never dream of actively promoting atheism - let alone defend it from the onslaught of Christian or other missionaries.

And whereas most Western and developed Latin and Asian societies can boast of a uniform civil code, India's "secular" communists and noncommunists (alike) treat such discussions as 'conspiratorial' or 'divisive'. So then, again, what is Indian "secularism"? If it isn't separation of church and state, if it isn't a uniform civil code, if it isn't a modern public education system run independent of all religious institutions, and if it isn't the progressive retreat of religion in public life as in Taiwan, Korea or Japan (let alone the espousal of atheism) - what is it? Most Indians would probably say it is respect and tolerance for all religions. From an idealist or liberal perspective, that appears to be a perfect fully reasonable and unobjectionable position, except that in practice, it has never been that. Some might then say that while it may be hard to achieve, it is a principle worthy of striving for.

But that too poses problems. Are all religions really all the same? Are they all equally meritorious and deserving of support and tolerance? Are there no rivalries or conflicts amongst competing religions that might make the whole notion of tolerance too difficult to implement? These are very important questions that Indian "secularism" insists on evading even as gross distortions in India's "secular" practice become more evident. Should that come as any surprise? First, it should be noted that in the realm of politics, "respect and tolerance" for all religions (without the separation of church and state) can degenerate into partiality towards one or more religion and stepmotherly treatment of other religions. Political coalitions can quickly evolve to favour one group of religions over another. Even if all religions derived the same level of state support, it would amount to an injustice towards atheists, agnostics and the nonreligious or to those who did not subscribe to any organized religion.

Second, by allowing religious institutions to control childhood (or even adult) education, there is a great danger in the inculcation of highly subjective, partisan and sectarian values that might make the goal of "respect and tolerance" for all religions extremely difficult to enforce. Third, implicit in this liberal and/or idealist perspective is the notion that all religions are essentially the same that ultimately they are but different paths to the same god. This is a noble and ecumenical Indic view that can be traced to Puranic and Vedic texts that has garnered enormous appeal throughout the Indian subcontinent and remains perhaps, one of the defining features of modern Indian society. The popular Indian belief that all life forms have a soul further reinforces such an ecumenical world view.

But unfortunately, these are extremely naive and untenable views of the world. For if all religions believed in such an edict, there would be no need for religious proselytizing or conversions, for religious crusades, or religious wars. Partition would not have taken place and there would be no religious terrorism. The very fact that Western secularism required the separation of church and state, a uniform civil code, the banning of the church from mass education (as in France), or an atheist revolution (as in Russia) implies quite clearly that the European church was incapable of peacefully coexisting with heterodox or unorthodox views. While practioners of several faiths might subscribe to the notion that all religions are essentially the same, such a notion would be a complete anathema to the textual foundations and socialization of Christianity and Islam. The very idea of saving the "heathens" from hell by teaching them the "love of Christ" makes it abundantly clear that traditional Christianity does not believe that all religions are the same. Those who refuse to accept the umbrella of Christ are "sinners" destined for eternal damnation.

Likewise, there is no tolerance for the "idolworshippers" in Islam. Unless one accepts that there is one God whose final prophet was Mohammed and submits unconditionally to "His Will" one is doomed to burning in hell. While modern day Muslim intellectuals can pretend otherwise, there are enough injunctions in the Quran (and the Hadith) that enjoin every good Muslim to convert the disbelievers, failing which there is sanction for both slavery and death for the "infidels". By the same token, apostasy is a very serious crime that requires Islamic authorities to take stringent action to prevent it. A "true" Muslim can therefore neither leave the faith, nor tolerate the faith of the "infidel". In both Islam and Christianity, God is One and it is Him. For Christianity, Jesus is His Son; for Islam, Mohammed is His last Apostle. Those who doubt these basic and essential tenets are unredeemable sinners who must either be saved (by the Christians) or risk enslavement or death (by the Muslims).

The Indian notion of 'all religions are equal - just different' is something that finds no real parallel in either Christianity or Islam, although it finds echoes in many ancient societies untouched by such religions of the book. (It may also have been the view of many early (and naive) converts to Islam and Christianity, but unfortunately, such liberal attitudes seldom inhibited the more sectarian elements from taking centre-stage). Christianity and Islam co-exist peaceably with each other and with the "heathens" or the "infidels" in the modern Western world only because the Western states are strong enough to enforce separation of church and state and react with an iron fist against even the slightest hint of armed religious violence.

Muslims might argue that in practice, not all "infidel" societies were enslaved or put to death, or even always subject to the Jazia (the "infidel" tax); but the fact remains that no "infidel" society was ever treated as equal. "Infidel" societies wee allowed to survive only under a condition of dominance and subjugation. Likewise, Christians could argue that they are not out to save the souls of all Hindus, but until they take a firm stand against aggressive missionaries, and disassociate themselves from the colonial church record, such claims cannot be taken seriously. This then is the context of Indian "secularism". It is a curious hangover from the violent conquest of invading forces attached to two predominantly alien religions first Islam, and then Christianity, each preaching a very similar gospel - that the original inhabitants of the Indian subcontinent were either "infidels" or "heathens" who needed to be "saved" from the gates of hell and/or be subjugated and exploited.

Modern day political, sociological, cultural and intellectual discourse merely echoes past colonial or imperial prejudices albeit in much more subtle and sophisticated terms.

The Hindu response is invariably defensive or apologetic. And when it is not, it is invariably treated as an unforgivable transgression. Consequently, Hindu intellectuals (particularly in their interaction with Westerners), are often embarrassed by the plethora of Indian gods and goddesses and the many seemingly juvenile or inane rituals associated with the Hindu faith. Few have the gumption to ask as to why it is any more logical to believe in just one male god than in multiple gods and goddesses. After all, there is no more proof that there is just one male god as there is proof for multiple male or female divinities.

Religious texts, no matter how "sacred" have been written and transmitted by mortals; as to their validity it is entirely a matter of ones own faith and speculation. Claims about Jesus being the "Son of God" or Muhammad being the "Last Prophet" are simply partisan, egotistical and sectarian claims that have no greater significance or relevance than Hindu assertions of the divinity of Ram or Krishna. But in India's "secularism" Mohammed and Jesus are sacred their holiness can neither be challenged nor questioned, but Ram or Krishna can be easily relegated to the level of myths. Thus, Islamic and Christian religious assertions become privileged over Hindu assertions. As for the illogic of idol worship faith is never logical. It is often psychosomatic, and for many Indians a deeply personal and spiritual experience. If believing in the mystic or magical powers of a divinity in the form of a clay idol is irrational, so is the belief in an unseen unheard unverifiable Christian or Islamic male "God".

Throughout the world, there is a benevolent tolerance towards the tribal rituals of Africa or Papua or the Native American people. Their belief in animal spirits, their totemic religious practices, their creation myths and legends are afforded a respect that is invariably withheld from very similar Indian practices. Even the positive gender connotations of India's reverence for Durga, Saraswati, Kali, Chamunda or the Ardhnareshwari are denied or obscured. Many traditional

Indian communities worshipped plant or animal divinities making them superb conservationists. But gender sensitive or ecologically conscious currents are rarely objects of appreciative study by Western indologists. Hence, Indian "secularists" must pretend as though such trends were either marginal or merely fleeting.

The Indian "secularist" is obliged to see Hinduism only in its most sordid form - it can never be seen as a reflection of anything positive or morally redeeming. For instance, it is often argued that whereas Christianity and Islam treat all human beings as equal, Hinduism treats its members as irrevocably divided by caste. This is perhaps the most serious and damning allegation that Hindus must confront. "Secularism" provides a convenient escape route for the Hindu who has no answer. But a more careful perusal of the Pauranic literature reveals a rather ecumenical view of the world in which all human beings have a soul and are capable of redemption by performing good deeds and doing adequate penance for ones sins. In the Vedic texts there are references to division of labour and the cooperation of different jatis but without mention of any hieraracy. In the Vaishnava literature, in the poetry of the numerous Bhakti saints, there are currents as ecumenical as any other.

In Tantric, Buddhist or Jain texts there is no question of caste discrimination and the same view prevails in many other Hinduidentified satsangi communities. More significantly, there is universality in the Indian ecumenical tradition that is actually absent in Christianity and Islam. For instance, all Christians are equal before Christ, but that is not the same as saying that all human beings have the same soulforce, or that all humans are equal before god. In Christianity, belief in Christ and the Bible presages equality. In Islam, all Muslim men have equal opportunity for salvation, but there is no universal view on human salvation. Equality is conditioned upon faith (and gender}. It is thus a sectarian and partisan approach to equality. In any case, in practice, neither Christian nor Islamic societies were particularly egalitarian (even amongst themselves). Christians and Muslims may have preached equality before "God" - but they certainly didn't preach equality before kings and emperors!

And even Hindu traditions that approved of caste divisions offered all castes an equal chance of liberation through the application of the concepts of Karma and Dharma. Besides, for almost five hundred years, India was ruled by Islamic invaders, and then for two hundred years, it was ruled by Christian colonizers. Missionaries and clerics accompanied both invasions. None of India's conquerors ever attempted to rid India of its caste system in spite of their supposed espousal of "egalitarian" faiths. If anything, they exploited and enhanced India's caste divisions instead of ameliorating them. Even today, the staunchest of India's Muslimaligned "secular" politicians swear by caste loyalties more than any other ism or modern philosophy. They campaign for votes based on caste and they frame policies that derive from caste.

Rather than fight to replace caste by modern parameters such as merit or work or social contribution, it is India's "secularists" who have fought more to keep the caste cauldron burning. Another common criticism of Hinduism in Christian and Islamic circles is how Hindus lack a philosophy of giving whereas they developed a strong tradition of charitable giving, conveniently forgetting how Christian and Muslim conquerors robbed and pillaged every land they conquered. In any case, the concept of the dharamshala, of providing alms to the Sadhus and Sadhvis, of "daan" or of charitable giving to the poor is as old as the Puranas and the Upanishads. "Give. Give with faith. Do not give without faith. Give with sensitivity. Give with a feeling of abundance. Give with right understanding." Taittiriya Upanishad Hindu scriptures are hardly devoid of hymns that consider the elimination of human suffering as a great virtue. The upliftment of the weak and less fortunate through *dâna* (charitable giving) and *sevâ* (selfless service) is praised and extolled. Charitable giving and selfsacrifice is lauded not only for its potential for the betterment of the lives of those suffering, but also for the giver's own spiritual growth.

In the *Upanishadic* view that avers that all beings are related because a soul or divinity dwells within all life forms, to see the suffering of another as something separate from oneself, or as "someone else's problem" is a form of delusion. Moreover, unlike in Islam and Christianity where rule books substitute for indepth discourses on how to resolve moral dilemmas, India developed numerous philosophical systems concerning human ethics, law and justice. The *NyayaSutras* built upon the radical and universal notion that in order to dispense true justice, one needed to discover the truth and nothing less than the whole truth. No moral codes can be efficacious if they are not accompanied by an all-encompassing search for the truth. To this day, the *Nyaya-Sutras* remain a unique and highly relevant treatise on how to determine the truth and how to recognise falsehoods and separate false arguments from genuine ones. Justice is an extremely important yardstick of social progress for any civilized society. That ancient India discovered that the administration of justice was intricately linked to ones knowledge and understanding of the whole truth speaks of its civilizational advance - something that Indian "secularists" are repeatedly asked to deny.

Unlike Islam or Christianity whose moral compass is limited to the Bible or the Quran, the concepts ingrained in the *NyayaSutras* are easily adapted across civilizations and across time. As long as a *Nyayavadi* is willing to discover all the truths as they unfold and emerge with the expansion of human knowledge, the *Nyayavadi* is much more likely to come to answers that are relevant to modern times than the Biblical Christian or the Quranic Muslim. Yet, the Indian "secularist" is asked to bow to the morality of the Biblical Christian or Quranic Muslim but to stay well aloof from the far more flexible and adaptable indic tradition. Instead of noting how the Christian and Islamic views on God lend themselves very conveniently to imperial projects of expansion and subjugation but India's polycosmological and heterodox philosophical systems fit in better with a multipolar view, India's "secularists" synchronise their attitudes with those of their former conquerors. While India's detractors see Hinduism through a very narrow lens, in actuality, India's plural tradition embraces a wide range of beliefs from the atheistic or agnostic, to the Gnostic, to beliefs in one god, or multiple gods of either gender or even bigender.

One can find belief in god as a supernatural entity (who is invisible, omnipotent and infinite) or as an abstract (or indescribable) lifegiving and lifesustaining force. Moreover, India's gods can take multiple life forms they can transform themselves depending on the situation and they provide parables that can be interpreted and reinterpreted with the passage of time. The gods of creation, preservation and destruction are all present their worship and their popularity can modify Indian society or preserve it.

When necessary, there can be a constant churning within the Indic religiospiritual ethos. It is neither static nor rigidly confined to some outdated ancient or medieval text. Sacred texts can be recontextualized and reinterpreted with fresh and original commentaries. Even the concepts of *dharma* and *karma* are amenable to dialectical transformation. Interpetreted properly, they can lead to mores that can be conducive to improved personal morality, enhanced professional ethics and advances in social harmony. In the ancient *Mimamsaka* view, ones actions (both accumulated and current) determined ones rewards.

This implied the cognition of a very important ethical notion that of causality and proportionality. Furthermore, in the *karmic* model, one could be absolved of ones crimes (or sins) only by penance, through selfawareness and acquisition of wisdom, by cleansing oneself of the source or mindset of the sin, and/or through an accumulation of good deeds. But in Christianity, sins can be absolved merely through the love of Christ. There is no strong injunction for penance, for self-realization, for the acquisition of knowledge and wisdom, and of compensating through good deeds. In the *karmic* model (which extends across several Indic streams of thought, including Tantrism, Jainism, Buddhism, Hinduism and Sikhism) redemption comes primarily from personal transformation and atonement. The notion that a third party (such as Christ) could bear your sins would seem as passing the buck almost as moral abdication. But in the typical "secular" mindset it is presented as the other way around - it is the Hindu who lacks the moral compass - who abdicates from personal responsibility as opposed to the "godfearing" Christian or Muslim who is obviously (and bydefinition) more morally worthy.

Even as European humanists saw through the limitations and weaknesses of Christian morality and thus created the climate for the modern European discourse on social democracy with its emphasis on fairness and equal opportunity and proportionality of reward, Indian "secularists" prefer not to see the struggles involved in the construction of European secular civilization. As a consequence Indian "secularism" remains mired in an amalgam of biblical edicts and Islamic authoritarianism. Thou shall never question the holiness and moral consistency of Christianity or Islam.

However, thou may find it acceptable not to take the sacredness of any Hindu god or goddess too seriously. Any aspect of Hindu faith may be vilified, distorted or represented as crude caricature but even honest and relevant criticism of Islam and Christianity must be absolute taboos. There are other unspoken rules: Christians will never try to convert Muslims (or Sikhs) but must have the unconditional right to convert Hindus. But if Hindus try to reconvert ex-Hindus, it will be seen as an unforgivable crime. The "secular" Indian state must spend enormous amounts of fixed and floating capital on the Hajj, but when Hindus demand a relatively small piece of land in Kashmir to facilitate an age-old pilgrimage - they are stoking "communal" passions.

Rabidly sectarian and violent Muslims in Kashmir must be shown "understanding" for they are merely "alienated", "oppressed", or "militant". But Hindus asking for equal treatment are unreconstructed and irreformable "fascists" and "Nazis". Hindus who resist illegal Muslim migrants from Bangladesh are communal racists as are Hindus who rake up the genocidal violence of partition. But Muslim migrants (or locals) who engage in violent land-grabbing (as in Assam), or aid and abet violent acts of mass terrorism (as all over India) are innocent even when demonstratably guilty. Muslims and Christians are always victims never perpetrators. The Godhra train burning was not a Muslim pogrom against Hindus. It was a conspiracy to "defame" Muslims. When Muslims throw stones at Hindus celebrating a festival in their own town they are "provoked" the Hindus are seen as "deliberately" causing trouble. When Muslims (such as Geelani) support Pakistan the perpetrator of a Hindu genocide or the Kashmiri terrorists (also perpetrators of a Hindu genocide) he is a respectable "secular" professor. When Hindus merely hint at the truth - they get branded as "rabid communalists".

When Muslims block traffic to pray, they are merely excercising their constitutional right to religious freedom and if Hindus object, they are denying them their "secular" rights. Imagine if Hindus demanded the same right to cause a nuisance? Imagine if Hindus threw stones at a Moharram procession or during Eid celebrations? When Christians proliferate hate literature against Hindus, it is a mere exception an action undertaken by a fringe group unrepresentative of the mainstream. Besides, why must Hindus agitate over every little insult? Why must they always take such exception? Yet, when Hindus critique the duplicitous and baneful role of Christian missionaries during colonization, they are charged with destroying the "secular" fabric of the country. In India's "secularism" one can exaggerate and embellish the historic injustices in the practise of Hindus but even the unvarnished truth about the Islamic invasions or Christian crimes during colonization are unacceptable.

In the Indian "secular" discourse, Akbar can be viewed as a great "secularist" because he took Rajput brides, entered into military alliances with Rajput rulers and hired Hindu consultants. That the Rajput brides were amongst several in a polygamous marriage doesn't raise any hackles. Nor is it worthy of noting that the alliances with the Rajputs were often forced and unequal, or that Hindus in Akbar's court were grossly underrepresented in proportion to their population. The modern Indian "secular" discourse presumes secondclass status for the Hindu and for the woman. But even such deformed logic is never extended to Hindu rulers.

The Rajputs of Bikaner and Jaipur who collaborated with Muslim emperors and also hired Muslims in their court are never credited for their "secularism". Nor are the countless Hindu rulers who routinely gave royal grants to Buddhist and Jain monasteries and hired Jain or Buddhist scholars in their courts given credit for being "secular".

In the "secular" discourse, Hindu society was so backward, it invited the invasions. If Hindus were conquered and subjugated by slavetrading marauders, it was their own fault. If the conquerors raped and pillaged, looted and destroyed, it was of no consequence. There is no opprobrium in the destruction of Hindu society. India's good little "secular" soldiers must not let such historical facts worry their tidy brains. Muslims do not commit crimes. If they conquered and destroyed, it must have been good reason. But a Babari Masjid cannot be destroyed - that is an abomination an unspeakable crime - a dark and odious stain on India's proud and pure "secular" heritage.

And so goes India's "secular" discourse - with all its attendant asymmetries and unrelenting assaults on the intelligence of every honest thinking Indian. It is such "secularism" that is inviting the pejorative of "sickularism". Rather than encourage more of India's Christians and Muslims to join with their Hindu brethren in moving towards a more progressive and genuine secularism where all Indians can draw upon the great reservoir of ancient wisdom that India offers, devious political leaders with their foolish cohorts have reduced secularism to a wicked game of communal domination which assumes that India's Hindus will once again pay homage to the ideologies of their former conquerors. But will they or will more of them stand up and say enough is enough? The next battle may not be about secularism at all. Which is too bad because India needs real secularism as much as any other modern nation? But it will be a lot about how Hindus see themselves, and how much they are willing to take from the modernday avatars of their earlier conquerors.

Bibliography

A.H. Armstrong, ed., *Classical Mediterranean Spirituality*, World Spirituality 15, New York: Crossroad, 1989.

Angelika Malinar, *The Bhagavadgita: Doctrines and Contexts*, Cambridge: Cambridge University Press, 2008

Annemarie Schimmel, *Mystical Dimensions of Islam*, Chapel Hill: University of North Carolina Press, 1975.

Babin, P., *The New Era in Religious Communication*, Minneapolis, MN: Fortress Press, 1991.

Barnstone, Willis (Ed.), *The Other Bible*, HarperSan Francisco, 1984.

Bavinck, J. H., *The Church between Temple and Mosque*, Grand Rapids: Eerdmans, 1966.

Bavinck, J. H., *The Impact of Christianity on the Non-Christian World*, Grand Rapids: Eerdmans, 1948.

Bruce, S., *Religion in the Modern World: from Cathedrals to Cults*, Oxford: Oxford University Press, 1996.

Chan, Wing-Tsit, trans. and ed. *A Source Book in Chinese Philosophy*. Princeton: Princeton University Press, 1963.

Charles S. Prebish & Damien Keown, *Introducing Buddhism*, World Religion Series, New York: Routledge, 2006.

Daniel Chanan Matt, ed., *Zohar: The Book of Enlightenment*, Classics of Western Spirituality, New York: Paulist Press, 1988.

Dawood, N.J., (translated with revisions) *The Koran*, Penguin Books: NY, 1997.

Donald S. Lopez, Jr., ed., *Religions of China in Practice*, Princeton Readings in Religion, Princeton: Princeton University Press, 1996.

Eichhoefer, Gerald W. *Enduring Issues in Philosophy.* San Diego: Greenhaven Press, Inc., 1995.

Gitlin, T., *The Whole World is Watching*, Berkeley, CA: University of California Press, 1980.

Holm, Jean and John Bowker, eds., *Human Nature and Destiny*, London: Printer Publishing, 1994.

John Esposito, Darrell Fasching & Todd Lewis, eds., *World Religions Today*, New York: Oxford University Press, 2001.

Joseph Dan, *Jewish Mysticism*, 4 vol., Northvale, NJ: Jason Aronson, 1998.

Kurtz, Lester R., *Gods in the Global Village*, Thousand Oaks, CA: Sage, 2007.

Lyden, John. *Enduring Issues in Religion.* San Diego: Greenhaven Press, Inc., 1995.

Malise Ruthven, *Islam: A Very Short Introduction*, New York: Oxford University Press, 2000.

Mark Juergensmeyer, *Global Religions: An Introduction*, New York: Oxford University Press, 2003.

McDannell, C., *Material Christianity: Religion and Popular Culture in America*, New Haven, CT: Yale University Press, 1995.

Michael A. Sells, ed., *Early Islamic Mysticism: Sufi, Quran, Miraj, Poetic and Theological Writings*, Classics of Western Spirituality, New York: Paulist Press, 1996.

Michael D. Coogan, ed., *The Illustrated Guide to World Religions*, New York: Oxford University Press, 2003.

Norman Solomon, *Judaism: A Very Short Introduction* (New York: Oxford University Press, 2000.

O'Flaherty, Wendy Doniger (ed. and trans.), *The Rig Veda: An Anthology*. Penguin Books, NY, 1981.

Pritchard, James B. (ed.), *The Harper Concise Atlas of the Bible*, HarperCollins: NY, 1991.

Rinpoche, Sogyal. *The Tibetan Book of Living and Dying.* New York: Harper Collins, 1993.

Seyyed Nasr Hossein, ed., *Islamic Spirituality I: Foundations*, World Spirituality 19 (New York: Crossroad, 1987.

Tu Weiming & Mary Evelyn Tucker, eds., *Confucian Spirituality*, World Spirituality 11, New York: Herder & Herder, 2002.

Warms, Richard, James Garber and Jon McGee, eds., *Sacred Realms: Essays in Religion, Belief & Society*, New York: Oxford University Press, 2004.

William A. Graham, David Burrell & R.J. McCarthy, eds., *Al-Ghazali's Path to Sufism: His Deliverance from Error (al-Munqidh min al-Dalal) and Five Key Texts*, Louisville: Fons Vitae, 2000.

William C. Chittick, *Ibn Arabi*, Makers of the Muslim World, Oxford: Oneworld, 2005.

Wuthnow, R., *Rediscovering the Sacred: Perspectives on Religion in Contemporary Society*, Grand Rapids, MI: Eerdmans, 1992.

Xinzhong Yao, *An Introduction to Confucianism*, Cambridge: Cambridge University Press, 2000.

Zaehner, R.C. (translation), *Hindu Scriptures*, J.M. Dent & Sons: London, 1966.

Index

S

T

V

W